African perspectives on selected marine, maritime and international trade law topics

Patrick Vrancken & Charl Hugo (Eds)

SUN PRESS

African perspectives on selected marine, maritime and international trade law topics

Published by African Sun Media under the SUN PReSS imprint
Place of publication: Stellenbosch, South Africa

This publication was subjected to an independent double-blind peer evaluation by the publisher.

The author and the publisher have made every effort to obtain permission for and acknowledge the use of copyrighted material. Refer all enquiries to the publisher.

Views reflected in this publication are not necessarily those of the publisher.

First edition 2020

ISBN 978-1-991201-06-5
ISBN 978-1-991201-07-2 (e-book)
https://doi.org/10.18820/9781991201072

Bembo Standard Regular 12/14

Cover design, typesetting and production by African Sun Media

SUN PReSS is an imprint of African Sun Media. Scholarly, professional and reference works are published under this imprint in print and electronic formats.

This publication can be ordered from:
orders@africansunmedia.co.za
Takealot: bit.ly/2monsfl
Google Books: bit.ly/2k1Uilm
africansunmedia.store.it.si *(e-books)*
Amazon Kindle: amzn.to/2ktL.pkL

Visit africansunmedia.co.za for more information.

Contents

PREFACE

The oceans and seas of the world link continents, islands and diverse countries and peoples. They affect the lives of all of us. Similarly, diverse fields of law are also linked to the sea, as reflected by this text you are holding in your hand or scrolling through on your computer, *African Perspectives on Selected Marine, Maritime and International Trade Law Topics.* Legal issues rooted in international law, environmental law, public law and international trade law - in which the common denominator is the sea – are brought together in this collaborative research project of Nelson Mandela University and the University of Johannesburg.

The initiative for this project can be traced back to an informal meeting between the deans of the two Universities, Professor Letlhokwa George Mpedi and Professor Avinash Govindjee in 2017. The editorial responsibility was assumed by two research bodies of the respective universities, namely, the South African Research Chair in the Law of the Sea and Development in Africa (housed at Nelson Mandela University) and the Centre for Banking Law (housed at the University of Johannesburg).

All contributions were subjected to a double-blind peer-review process by independent reviewers. The remarks of the reviewers were communicated to the authors who then improved their contributions with reference to the comments of the reviewers to the satisfaction of the editors. We would like to extend our warm gratitude to the three reviewers who were willing to offer their time and expertise on the altar of academia.

We would also like to thank the publisher, African Sun Media, mainly in the person of Wikus van Zyl.

The editors
30 December 2020

SLIPPING THROUGH THE NET: REFORMING SOUTH AFRICAN FISHERIES LAW ENFORCEMENT

HENNIE VAN AS*

CAMERON CORDELL**

* Professor in Public Law and Director of the FishFORCE Fisheries Law Enforcement Academy, Nelson Mandela University, and Honorary Senior Fellow, Australian National Centre for Ocean Resources and Security (ANCORS), Faculty of Law, Humanities and the Arts, University of Wollongong, Australia.

** LLM candidate and research assistant, FishFORCE Fisheries Law Enforcement Academy, Nelson Mandela University.

INTRODUCTION

The first annual review of organised crime in Southern Africa[1] showed that the smuggling and illegal importation of goods and counterfeit commodities is one of the most prevalent organised criminal activities in the region.[2] In many instances, these activities are undertaken by so-called "professionals"[3] as part of a system that sees marine living resources being smuggled out of the country while drugs and other wares, such as cigarettes, are being smuggled into the country. The link between the illegal wildlife trade (and marine living resources in particular) and drug trafficking is strong. In the Western Cape, the relationship between abalone poaching and crystal methamphetamine, known as "*tik*", has been called a "marriage of convenience".[4]

Criminal activities in the fisheries sector are often regarded as synonymous with illegal fishing, which many countries do not view or prosecute as criminal offences, but rather as a fisheries management concern, attracting low, and usually administrative, penalties.[5] As a result, organised criminal syndicates engage in fisheries crime with relative impunity due to low risk and high profits as well as uncoordinated and ineffective domestic and cross-border law enforcement efforts.

South Africa's law enforcement agencies, in particular its fisheries control officers (FCOs), have been struggling to curb the illegal harvesting of abalone at the hands of poachers and transnational crime syndicates.[6] The country's stock of wild abalone is on the brink of extinction[7] due predominantly to wide-scale illegal harvesting by poachers. Annually, tons of poached abalone are confiscated along with numbers of people being arrested and property seized, yet the plundering

---

1   Hübschle *Organised Crime in Southern Africa: First Annual Review* (2010).

2   ibid 13.

3   ibid 14.

4   ibid 30.

5   UNODC "Bringing to light the perfect storm of illegal activities in the fishing sector" (undated) https://www.unodc.org/unodc/about-unodc/campaigns/fisheriescrime.html (20-01-2019).

6   Redpath "Poached close to extinction" 2002 *Focus* http://hsf.org.za/resource-centre/focus/issue-25-first-quarter-2002/poached-close-to-extinction (20-01-2019).

7   Villette "Abalone poaching 'seen as easy way out of poverty for youth'" IOL (15-06-2017) https://www.iol.co.za/capetimes/news/abalone-poaching-seen-as-easy-way-out-of-poverty-for-youth-9794638 (20-01-2019).

of abalone continues unabated.[8] The involvement of organised crime and the high value of abalone has resulted in poachers resorting to more desperate and violent measures,[9] operating in dangerous waters without proper scuba training or equipment.[10] If caught, South Africa has a low rate of detention of abalone poachers and its justice system has been criticised for providing weak deterrence due to low fines and penalties as well as poor conviction rates.[11] These issues are exacerbated by the prevalence of corruption and non-compliance within the agencies meant to combat such criminal activity.[12]

This chapter begins by briefly examining the environment of abalone poaching, why it is so difficult to combat it and why administrative corruption and a culture of non-compliance has taken root within the agencies involved. To do this, a brief foray into the development and entrenchment of poaching syndicates in South Africa's vulnerable coastal communities is necessary. Reference will then be made to the legislative instruments that give FCOs their powers as well as the legislation that seeks to prevent corrupt activities. A discussion of how to treat administrative corruption effectively will follow before possible solutions to attempt to remedy the situation are provided in the conclusion.

It should be noted at the outset, however, that the focus is not on providing a solution to the abalone poaching crisis itself, but rather on improving the efficacy of the (currently) ineffectual FCOs who are meant to combat that activity. From that perspective, the main issues discussed are the nature of administrative corruption and non-compliance, why the latter have become so entrenched within the ranks of those meant to uphold the laws and regulations and which reforms might address those problems, acknowledging immediately that any solution suggested will not be a panacea to corruption and non-compliance.

---

8 Hyman "The wild, wild Western Cape – where poachers are robbed by gangsters" *Times Live* (23-08-2017) https://www.timeslive.co.za/news/south-africa/2017-08-23-the-wild-wild-western-cape-where-poachers-are-robbed-by-gangsters/ (20-01-2019).

9 Hopkinson "Pleasures of perlemoen poaching" *Business Day* (29-10-2014).

10 De Greef "The poachers and the treasures of the deep: diving for abalone in South Africa" *Guardian* (19-08-2018) https://www.theguardian.com/environment/2018/aug/19/poachers-abalone-south-africa-seafood-divers (07-02-2019).

11 De Greef "Fishing for answers at poaching's ground zero" *Mail and Guardian* (15-08-2014) https://mg.co.za/article/2014-08-14-fishing-for-answers-at-poachings-ground-zero (20-01-2019).

12 Specific instances will be dealt with below.

ABALONE POACHING AND ORGANISED CRIME: AN INTRINSIC CONNECTION

The rise of abalone poaching in South Africa is a relatively recent phenomenon. As a result, there was little to no legal limitation on the capture of abalone until it was realised during the mid-90s that South Africa's stocks were depleting beyond the point of sustainability. This explains why the Marine Living Resources Act (MLRA),[13] which was developed in line with the 1982 United Nations Convention on the Law of the Sea (LOSC),[14] recognises abalone (*Haliotis midae*) as one of the most vulnerable stocks. Nevertheless, rampant illegal fishing between 1996 and 2003 has decimated the abalone resource, necessitating restrictions upon the total allowable catch (TAC) as well as limitations on the size of the abalone caught. This led to the setting of a TAC of just 282 tons in 2003[15] and the total closure of the fishery in 2008.[16] The fishery was subsequently reopened in July 2010, with TAC allocations of 150 tons in the 2009/2010 and 2010/2011 seasons that were conditional on a 15% per annum reduction in poaching. However, the required reduction in illegal harvesting has not been achieved. In fact, it increased substantially. By 2014, it was estimated that poaching had increased by some 150%, whilst a net 50% reduction in poaching was required under the rebuilding plan.[17]

When placing such restrictions upon the harvesting of abalone, the government failed to consider two factors adequately. First, the imposition of the restrictions on fishing placed restrictions upon the small-scale fishers[18] living in or near coastal communities that required the resources for sustenance. Second,

---

13 18 of 1998.

14 1833 *UNTS* 3, (1982) 21 *ILM* 1261. Adopted: 10-12-1982; EIF: 16-11-1994.

15 Department of Environmental Affairs "Seas of change" (undated) https://www.environment.gov.za/sites/default/files/docs/10ytearsreview_marine_coast.pdf (06-02-2019).

16 Department of Agriculture, Forestry and Fisheries (DAFF) *Status of the South African Marine Fishery Resources* (2014) 5.

17 ibid 7.

18 In terms of s 1 of the MLRA, the term "small-scale fisher" means "a member of a small-scale fishing community engaged in fishing to meet food and basic livelihood needs, or directly involved in processing or marketing of fish, who[:] (a) traditionally operates in near-shore fishing grounds; (b) predominantly employs traditional low-technology or passive fishing gear; (c) undertakes single day fishing trips; and (d) is engaged in consumption, barter or sale of fish or otherwise involved in commercial activity, all within the small-scale fisheries sector".

abalone (and in particular the South African variety) is considered to be a delicacy in the Far East,[19] resulting in increased demand for a scarce resource.

The rise of criminal poaching networks resulted from the overlap of those two issues. A culmination of factors, including the high prices on offer as well as the socio-political climate and attitudes around the rights and legalities of abalone fishing, fostered an environment for the illegal fishery to grow.[20] When Far-Eastern crime syndicates moved into coastal communities that had been prohibited from fishing, offering competitive financial incentives to poach abalone, the traditional informal abalone fishery grew into a highly organised illegal fishery facilitated by international networks[21] exporting the product to Hong Kong. This, in turn, led to the development of organised crime syndicates. This is, of course, a very simplified description of a complex and vast series of factors, which have resulted in the entrenchment of poaching syndicates that are also involved in gangsterism as well as drug and human trafficking.

Many of the factors that gave rise to the prevalence of abalone poaching within South Africa's coastal communities could have been avoided had the implications of the existing fisheries-law framework been considered, particularly regarding the role of the FCOs, who are often members of the communities in which the poaching syndicates have taken root.

There is a body of work that confirms that abalone poaching in South Africa is linked to organised and transnational crime, the fact that the latter is also involved in the smuggling of poached abalone out of South Africa being known for years.[22] Steinberg notes that there is a large and highly efficient Chinese organised-crime network involved in the South African illicit trade in abalone.[23] According to De Greef, the "international criminal groups, in particular the so-

---

19 DAFF (n 16) 5.

20 De Greef and Raemaekers *South Africa's Illicit Abalone Trade: An Updated Overview and Knowledge Gap Analysis* (2014) 6-9.

21 Okes, Bürgener, Moneron and Rademeyer *Empty Shells: An Assessment of Abalone Poaching and Trade from Southern Africa* (2018) 5.

22 Gastrow "Triad societies and Chinese organised crime in South Africa" *Organised Crime and Corruption Programme, Institute for Security Studies* Occasional Paper No 48 (2001).

23 Steinberg "The illicit abalone trade in South Africa" *Institute for Security Studies* (2005) 16.

called 'triad gangs' are from East Asia and they are heavily involved in the illegal trade of abalone".[24] South Africa is viewed by these criminal organisations as a gateway into the African continent for their expansion of smuggling networks.[25] The illicit trade of abalone is one of the triad-organised criminal activities pursued in this country.[26] An occasional paper entitled "Triad societies and Chinese organised crime in South Africa" illustrated the link between these triads and abalone poaching when it stated that

> "[t]he Taiwanese-linked criminal group active in Cape Town was referred to as the 'Table Mountain Gang' at that stage. Police soon discovered that members of these triad societies were also operating in the Johannesburg/Pretoria area as well as in every harbour city in South Africa. Police investigations also revealed that the illicit trade in abalone constituted a major component of the Chinese organised criminal groups".[27]

It is alleged that there are Chinese nationals, who are based in South Africa, who coordinate the poaching of abalone between local communities and importers in Asia.[28] They are also responsible for controlling the flow and prices of poached abalone.[29]

This research is backed up by the recent case involving a poaching syndicate operating from Port Elizabeth. In *S v Blignault*,[30] the court stated that "[t]he scale of [this] enterprise's activities extended far beyond provincial boundaries and establishes the reach of its organisational tentacles".[31] Of the nine persons arrested in this matter, two were Chinese citizens, who claimed to be economic migrants. The testimony of these foreign nationals given in a separate trial[32] demonstrates

---

24 De Greef and Raemaekers (n 20) 6. "Triads" are defined as "ancient secret criminal societies which trace their roots to 17th century China" (Snyman and Wagener "The role of the Chinese triads in South African organised crime" 1997 *Acta Criminologica* 107).

25 Snyman and Wagener (n 24) 112.

26 ibid.

27 Gastrow (n 22) 2.

28 Lau "An assessment of South African dried abalone *Haliotis midae* consumption and trade in Hong Kong" *TRAFFIC International* (2018) 15.

29 Gastrow (n 22) 5–6.

30 [2019] JOL 44135 (ECP).

31 par 9.

32 *S v Blignault* 2018 (1) SACR 587 (ECP) par 5-6.

that human trafficking may also be taking place to fuel the abalone poaching trade. Indeed, it was shown in evidence that the Chinese nationals involved were from impoverished communities in China, were promised well-paid jobs in South Africa and were then kept in "horrific conditions".[33] In addition, it was shown that a lot of the abalone being processed by the syndicate did not originate from the Eastern Cape's coastal waters, but rather from the waters off the shores of the neighbouring Western Cape.[34] In evidence, the link between abalone and drug trafficking was further confirmed, with some of the "workers" at the processing plant being paid in drugs rather than money.[35]

The case also suggests that the operation of the law regarding the poaching of abalone, in particular, appears not to be a deterrent against the activities of poaching syndicates. Indeed, Blignault himself was the subject of previous convictions for possession of abalone, but had continued with his illegal activities.[36] The court viewed the matter in such a serious light that it stated that "[t]he time had arrived for a complete reassessment of sentencing options … The plunder continues unabated and the stage has been reached for appropriate sentences to stem the poaching tide".[37]

The entrenchment of the syndicates inside the coastal communities has created an environment of perceived impunity within these areas. As a result, poaching activities, that were once clandestine operations taking place under cover of night, are now widely practised in the light of day, in full view of the public and law enforcement officials.[38]

---

33 ibid 6.

34 *Blignaut* (n 30) par 6.

35 Dorfling "Perlemoen-sindikaat: Baasbrein het met dwelms betaal" *Die Burger* (24-01-2019) https://www.netwerk24.com/Nuus/Hof/perlemoen-sindikaat-baasbrein-het-met-dwelms-betaal-20180920 (28-01-2019).

36 *Blignault* (n 30) par 7.

37 ibid.

38 SA People News "Shocking Revelations of Blatant Abalone Poaching in South Africa" (30-12-2018) https://www.sapeople.com/2018/12/30/shocking-revelations-on-blatant-abalone-poaching-in-south-africa/ (24-01-2019).

In addition, there is ample evidence that abalone from South Africa has traditionally been bartered for the ingredients of Mandrax[39] and later "*tik*",[40] imported from Asia. This straight exchange of commodities leaves no paper trail because there is no exchange of money, making it harder to track criminals involved in such dealings. There is a hierarchy and culture that has developed around these illicit trafficking activities, with the Chinese triads sitting at the apex and local dealers at street level selling the drug. Similarly, the poaching of abalone is done by local fishermen. This system is a highly effective one, particularly because the drug dealers and poachers do not know the identities of those above them in the chain. As a result, higher ranks of the abalone syndicate remain largely untouched due to each level of this complex system working in anonymity. In other words, the higher-ranking members of the syndicates remain above any consequences because there is usually insufficient evidence against them.

THE CORRUPTION AND INEFFICIENCY OF FISHERIES LAW ENFORCEMENT

Abalone poaching in South Africa remains one of the most serious and entrenched forms of fisheries-crime violations. In March 2018, the Western Cape High Court handed down judgment in *S v Miller*,[41] where the learned judge noted that

> "[i]t must be said that the alarming fact is that poaching of large quantities of undersized abalone continues unabated. The sentences handed down by the lower courts…seem to have been no more than an occupational hazard taken into account by the unlawful enterprises as part of their necessary running expenses".[42]

The fact that court-imposed sanctions do not act as a deterrent to the continued poaching of abalone stocks in the South African coastal waters is an inefficiency mirrored throughout the fisheries law enforcement chain. In the same month as the *Miller* judgment, nine FCOs who were employed as compliance

39   a combination of methaqualone, cannabis and tobacco.

40   Okes (n 21) 5.

41   2018 (2) SACR 75 (WCC).

42   *S v Miller and Others* [2018] 2 All SA 488 (WCC) 33.

officers by the Department of Agriculture, Forestry and Fisheries (DAFF) were arrested by the Directorate for Priority Crimes Investigation ("the Hawks") on charges of being directly involved in organised crime syndicates pertaining to abalone poaching.[43]

The presence of corruption within DAFF is not limited to ground-level FCOs but seems to have spread throughout the entire chain of command, with allegations of corruption within the fisheries sector even being levelled at the Presidency. In 2018, it was alleged that former President Jacob Zuma had, during the course of his tenure, received a bribe of R1 million aimed at him not replacing the Minister of Agriculture, Forestry and Fisheries, who was in turn implicated in corrupt activity involving the sale of confiscated abalone.[44] The operations of DAFF have further been hampered by prolonged in-fighting between the heads of department, with the result that

> "[t]he department has spent tens of millions of rands on legal fees for both officials, in some cases hiring opposing sets of counsel. In the last two years, the department has also commissioned at least three forensic reports into corruption, although even these have been tainted by allegations of improper influence.
>
> From both sides, there are claims that the department has been 'captured' by private interests, ranging from tenderpreneurs to abalone poaching syndicates".[45]

While this evidence demonstrates the presence of active organised crime, corruption and misadministration within the department that is expected to protect the marine living resources, passive corrupt acts have also taken root among FCOs, in most cases via non-compliance with regulations. This can take the form of overlooking a violation or failing to inspect vessels with due diligence, often in

43 Du Plessis "Hawks swoop on syndicates" *Netwerk24* (12-032018) https://www.netwerk24.com/ZA/Hermanus-Times/Nuus/hawks-swoop-on-syndicates-20180307-2 (20-01-2019).

44 News24 "'R1m bribe' for Zuma exposes crisis levels of abalone poaching DA" *News24* (25-03-2018) https://www.news24.com/SouthAfrica/News/r1m-bribe-for-zuma-exposes-crisis-levels-of-abalone-poaching-da-20180325 (30-01-2019).

45 De Greef "Fisheries department rots from the top" *GroundUp* (12-11-2018) https://www.groundup.org.za/article/fisheries-department-rots-top/ (30-01-2019).

exchange for gratification.[46] This "culture of non-compliance"[47] has had negative consequences on several fronts.

First, a failure to combat the spread of abalone poaching syndicates effectively has allowed them to take root within coastal communities, increasing connected crimes such as drug trafficking, money laundering, tax evasion[48] and gang violence within their areas of operation. The long-term involvement of so many individuals in this illicit economy and their exposure to other related crimes makes them highly vulnerable to a collapse in this economy, leaving them without the skills, relationships and networks to secure lawful employment.[49]

Second, apart from the environmental damage caused by the removal of the abalone stocks, the failure could be catastrophic for the South African fisheries industry as a whole because it robs the economy of potential revenue that could be gained through a sustainable abalone fishery.

Third, the lack of consequences for corrupt activities and organised crime has meant that the systems in place cannot effectively deal with curbing the theft of abalone stocks. As a result, extensive reform is required regarding how abalone poaching is investigated and how the officials meant to combat the crime are selected and trained.

Corruption (in brief)

It is often overlooked that, at the theoretical level, "corruption" is a catch-all term for different types of conduct that contribute to personal gratification at the expense of ethical or moral duty.[50] "Corruption" within the South African government is an issue which has been at the forefront of public consciousness over at least the past decade. This is predominantly due to large-scale corruption

---

46   Sundström "Covenants with broken swords: Corruption and law enforcement in governance of the commons" 2015 *Global Environmental Change* 253 256–258.

47   See below. See also Villegas "Disobeying the law: The culture of non-compliance with rules in Latin America" 2012 *Wisconsin International Law Journal* 263.

48   Okes *Traffic* (2018) 6.

49   ibid.

50   See, for example, Transparency International "What is corruption?" (undated) https://www.transparency.org/what-is-corruption (2018-07-28).

scandals that have shaken even the highest levels of government, such as allegations of state capture,[51] the near collapse of the South African Social Security Agency through corrupt dealings[52] as well as the deaths of mentally-ill patients in state care caused by corrupt and administrative mismanagement in the *Life Esidimeni* saga.[53] These are, however, all examples of what is known as "grand corruption", which can be defined as "high-level power that benefits the few at the expense of the many, and causes serious and widespread harm to individuals and society".[54]

At the other end of the corruption spectrum is so-called "petty corruption", defined as "[e]veryday abuse of entrusted power by public officials in their interactions with ordinary citizens, who often are trying to access basic goods or services in places like hospitals, schools, police departments and other agencies…".[55] This is most commonly illustrated with reference to small bribes being paid to traffic officials upon being pulled over. Clearly, petty corruption fits the actions of corrupt FCOs more than grand corruption, where bribes are paid to corrupt officials to overlook abalone catches or warn poaching syndicates of police raids (although it will be shown later that grand corruption within DAFF is also an issue).

Corruption within FCOs also takes the form of "administrative corruption" or "the abuse of roles, powers, or resources found within public bureaucracies".[56] In terms of the regulation of fisheries, FCOs can commit corrupt acts by, for example, approving illegal catches or allowing permits to fish in marine-protected areas (MPAs) to known members of poaching syndicates. According to the UN

---

51   See, generally, Public Protector *State of Capture Report* (2016).

52   Munusamy "Sassa crisis in concourt: The guardians, the people and the predator state" *Daily Maverick* (16-03-2017) https://www.dailymaverick.co.za/article/2017-03-16-sassa-crisis-in-concourt-the-guardians-the-people-and-the-predator-state/ (28-07-2017).

53   Malan and Msomi "#LifeEsidimeni judge: 'Government violated the Constitution'" *Bhekissa* (19-03-2018) https://bhekisisa.org/article/2018-03-19-00-lifeesidimeni-settlements-for-families-announced (28-07-2018).

54   Transparency International "Anti-corruption glossary: grand corruption" (undated) https://www.transparency.org/glossary/term/grand_corruption (20-01-2019).

55   ibid.

56   Johnson "Administrative corruption" in Badie, Berg-Schlosser and Morlino (eds) *International Encyclopaedia of Political Science* (2011) 481.

Office on Drugs and Crime (UNODC),[57] corruption in the fisheries sector can manifest itself as:

"Active bribery – the promise, offering or giving to a national public official…of an undue advantage, in order to act or refrain from acting in matters relevant to official duties.

Passive bribery – the solicitation or acceptance by a public official … of an undue advantage, in order to act or refrain from acting in matters relevant to official duties.

Embezzlement – theft or misappropriation of property, funds, securities or any other item of value entrusted to a public official in his or her official capacity.

Abuse of functions – performance of, or failure to perform, an act in violation of the law by a public official in order to obtain an undue advantage.

Trading in influence – abuse of a public official's influence with an administration, public authority or State authority in order to gain an advantage.

Illicit enrichment – a significant increase in assets of a public official that cannot reasonably be explained as being the result of his or her lawful income.

Money laundering – the concealment of the origins of corruptly obtained money, often by means of transfers involving foreign banks or legitimate businesses.

Concealment – hiding or continued retention of property that has resulted from corruption".[58]

The above does not mean that the lines between the types of corruption are clear cut. Rather, the different types of corruption live in a symbiotic relationship, feeding and nourishing each other.[59] As such, low-ranking officials who perceive high-ranking members of the executive as partaking in corrupt acts without sanction are thereby encouraged to indulge in petty corruption. After being promoted (assuming a situation where corruption is endemic), they then turn to administrative corruption, routinely departing from the prescribed administrative

---

57   UNODC *Rotten Fish: A Guide on Addressing Corruption in the Fisheries Sector* (2018) 3.

58   ibid.

59   See Mashali "Analyzing the relationship between perceived grand corruption and petty corruption in developing countries: case study of Iran" 2012 *International Review of Administrative Sciences* 775.

procedure for personal gain. Finally, if and when appointed to high-level posts in government, they perpetuate the culture of grand corruption, which in turn feeds the cycle from the base again.[60]

Culture of non-compliance

Non-compliance occurs when state officials choose not to enforce legal requirements and obligations. This can be for personal benefit (in which case the act could be said to be corrupt in nature) or for a number of sociological reasons. When such acts of non-compliance reach a stage that a failure to abide by a rule or regulation is systematic, then it can be said that a "culture of non-compliance" has developed.

In other words, a "culture of non-compliance" exists where the enforcement of a law is routinely abandoned to the point that the existence of the law can be said to be nothing more than fiction. With the entrenchment of this disregard of rules and procedures, particularly within the law enforcement agencies, it becomes increasingly difficult to combat criminal activities because the officers meant to investigate crimes are generally compromised. Corrupt acts perpetrated by state officials within structures where a culture of non-compliance prevails have generally been normalised to the extent that the act in question (for example, taking a bribe or doctoring inventories) is no longer viewed as morally or legally wrong by those within the system.[61]

Villegas, writing within a South American context, notes that there are three perspectives on how cultures of non-compliance develop.[62] The first is the strategic perspective, whereby an actor weighs up the pros and cons of obeying and abandoning a rule or procedure and concludes that the benefit of disobedience is greater or that the cost of compliance is too great.[63] Secondly, cultural norms might make actors consider their duty to their community to be greater than the duty to obey a rule viewed as being imposed upon the members

---

60   ibid 785.

61   Passas "Fighting corruption" (16-08-2015) https://www.youtube.com/watch?v=d4Dj0qdWLnk (20-01-2019).

62   Villegas (n 47) 263.

63   ibid 264.

of that community.[64] Finally, non-compliance can be a political act of resistance to a government considered to be corrupt.[65] It seems that the development of the culture of non-compliance within the ranks of FCOs has resulted from a combination of the first two perspectives. Indeed, corrupt officials are often working towards the preservation of self-interest and otherwise feel more affinity towards the community members, the activities of whom they are meant to investigate, than the agency that employs them.

A culture of non-compliance has been said to exist within the ranks of marine living resources inspectors since as early as 2001, when 18 Marine and Coastal Management (MCM) officials[66] were implicated in a trial involving the poaching of West Coast rock lobster by the Hout Bay Fishing Company (belonging to one Bengis).[67] The extent of corrupt activities among government officials expected to combat fisheries crime was revealed when a large number of officials turned out to be implicated in such a high-profile case. In research conducted in 2015 by Sundström,[68] during which senior officials were interviewed on the prevalence of corruption within the ranks of FCOs, it was stated that "respondents give a uniform image of the almost endemic state of bribery".[69] Those interviewed claimed that inspectors were primed with gifts of fish by fishers seeking to avoid complying with the MLRA Regulations.[70] The amount of the fish given would then increase over time, before monetary gratification is utilised.[71] Furthermore, FCOs are often friends and family of local fishers who are involved with poaching syndicates, particularly in problem areas such as Gansbaai.[72] At the street level, most of these violations appear to be simply inaccurate declarations of catches. When

---

64   ibid 265.

65   ibid.

66   the forerunners of the FCOs under DAFF.

67   Hauck and Kroesser "Fisheries compliance in South Africa: A decade of challenges and reform 1994–2004" 2006 *Marine Policy* 74 75. The *Bengis* matter would go on to have serious implications for the transnational combating of fisheries crime, but that aspect is not relevant to the subject at hand.

68   Sundström (n 46) 253.

69   ibid 257.

70   GN R1111 in *GG* 19205 of 02-09-1998.

71   ibid.

72   ibid.

poaching syndicates are involved, however, the service rendered in exchange for gratification is often far more sinister, with FCOs informing poachers of police raids, removing or tampering with evidence to scupper a case against a poacher or hiding poached stocks from the police.[73] As recently as 2018, 18 DAFF officials were arrested for being actively involved in abalone poaching syndicates, not only selling seized abalone stocks back to the people they were taken from, but also escorting poached abalone through police roadblocks to evade detection.[74]

The culture of non-compliance that has taken root in DAFF is, based upon the above evidence, both strategic and cultural in nature. It is strategic in that FCOs weigh up the cost of either obedience or disobedience and decide that violating their duty is the more beneficial option. During Sundström's interviews, FCOs stated in their responses that officers caught with illegal abalone on their persons continued to work unfettered within the department, while whistle-blowers were usually ousted.[75] This lacklustre approach to combating corruption within the department has resulted in it being more beneficial for FCOs to either ignore or participate in corrupt activity than to combat it.[76] This is not helped by the lack of potential career advancement. Furthermore, the perception that even officials at the top of the hierarchy are committing corrupt acts has led to a perception that corruption is a necessary part of the job. From a cultural perspective, it has already been pointed out that FCOs often have close connections with friends and families within the coastal communities where poaching syndicates operate. This creates a conflict of interest where officials may be tempted to support these connections rather than uphold their duty to the State. A discussion of the legal instruments in place to combat corrupt activity must take place against this background of corruption and a culture of non-compliance.

73   ibid.

74   Pitt "Marine inspectors bust for allegedly aiding abalone syndicate" *News24* (06-03-2018) https://www.news24.com/SouthAfrica/News/marine-inspectors-bust-for-allegedly-aiding-abalone-syndicate-20180306 (20-01-2019).

75   Sundström (n 46) 259.

76   ibid.

LAW

Marine Living Resources Act

The main statute governing the South African fisheries is the MLRA, which deals predominantly with "the conservation of the marine ecosystem, the long-term sustainable utilisation of marine living resources and the orderly access to exploitation, utilisation and protection of certain marine living resources...".[77] It does this by providing for the management and control of fishing rights on both a micro and macro level. Section 9 of the MLRA gives the Minister responsible for fisheries the power to appoint officials known as FCOs.[78] These FCOs may be appointed from "any organ of state".[79] In practice, these officials are found as a unit within DAFF. The powers of FCOs are defined in section 51 of the MLRA. While they are able to enter, search and seize the property of "any vessel" with a warrant,[80] they are also granted extensive powers that they are able to exercise without a warrant. Those powers include the power to stop vessels,[81] muster the crew, [82] require the master to produce a licence and the records of fish caught[83] as well as escort a vessel to port for the purposes of investigating a violation of the MLRA or its Regulations, where there is a reasonable suspicion that such a violation has occurred.[84] FCOs also have powers of search and seizure of any vessel they reasonably suspect has committed illegal fishing activity in terms of the Act.[85]

The MLRA Regulations complement the Act by providing, for instance, that the master of a vessel must comply with any legitimate order by an FCO[86] and that the costs incurred by an FCO while supervising the offloading or

---

77 long title of the MLRA.

78 s 9.

79 s 9(1).

80 s 51(1).

81 s 51(2)(a).

82 s 51(2)(e).

83 s 51(2)(f).

84 s 51(2)(j).

85 See, generally, s 51(3).

86 See, generally, reg 83(1).

transhipment of goods or fisheries stocks are to be borne by the captain of the vessel.[87] The FCOs are themselves subject to regulations in that, for instance, they are required to notify a vessel of their intention to board via radio or any other appropriate signal[88] and they may not require vessels to stop or manoeuvre while they are in the process of fishing, shooting or hauling.[89]

The restrictions on the harvesting of abalone are also of import in terms of this discussion. While abalone as a species is not mentioned within the main body of the MLRA itself, the Minister is given the power to determine the TAC of a particular species with regard to small-scale, recreational, local commercial and international commercial fishing.[90] It is in the exercise of that power that the Regulations for the Protection of Wild Abalone ("the Abalone Regulations")[91] were promulgated. The Regulations seek not only to suspend the activities of the abalone industry, but also to provide for the implementation of measures to bolster the failing abalone stocks.[92] In addition, the Regulations set out specific areas[93] wherein diving and the possession of prohibited materials is prohibited without the specific authorisation from the Minister.[94] The penalty for committing an act that constitutes an offence in terms of the Abalone Regulations is either a fine of up to R 500 000 or imprisonment not exceeding two years.[95] As far as the activities listed under regulation 3(3)[96] are concerned, should they be conducted

---

87   reg 83(3).

88   reg 84(1).

89   reg 84(2).

90   s 14 of the MLRA.

91   GN R62 in *GG* 30716 of 01-02-2008.

92   reg 2.

93   annexure 1 of the Abalone Regulations. The areas are: the Bird Island Marine Protected Area; Quoin Point to Danger Point, extending two nautical miles seaward from the high watermark; Dyer Island, extending one nautical mile from the high watermark; Venus Pool to Cape Point and from Cape Point to Olifantsbospunt, extending 2 nautical miles seaward from the high watermark, but excluding Bellows Rock; and Robben Island, extending 1 nautical mile from the high watermark.

94   reg 3. See, however, the exceptions in reg 4.

95   reg 5(1).

96   The activities include: "(a) scientific research and monitoring; (b) white shark-cage diving; (c) commercial kelp harvesting; (d) sea ranching; (e) salvage operations; [and] (f) maintenance of legal underwater infrastructure …".

without having obtained a permit from the Minister as per the Regulations, the fine is R 100 000 with the alternative of one year imprisonment.[97]

Prevention of Organised Crime Act

The Prevention of Organised Crime Act (POCA)[98] is often utilised in conjunction with the MLRA when combating abalone poaching. The reasons for this are fairly self-explanatory when one considers the prevalence of organised poaching syndicates having taken root within coastal communities in South Africa. POCA not only provides for the offences of racketeering and money laundering but goes further in that it provides for the seizure of property and profits derived from illicit activities.

Of primary importance with regard to abalone poaching are the provisions relating to racketeering activities. Section 2 of POCA lays out a wide-ranging framework whereby any person who retains any property that amounts to the proceeds of "a pattern of racketeering activity", and who knows that such property is so derived, is guilty of an offence. "A pattern of racketeering activity" is defined for the purposes of POCA as

> "the planned, ongoing, continuous or repeated participation or involvement in any offence referred to in Schedule 1 [of POCA], and includes at least 2 offences…, of which one of the offences occurred after the commencement of the Act… ".[99]

As far as criminal gang activities are concerned, POCA makes it an offence, for instance, for any person who actively participates in or is a member of a criminal gang to wilfully aid and abet "any criminal activity committed for the benefit of, at the direction of, or in association with any criminal gang".[100]

POCA also provides extensively for the offence of corruption. It does this by setting out a general offence of corruption combined with specific offences

---

97 reg 5(2).

98 121 of 1998.

99 s 1. Schedule 1 lists "dealing in, being in possession of or conveying endangered, scarce or protected game or plants or remains thereof in contravention of a statute of official ordinance".

100 s 9(1)(a).

pertaining to public officials. In terms of these provisions, any persons within public office (such as FCOs in the employ of DAFF) are guilty of an offence of corruption if they accept, agree or offer to accept any gratification in exchange for committing an illegal or unethical dereliction of duty.[101] The "gratification" can amount to money, goods or services.[102] It should be noted that both parties within a corrupt act, the briber and bribee, fall within the prohibition of corrupt activity.[103]

It must also be pointed out that POCA provides for confiscation and preservation orders,[104] which assist in preserving evidence of the commission of poaching activities prior to and during prosecution or forfeiting the proceeds of unlawful activities to the State.

ISSUES

Despite the comprehensive attempts to control and regulate the South African fishing industry, the issue of non-compliance by both the public and the FCOs themselves has demonstrated that the existing legislative framework is insufficient to combat fisheries crimes effectively. This has several knock-on effects.

First, the failure of DAFF to secure compliance with fisheries regulations and the existing tensions within the communities in which the FCOs operate have resulted in the entrenchment of poaching syndicates in these communities. As a further result, this has led to increased gangsterism as well as the introduction of drugs and, in some cases, human trafficking.

Second, the failure to ensure compliance has been shown to have a negative effect on the delicate ecosystems that exist in South Africa's coastal waters. The removal of the species from its native habitat has been cited as "detrimental",[105]

---

101 s 3.

102 s 1.

103 s 3 clearly states that both offering and receiving gratification are prohibited.

104 ss 18 and 38 respectively.

105 Pariona "The ill effects of abalone poaching in South Africa" (01-08-2017) https://www.worldatlas.com/articles/the-ill-effects-of-abalone-poaching-in-south-africa.html (20-01-2019).

having knock-on effects on other species, which in turn cause further difficulties for the members of local communities who rely upon the sea for livelihood and sustenance.

Third, while FCOs' powers seem quite effective when one reads the legislation, those powers are in reality exceptionally weak and reliant upon the support of the members of the South African Police Services (SAPS). While FCOs are able to enter vessels and premises as well as search and seize property, any evidence collected needs to be handed over to the police as soon as possible. Furthermore, there are holes within the MLRA in terms of how FCOs are able to operate. The best example is the question of whether FCOs (as peace officers) are able to apply for a search warrant in terms of the Criminal Procedure Act (CPA).[106] It seems reasonable to think that, when FCOs are given the power to enter premises or board a vessel with a warrant, they should be able to apply for the warrant in question. However, this does not appear to be the case. In practice, some magistrates entertain applications from FCOs but, in many instances, they require SAPS officials to apply for the warrants on behalf of the FCOs, a task that is, in many instances, completed with difficulty.[107] For that reason, it can be argued that FCOs are largely ineffective and dependent on the SAPS in the fulfilment of their legislative mandate.

In addition, FCOs have no powers to investigate. In practice, it means that, after they have apprehended suspects and completed statements, they have to hand the case over to the SAPS. In most instances, they have no idea of how, or even whether, cases are progressing. The demoralising effect of this lack of inter-agency cooperation is well documented.[108] Furthermore, there is a proliferation of law enforcement agencies attempting to address abalone poaching. In the South-Western Cape, there are the SAPS, DAFF, Cape Nature, SANParks and the Overstrand Municipality Law Enforcement Unit. In addition, the City of Cape Town has marine units in its Metro Police as well as in its Law Enforcement

---

106 51 of 1977.

107 Snijman and Van As (2018) (Unpublished legal opinion to DAFF).

108 e-mail dated 13-07-2018 from a Senior FCO to the Director of FishFORCE and interviews with senior officials at DAFF in 2017/18.

Department. However, these units do not collaborate, they do not liaise with each other and they do not have common objectives.[109] In the words of one official employed by the City of Cape Town: "We chase numbers. CIVOC[110] wants numbers. They are not interested in quality".

All of the above speaks towards the failure of the MLRA to provide an effective and independent framework to deal with illegal fishing. The lack of clear powers given to FCOs has resulted in poaching syndicates feeling that they can commit their crimes with impunity while also leading FCOs themselves to be non-compliant in the fulfilment of their duties. It is noteworthy that this is not a problem unique to South Africa. Indeed, Njaya notes in the Malawian context that "co-management arrangements are characterized by unequal power distribution among these different actors, often resulting in the marginalization" of subsistence fishers.[111]

POSSIBLE SOLUTIONS

Legal reform is the only way forward to make FCOs more effective. This can be done by clarifying the powers already granted by the MLRA, such as the ability of FCOs to apply for search warrants, but also extending their powers of search, seizure and arrest as well as their power to set up roadblocks in order to make them more effective. This is especially important in view of the fact that inter-agency collaboration is required to set up such blockades and that the ability and availability of the agencies required to make this possible are often a source of frustration. This would also require the MLRA and its regulations setting a minimum standard of formal training. This is confirmed by a number of international bodies, which have identified proper training as a prerequisite for combating fisheries crime. Those bodies include the World Wide Fund for

---

109 interviews with members of the various units conducted on behalf of FishFORCE on 03-7-2018 and 17-08-2018 by HJ van As.

110 the Civilian Oversight Committee established in terms of s 64J of the South African Police Service Act (68 of 1995, SAPSA).

111 Nadya "Analysis of power in fisheries co-management: Experiences from Malawi" 2012 *Society and Natural Resources* 652.

Nature (WWF),[112] the Food and Agriculture Organization of the United Nations (FAO)[113], Interpol[114] and UNODC.[115]

Another question to be answered, considering the current situation and the urgency of combating illegal fishing, is whether FCOs are best suited as a unit of DAFF or whether the body should be moved to a specialised unit of the SAPS dedicated to addressing fisheries crime as an element of organised crime. While it would seem prudent to house FCOs within the department responsible for fisheries, these officials are primarily fulfilling a policing function. Placing the agency within the SAPS would also solve some of the issues facing FOCs currently by formalising training in fitness, investigation and arrest,[116] allocating powers such as applying for warrants[117] and bringing expertise on the fisheries industry to other SAPS units such as the Hawks. Such a move might also assist in combating the culture of non-compliance and corruption that has taken root among the FCOs by bringing the unit under the oversight of bodies such as the Independent Police Investigative Directorate (IPID).[118]

An alternative is to designate FCOs as environmental management inspectors (EMIs) in terms of the National Environmental Management Act (NEMA).[119] Such a move would result in minimum training requirements being set as well as an extension and clarification of the FCOs' powers, including the use of force for the purpose of stopping vessels, vehicles and aircraft.[120] It would also confer upon the FCOs "all the powers of a member of the South African

---

112 WWF *2015 Annual Report* (2015) 32 https://c402277.ssl.cf1.rackcdn.com/publications/832/files/original/WWF_EFN_Annual_Report_FINAL_SPREAD.pdf?1445869889 (13-05-2020).

113 FAO *Recent Trends in Monitoring, Control and Surveillance Systems for Capture Fisheries* (2018) 58.

114 Interpol hosts annual police training symposiums, which include sessions aimed at improving marine law enforcement.

115 In 2016, Nelson Mandela University became a founding member of the UNODC's LETrainNET initiative, which promotes the exchange of training materials and courses between law enforcement organisations and tertiary institutions.

116 s 32 read with s 37 of the SAPSA.

117 s 25(1) of the CPA.

118 established by s 3(1) of the Independent Police Investigative Directorate Act (1 of 2011).

119 107 of 1998.

120 s 31J(4)(b) of NEMA.

Police Service in terms of section 13(8) of the South African Police Service Act, 1995".[121] That would include the power to set up and conduct roadblocks in terms of the SAPSA.[122] EMIs are also granted specific permission to apply to a court for a warrant.[123] In addition, and most importantly, NEMA provides that EMIs may issue compliance notices,[124] which must state that a person has failed to comply with relevant legislation and indicate the steps that must be taken to rectify the situation.[125] Failure to comply with a compliance notice can result in a permit being revoked and the imposition of a fine not exceeding five million rand, with an alternative of 10 years imprisonment.[126]

In whatever form, legislative reform is required to secure the country's marine living resources for current and future generations through effective enforcement of the law.

---

121 See s 31J(7) of NEMA.

122 s 13(8)(c) of the SAPSA.

123 s 31K(4) of NEMA.

124 s 31L(1) of NEMA.

125 s 31L(2) of NEMA.

126 s 31N(2) of NEMA.

THE PROTECTION OF SELECTED LABOUR CONDITIONS OF FISHERS IN NAMIBIA

HASHALI HAMUKUAYA*

PATRICK VRANCKEN**

* LLD candidate, Nelson Mandela University

** Professor in Public Law and holder of the NRF Research Chair in the Law of the Sea and Development in Africa, Nelson Mandela University.

INTRODUCTION

> "For fishers, their ship is their home, and for many, the crew is their only family".[1]

The International Labour Organization (ILO) was established in 1919[2] as an independent body devoted to promoting social justice and improving labour rights internationally. Its main strategic objective is to seek the improvement of social conditions throughout the world and to ensure decent work.[3]

The ILO "considers fishing as a hazardous occupation when compared to other occupations".[4] Workers on board fishing vessels are known as "fishers".[5] Indeed, while fishers are out at sea, they are exposed to significant hazards, including rough weather, crushing waves, powerful and dangerous machinery as well as sea-related health issues.[6] The level of exposure to those hazards amongst fishers varies considerably depending on, but not limited to, the number of crew on the vessels to execute occupational functions, the design of the fishing vessels, the gear used as well as the type, and availability and quality of the catch, all of which have an impact on the amount of time spent offshore.[7] As a result, those factors play an important role in the hours of work of fishers and how much fishers earn over any specific period of time.

Fishers have many of the labour rights common to all workers, depending on the scope of the definitions given in relevant instruments. For example, fishers have fundamental core rights and freedoms such as the right not to be compelled

---

1   See ILO "News" available at http://www.ilo.org/global/about-the-ilo/newsroom/news/WCMS_083074/lang--en/index.htm (13-08-2019).

2   by art 387 of the 1919 Treaty of Peace between the Allied and Associated Powers and Germany (225 *CTS* 189, (1919) 13 *AJIL Suppl* 151; adopted: 28-06-1919; EIF: 10-01-1920).

3   preamble of the Constitution of the International Labour Organization (15 *UNTS* 40; adopted: 01-04-1919; EIF: 28-06-1919).

4   seventh preambular par of the 2007 Work in Fishing Convention (No 188) (WIFC) (adopted: 14-06-2007; EIF: 16-11-2017; https://treaties.un.org/doc/Publication/UNTS/No%20Volume/54755/Part/I-54755-080000028005f62c.pdf (13-08-2019)). Namibia and South Africa ratified the Convention in 2018 and 2013 respectively.

5   art 1(e) of the WIFC.

6   Jepsen and Van Leeuwen "Seafarer fatigue: a review of risk factors, consequences for seafarers' health and safety and options for mitigation" 2015 *International Maritime Health* 106

7   Couper, Smith and Ciceri *Fishers and Plunders Theft, Slavery and Violence at Sea* (2015) 30.

to undertake forced labour,[8] the freedom of association[9] and the effective recognition of collective bargaining,[10] to name just a few.[11] However, the ILO has long recognised the unique nature of the living and hazardous working conditions of fishers and adopted over the years a number of dedicated instruments, such as the 1959 Minimum Age (Fishermen) Convention (No 112),[12] the 1959 Medical Examination (Fishermen) Convention (No 113),[13] the 1959 Fishermen's Articles of Agreement Convention (No 114)[14] and the 1966 Accommodation of Crews (Fishermen) Convention (No 126).[15] It is to bring those instruments up to date and to reach a greater number of the world's fishers that the ILO adopted the 2007 Work in Fishing Convention (No 188) (WIFC).[16] The Convention establishes minimum international standards relating to fishers' conditions of employment

8   1930 ILO Forced Labour Convention (No 29) (adopted: 28-06-1930; EIF: 01-05-1932; https://www.ilo.org/dyn/normlex/en/f?p=NORMLEXPUB:12100:0::NO::P12100_ILO_CODE:C029 (13-08-2019)) and 1957 ILO Abolition of Forced Labour Convention (No 105) (adopted: 25-06-1957; EIF: 17-01-1959; https://www.ilo.org/dyn/normlex/en/f?p=1000:12100:0::NO::P12100_ILO_CODE:C105 (13-08-2019)).

9   1948 ILO Freedom of Association and Protection of the Right to Organise Convention (No 87) (adopted: 09-07-1948; EIF: 04-07-1950; https://www.ilo.org/dyn/normlex/en/f?p=NORMLEXPUB:12100:0::NO::P12100_INSTRUMENT_ID:312232 (13-08-2019)).

10   1949 ILO Right to Organise and Collective Bargaining Convention (No 98) (adopted: 01-07-1949; EIF: 18-07-1951; https://www.ilo.org/dyn/normlex/en/f?p=NORMLEXPUB:12100:0::NO::P12100_ILO_CODE:C098 (13-08-2019)).

11   The other four fundamental conventions of the ILO are: the 1973 ILO Minimum Age Convention (No 138) (adopted: 26-06-1973; EIF: 19-06-1976; https://www.ilo.org/dyn/normlex/en/f?p=NORMLEXPUB:12100:0::NO::P12100_ILO_CODE:C138 (13-08-2019)); the 1999 ILO Worst Forms of Child Labour Convention (No 182) (adopted: 17-06-1999; EIF: 19-11-2000; https://www.ilo.org/dyn/normlex/en/f?p=NORMLEXPUB:12100:0::NO::P12100_ILO_CODE:C182 (13-08-2019)); the 1951 ILO Equal Remuneration Convention (No 100) (adopted: 29-06-1951; EIF: 23-05-1953; https://www.ilo.org/dyn/normlex/en/f?p=NORMLEXPUB:12100:0::NO::P12100_ILO_CODE:C100 (13-08-2019)); and the 1958 ILO Discrimination (Employment and Occupation) Convention (No 111) (adopted: 25-06-1958; EIF: 15-06-1960; https://www.ilo.org/dyn/normlex/en/f?p=NORMLEXPUB:12100:0::NO::P12100_ILO_CODE:C111 (13-08-2019)). The International Labour Conference declared in par 2 of the 1998 Declaration on Fundamental Principles and Rights at Work and its Follow-up (https://www.ilo.org/wcmsp5/groups/public/---ed_norm/---declaration/documents/publication/wcms_467653.pdf (23-08-2019)) that ILO Member States that have not ratified those conventions nevertheless "have an obligation, arising from the very fact of membership in the Organization, to respect, to promote and to realize, in good faith and accordance with the Constitution [of the ILO], the principles concerning the fundamental rights which are the subject of those conventions, namely: (a) freedom of association and the effective recognition of the right to collective bargaining; (b) the elimination of all forms of forced or compulsory labour; (c) the effective abolition of child labour; and (d) the elimination of discrimination in respect of employment and occupation".

12   adopted: 19-06-1959; EIF: 07-11-1961; https://www.ilo.org/dyn/normlex/en/f?p=NORMLEXPUB:12100:0::NO::P12100_ILO_CODE:C112 (13-08-2019).

13   adopted: 19-06-1959; EIF: 07-11-1961; https://www.ilo.org/dyn/normlex/en/f?p=NORMLEXPUB:12100:0::NO::P12100_ILO_CODE:C113 (13-08-2019).

14   adopted: 19-06-1959; EIF: 07-11-1961; https://www.ilo.org/dyn/normlex/en/f?p=NORMLEXPUB:12100:0::NO::P12100_ILO_CODE:C114 (13-08-2019).

15   adopted: 21-06-1966; EIF 06-11-1968; https://www.ilo.org/dyn/normlex/en/f?p=NORMLEXPUB:12100:0::NO::P12100_ILO_CODE:C126 (13-08-2019).

16   n 5.

with the objective of realising decent work for fishers and recognises, amongst others, the importance of the right to freedom of association and the effective recognition of the right to collective bargaining.[17]

The conditions of employment of fishers in Namibia have recently come under scrutiny with numerous complaints relating to hours of work and wages being lodged before the Director of Labour Services.[18] In the process of dealing with those complaints, the Director held numerous consultative meetings with all fishing companies and trade union representatives in 2014. Unfortunately, there was conflict amongst the different trade unions and between trade union members, with the result that no consensus could be reached and, eventually, unprotected ("wildcat") strikes broke out. These strikes cost the economy millions of Namibian dollars in lost revenue.[19]

This contribution examines the regulation of fishers' hours of work before it examines that of wages. It does so by comparing Namibia's standards with those of the WIFC, keeping in mind that Namibia is as yet not a party to the WIFC and has no legal obligation to implement its provisions. The contribution also includes an examination of the position in South Africa because the latter shares the same labour-law history as that of Namibia and is a party to the WIFC.[20]

REGULATION OF HOURS OF WORK

The international position

The ILO has recognised since its establishment in 1919 the importance of regulating the hours of work for all employees in different industries, including employees working on board vessels. That importance is illustrated by article 427

---

17   ibid.

18   New Era "Kaaronda tears into fishing industry" (undated) https://www.newera.com.na/2015/11/11/kaaronda-tears-fishing-sector/ (13-08-2019)

19   New Era "Seaman strike implications – Esau" (undated) https://www.newera.com.na/2015/11/05/seamen-strike-implications-esau/ (20-04-2016) One Namibian dollar is equivalent to one rand.

20   South Africa ratified the Convention in 2013

of the 1919 Versailles Peace Treaty,[21] which envisaged an eight-hour day or forty-eight-hours week as the standard to which to aim in every industry.

Prior to the adoption of the WIFC, the only instrument relating to fishers' hours of work was the 1920 Hours of Work (Fishing) Recommendation (No 7),[22] which called upon all the ILO member States to adopt national legislation limiting the hours of work of all employees in the fishing industry, while acknowledging that special provisions might be necessary to meet the conditions peculiar to the fishing industry in each country, and, when drafting those provisions, to consult with the employers' organisations and the workers' organisations concerned. As its name indicates, the Recommendation is not mandatory and, as a result, fishers often continued to be exploited by having to work excessive hours without being remunerated accordingly.

The WIFC is thus the first binding international instrument intended to regulate the hours of work for fishers.[23] However, it only does so indirectly by providing for "hours of rest". The general standard provided for in the WIFC is that fishers should be given regular and sufficient rest to ensure their safety and health as well as to limit fatigue, regardless of the vessel size and the period during which the vessel is at sea.[24] In addition to that general standard, the WIFC prescribes that minimum hours of rest for fishers who remain at sea for more than three days must be set by the competent authority[25] in each State and that those hours may not be less than ten hours in any 24-hour period and 77 hours in any seven-day period.[26] Temporary exceptions to those entitlements may be permitted "for limited and specified reasons", but fishers must then be granted "compensatory periods of

---

21   n 2.

22   adopted: 30-06-1920 https://www.ilo.org/dyn/normlex/en/f?p=1000:12100:14100203119983::NO::P12100_
SHOW_TEXT:Y: (09-08-2019).

23   ILO *Application of International Labour Standards 2008 (II)* (2008) 5. For a full discussion of the unique working
conditions of fishers and the reasons why it took so long to create an international standard, see ch 1 and ch 2 of
Hamukuaya *Labour Rights of Fishers in Namibia* (2018 LLM dissertation, Nelson Mandela University).

24   art 13(b)

25   In terms of a 1(b), the term "competent authority" means "the minister, government department or other authority
having power to issue and enforce regulations, orders or other instructions having the force of law in respect of the
subject matter of the provision concerned".

26   art 14(1)(b)

rest as soon as practicable".[27] "Substantially equivalent" alternative arrangements may be adopted after consultation with the representatives of fish workers and employers.[28] In addition, the WIFC does not

> "impair the right of the skipper of a vessel to require a fisher to perform any hours of work necessary for the immediate safety of the vessel, the persons on board or the catch, or for the purpose of giving assistance to other boats or ships or persons in distress at sea. Accordingly, the skipper may suspend the schedule of hours of rest and require a fisher to perform any hours of work necessary until the normal situation has been restored. As soon as practicable after the normal situation has been restored, the skipper shall ensure that any fishers who have performed work in a scheduled rest period are provided with an adequate period of rest".[29]

The Namibian position

The position in Namibian common law is that parties to an employment contract are free to determine the hours of work.[30] In practice, however, the prospective employee is often at a disadvantage at the negotiation table. This is primarily due to the employer knowing that the prospective employee is desperate for employment and would accept almost any terms and conditions for the sake of being taken on board. In the cases where the contract of employment does not regulate the hours of work, the courts apply the norm of the applicable industry to determine whether the working hours demanded of the employee are too harsh and unreasonable. This was the situation in *Namibia Foods and Allied Workers' Union v Novanam Limited and Another*, where the fishers of Novanam[31] were required to work excessive hours far above the industry standards set by the Minister of Labour, Industrial Relations and Employment Creation.[32]

---

27   art 14(2). There is no indication in the WIFC as to the duration of the compensatory periods of rest.

28   art 14(3) read with a 1(c)

29   art 14(4).

30   Parker *Labour Law in Namibia* (2012) 79.

31   Novanam Limited is a juristic person having its principal place of business in Lüderitz, Namibia. It is involved in many commercial activities, including fishing.

32   HC-MD-LAB-APP-AAA-2017/00015 par 28–31.

Fishers who are not independent contractors are employees as defined in section 1 of the Labour Act (LA).[33] In terms of the LA, an employer is prohibited from requiring or permitting an employee to work for more than 45 hours in any week.[34] In addition, an employer may not require an employee to work: (a) more than nine hours in any day when the employee works for five days in a week; (b) more than eight hours in any day when the employee works for more than five days in a week; or (c) more than the maximum number of hours prescribed by the Minister responsible for Labour for that employee's shift when that employee works in continuous operation.[35]

As a general rule, an employee who belongs to a class designated by the Ministry responsible for Labour may not be required or permitted to work more than 60 hours in a week,[36] divided into not more than 12 hours in any day, if the employee works for five days or fewer in a week, or 10 hours in any day, if the employee works for more than five days in a week.[37] In the case of fishers, the maximum is 54 hours in a week, divided into not more than 9 hours a day if the fisher works six or fewer days a week.[38]

The LA permits overtime only in accordance with an agreement, which "may not require a fisher to work more than 35 hours of overtime in a week and in any case not more than five hours overtime in a day".[39] However, maximum

---

33 11 of 2007. In 2016, the Minister of Labour, Industrial Relations and Employment Creation varied certain provisions of ch 3 of the Act (which deals with the basic conditions of employment) in so far as those provisions apply to employers and employees in the fisheries industry and, to that end, inserted a definition of the word "fisher" that reads as follows: "a person employed or engaged in any capacity or carrying out an occupation on board a fishing vessel, including persons working on board paid on the basis of as share of the catch but excluding pilots, naval personnel, shore-based persons carrying out work aboard a fishing vessel and fisheries observers" (see GN 250 in *GG* 6149 of 14-10-2016).

34 s 16(1). This rule is subject to any contrary provisions of ch 3 of the Act, which deals with the basic conditions of employment.

35 s 15(2).

36 s 16(3)(a).

37 s 16(3)(a)(i)-(ii).

38 In 2016, the Minister of Labour, Industrial Relations and Employment Creation made fishers a designated class when he varied certain provisions of ch 3 of the Act (which deals with the basic conditions of employment) in so far as those provisions apply to employers and employees in the fisheries industry (hereinafter "the 2016 Ministerial Variation"). To that end, he inserted a definition of the word "fisher" that reads as follows: "a person employed or engaged in any capacity or carrying out an occupation on board a fishing vessel, including persons working on board paid on the basis of as share of the catch but excluding pilots, naval personnel, shore-based persons carrying out work aboard a fishing vessel and fisheries observers" (see GN 250 (n 33)).

39 s 17(1) as amended by the Minister in 2016 This is more than the general limits of 3 hours in a day or 10 hours in a week.

overtime may be increased provided that the employer applies to the Permanent Secretary responsible for Labour to that effect and the affected employees agree.[40] When the Permanent Secretary grants the application,[41] he or she must issue a notice indicating the class of employees to whom the notice applies, the new limits on overtime work, any conditions concerning the working of the overtime and the duration of the approved overtime.[42] The provisions regarding overtime do not apply to fishers who are performing urgent work, including both "emergency work, which if not attended to immediately, ... could cause serious damage or destruction to property"[43] or "work connected with the arrival, departure, loading, unloading, provisioning, fuelling or maintenance of ... a ship ... used to transport ... perishable goods".[44] However, the spread-over[45] of working hours may not exceed 14 hours.[46] At the same time, the provision that an employee must not be required or permitted to work without a weekly interval of at least 36 consecutive hours of rest[47] does not apply in the case of fishers. Instead, "[u]pon the return of a fisher from sea, the employer must grant the fisher paid shore leave, calculated as follows: (i) one full day for every seven days worked at sea; and (ii) a fraction of a day calculated on a pro rata basis for less than seven days worked at sea".[48] This special dispensation makes room for the fact that fishers are at sea for different durations per cycle and it is often not possible for fisheries employers to give fishers a weekly rest period in terms of the LA. In addition, fishers would be exempted from the prohibition of work on Sunday[49] on the ground that fishers are engaged in "work in which continuous

---

40 s 17(3).

41 The Permanent Secretary may at any time amend or withdraw the notice.

42 s 17(4).

43 s 8(1)(k)(i).

44 s 8(1)(k)(ii).

45 In terms of s 8(1)(j), the term "spread-over" means "the period from the time an employee first starts work in any one 24 hour-cycle to the time the employee finally stops work in that cycle".

46 s 20(1) as amended by the Minister in 2016 This is more than the general limit of 12 hours. Any inconsistency with the WIFC is avoided as a result of the lack of application of the urgent-work exception in the case of fishers.

47 s 20(2).

48 s 20(2) as amended by the Minister in 2016

49 s 21(1).

shifts are worked",[50] were the Minister to declare fisheries-related operations to be continuous operations and "permit the working of continuous shift in respect of those operations".[51]

The position with regard to public holidays is different in that an employer may not require or permit an employee to perform any work at all on such days, unless the employer is exempted from this prohibition.[52] Two of the exceptions are "urgent work" and "work in which continuous shifts are worked",[53] the former being at the moment, as already indicated earlier, the only ground that is relevant as far as fishers are concerned. In addition, "[a]n employer may apply in writing to the Permanent Secretary to approve work on a public holiday if the employees affected by the application agree".[54]

Finally, the LA requires that an employer "give an employee who works continuously for more than five hours a meal interval of at least one hour".[55] In the case of fishers, that requirement was reduced to "at least 30 minutes for every five hours of continuous work".[56] The WIFC is silent in that regard.

The South African position

In South Africa, the Basic Conditions of Employment Act (BCEA)[57] sets minimum terms and conditions for employment, including hours of work, that are generally applicable to all employees.[58] However, chapter 2 of the BCEA, which relates to the regulation of working time, does not apply to persons employed on

---

50 s 21(2)(f). See also s 21(2)(g), which allows for exemptions to be granted by the Permanent Secretary.

51 s 15(1).

52 s 22(1).

53 s 22(2)(a) and (f).

54 s 22(3) In terms of s 22(4), "[i]f the Permanent Secretary grants the application, the Permanent Secretary must issue a notice in writing stipulating[:] (a) the nature of the work to which the notice applies; and (b) any conditions that may apply".

55 s 18(1).

56 ibid as amended by the Minister in 2016

57 75 of 1997.

58 Du Toit, Godfrey, Cooper, Giles, Cohen, Conradie and Steenkamp *Labour Relations Law* (2015) 588. The word "employee" is defined in s 1 of the Act to mean: "(a) any person, excluding an independent contractor, who works for another person or for the State and who receives, or is entitled to receive, any remuneration; and (b) any other person who in any manner assists in carrying on or conducting the business of an employer…".

vessels at sea in respect of which the Merchant Shipping Act (MSA-SA)[59] applies,[60] that is, primarily, "vessels which are registered or licensed in the Republic or which in terms of [the MSA-SA] are required to be so licensed[,] wherever such vessels may be".[61] As far as those vessels are concerned, hours of work are regulated by the Merchant Shipping (Safe Manning, Training and Certification) Regulations, 2013,[62] as amended in 2015.[63] Regulation 93 compels masters and owners to "take account of the danger posed by fatigue of seafarers, especially those whose duties involve the safe and secure operation of that ship".[64] With this imperative in mind, "[a]ll persons who are assigned duty as officer in charge of a watch or as a rating forming part of a watch and those whose duties involve designated safety, prevention of pollution and security duties" must "be provided with a rest period of not less than: (a) a minimum of 10 hours of rest in any 24-hour period; and (b) 77 hours in any 7-day period".[65] Hours of rest may not be divided into "more than two periods, one of which [must] be at least six hours in length", while "the intervals between consecutive periods of rest [may] not exceed 14 hours".[66] Those requirements "need not be maintained in the case of an emergency or in other overriding operational conditions".[67] In this regard, the regulation makes it clear that it does not

> "impair the right of the master of a ship to require a seafarer to perform any hours of work necessary for the immediate safety of the ship, persons on board or cargo, or for

---

59 57 of 1951.

60 s 3(3) of the BCEA.

61 s 3(4) of the MSA-SA. Fishers were excluded from the BCEA in view of their unique working conditions, which do not make the Act compatible with the fishing industry.

62 made in terms of s 356 of the MSA-SA and published under GN R511 in GG 36688 of 23-07-2013.

63 See the Merchant Shipping (Safe Manning, Training and Certification) Amendment Regulations, 2015 (GN R544 in GG 38912 of 25-06-2015).

64 reg 93(1).

65 reg 93(2). See also reg 93(5).

66 reg 93(3). Compare reg 93(11), in terms of which "[t]he hours of rest provided for in subreg 2 may be divided into no more than three periods, one of which shall be at least six hours in length and neither of the other two periods shall be less than one hour in length. The intervals between consecutive periods of rest shall not exceed 14 hours. Exceptions shall not extend beyond two 24-hour periods in any 7-day period".

67 reg 93(4), which adds that "[m]usters, fire-fighting and lifeboat drills, and drills prescribed by national laws and regulations and by international instruments, shall be conducted in a manner that minimizes the disturbance of rest periods and does not induce fatigue". In terms of reg 93(6), "[i]f a seafarer is on call, such as when a machinery space is unattended, the seafarer shall have an adequate compensatory rest period if the normal period of rest is disturbed".

the purpose of giving assistance to other ships or persons in distress at sea. Accordingly, the master may suspend the schedule of hours of rest and require a seafarer to perform any hours of work necessary until the normal situation has been restored. As soon as practicable after the normal situation has been restored, the master shall ensure that any seafarers who have performed work in a scheduled rest period are provided with an adequate period of rest".[68]

In addition, "[t]he master or owners may allow exceptions from the required hours of rest [...] provided that the rest period is not less than 70 hours in any 7-day period".[69] However, "[e]xceptions from the weekly rest period [may] not be allowed for more than two consecutive weeks" and "[t]he intervals between two periods of exceptions on board [may] not be less than twice the duration of the exception".[70]

A comparison of regulation 93 with articles 13 and 14 of the WIFC shows that the former is consistent with the latter. Although regulation 93 aims at incorporating into South African law the provisions of regulation 2.3 of the 2006 Maritime Labour Convention,[71] which does not apply to fishers,[72] there is no doubt that it applies to fishers because, for instance, it contains an Annex 2, which governs the watchkeeping principles and arrangements for fishing vessels.[73] In addition, fishers' working hours may be governed by sectoral determinations made by the Minister in accordance with chapter eight of the BCEA and published by notice in the *Gazette*.[74] Because no determination has been made to date with regard to fishers, hours of work for fishers are regulated by contractual agreement between employer and employee, the latter's freedom in that regard being limited when they are part of the Bargaining Council for the Fishing Industry or the Statutory Council for the Squid industry.[75]

---

68   reg 93(8). See par 2.1 above.

69   reg 93(9).

70   reg 93(10). See further reg 93(7) and (12)–(16).

71   (2014) 53 *ILM* 937. Adopted: 23-02-2006; EIF: 20-08-2013. The Regulations are mandatory in terms of art VI(1) of the Convention.

72   See art II(4).

73   See also Marine Notice No 13 of 2018.

74   s 3(3).

75   See par 4.3 below.

REGULATION OF REMUNERATIONS

The international position

The WIFC is silent on wages and commissions. The only indirect reference to wages is to be found in two provisions that relate to payment of fishers. Article 23 requires that States that have ratified the WIFC "adopt laws, regulations or other measures providing that fishers who are paid a wage are ensured a monthly or other regular payment". Article 24 requires that all fishers working on board fishing vessels "be given a means to transmit all or part of their payments received, including advances, to their families at no cost".

The silence of the WIFC may be explained by the fact that the manner in which wages of fishers are calculated makes it difficult to regulate them. Indeed, there are two types of payment systems, as well as a combination of both, in the commercialised fishing industry. In the flat wage system, a fixed salary is paid per pay period. In the share system, "fishers earn a percentage of the gross revenue or profit of the particular fishing trip. Sometimes fishers may be paid a low minimum wage, with the rest of their pay being based on a share of the catch or on bonuses (for example, for finding fish)".[76]

The Namibian position

One of the complaints of Namibian fishers has been that they are paid wages too low for the work done. They can find no assistance in that regard in the LA because it does not contain any provision relating to the minimum wage. Such a wage has been set in a few sectors by means of collective agreements, some of which have been prescribed for the whole sector either by means of an extension by the Minister[77] or by means of a wage order.[78] However, no such agreement exists in the case of the fisheries sector.

---

76 ILO "International Labour Standards on Fishers" (undated) https://www.ilo.org/global/standards/subjects-covered-by-international-labour-standards/fishers/lang--en/index.htm (25-08-2019).

77 in terms of s 71(5) of the LA. See, for instance, the 2018 Exten[s]ion of Collective Agreement on Conditions of Employment for Construction Industry (GN 65 in GG 6567 of 11-04-2018).

78 in terms of s 13(1) of the LA. See, for instance, the 2017 Wage Order for Setting Minimum Wage and Supplemental Minimum Conditions of Employment for Domestic Workers (GN 258 in GG 6428 of 29-09-2017).

The LA only goes as far as to provide that an employee is entitled to an additional payment of 6 percent of his basic hourly wage, excluding overtime work, for each hour of work the employee performs between 20:00 and 07:00.[79] There appears to be no reason why fishers who have shifts at night should not also be entitled to such a benefit. Likewise, the LA applies to fishers when it provides that an employee who works on Sundays is entitled to double his basic hourly wage for each hour worked,[80] unless the employee agrees to being paid only one and a half of his or her hourly basic wage in exchange for being granted an equal period of time away from work during the next succeeding working week.[81] By contrast, an employee who ordinarily works on Sundays, which does not appear to be the case of fishers, is entitled to his or her "daily remuneration plus the basic hourly wage for each hour worked".[82]

A public holiday is a paid holiday in terms of the LA. Fishers who are paid a monthly wage, and would therefore ordinarily work on a day on which a public holiday falls, are entitled either, when they do not work on such a public holiday, to no less than their daily remuneration[83] or, when they do work on such a public holiday, to their normal daily remuneration plus their hourly basic wage for each hour worked.[84] However, in the latter case, the employee and the employer may agree that the employee will be paid his or her "normal daily remuneration plus one half of that employee's hourly basic wage for each hour worked" and will be granted "an equal period of time from work during the next working week".[85] It is clear that the above only applies to fishers who are paid a wage per voyage when

---

79   s 19(1).

80   s 21(5).

81   s 21(6).

82   s 21(7). In terms of s 21(8), "if the majority of the hours worked on a shift that extends into or begins on a Sunday falls on[:] (a) the Sunday, all the hours on that shift are deemed to have been worked on Sunday; or (b) the Saturday or Monday, all the hours on that shift are deemed to have been worked on that Saturday or Monday".

83   s 22(5)(a)(i). In terms of s 22(6), "[i]f an employee who does not work on a public holiday fails, without a valid reason, to work on either the day immediately before, or the day immediately following, that public holiday, the employer is not required to pay that employee the amount otherwise required in terms of subsection (5)(a)(i)".

84   s 22(5)(a)(ii). In terms of s 22(7), "[i]f an employee works on a public holiday that falls on a day other than the employee's ordinary work day, the employer must pay double that employee's hourly basic wage for each hour worked".

85   s 22(5)(b)(ii). See further s 22(8).

a public holiday falls during the voyage and, inevitably, they are expected to work on that day.

The LA does provide that, where an employee works overtime, the employer must pay the employee "for each hour of overtime worked at a rate of at least one and a half times the employee's hourly basic wage", the rate being at least double that employee's hourly basic wage when the employee works ordinarily on a Sunday or public holiday and does work overtime on such a Sunday or public holiday.[86] This means that fishers must be paid at least one and a half times their hourly basic wage for at most the 35 hours of overtime in a week that they are normally allowed to work. It is doubtful that fishers are ever entitled to the rate applying to overtime work on a Sunday because either they are not expected to work regularly on such days or fisheries operations may be regarded as "continuous operations"[87] during which Sundays are treated as normal working days.[88]

As far as remunerated shore leave is concerned, the LA provides, "[u]pon the return of a fisher from sea, the employer must grant the fisher paid shore leave, calculated as follows: (i) one full day for every seven days worked at sea; and (ii) a fraction of a day calculated on a pro rata basis for less than seven days worked at sea".[89]

Fishers' commissions are determined at the company level, resulting in some fishers being paid higher commissions than those paid to other fishers. This has, to various degrees, a negative impact on compliance with the provisions relating to hours of work because fishers are prepared to work longer hours than permitted in order to catch as much quality fish as possible with a view to earning a higher commission.

With regard to the settlement of wages and commissions, the LA requires that an employer

"pay to an employee any monetary remuneration to which the employee is entitled –

---

86   s 17(2)

87   See s 15(1)

88   See minutes of meeting in authors' file

89   See s 20(2) as varied by the 2016 Ministerial Variation

(a) not later than one hour after completion of the ordinary hours of work on the normal pay day, which may be daily, weekly, fortnightly or monthly;

(b) in cash, or, at the employee's option, by cheque, and the payment must be either –

(i)   to the employee; or

(ii)   by direct deposit into an account designated in writing by that employee…".[90]

The Merchant Shipping Act (MSA-NA),[91] which applies, primarily, to "vessels which are registered or licensed in Namibia or which in terms of [the MSA-NA] are required to be so licensed[,] wherever such vessels may be",[92] goes some way towards ensuring consistency between Namibian law and article 24 WIFC when it provides that

"[i]f the balance of wages earned by but not yet payable to a seaman[93] of a Namibian ship is more than 50 rand and the seaman expresses to the master of the ship his desire to have facilities afforded to him for remitting all or any part of the balance to a savings bank, or to a near relative in whose favour an allotment note may be made, the master [must] give to the seaman all reasonable facilities for so doing so far as regards so much of the balance as is in excess of 50 rand, but shall be under no obligation to give those facilities while the ship is in port if the sum will become payable before the ship leaves port, or otherwise than conditionally upon the seaman going to sea in the ship".[94]

Thus, while the MSA-NA gives fishers working on board fishing vessels "a means to transmit all or part of their payments received, including advances, to their families", it does not go as far as requiring that it be "at no cost" as stated in article 24 WIFC.

---

90   See s 11(1)(a)–(b) See further ss 11(1)(c) and (2)–(4).

91   57 of 1951·

92   s 3(4).

93   In terms of s 2(1), the word "seaman" means "any person (except a master, pilot or apprentice-officer) employed or engaged in any capacity as a member of the crew of a ship".

94   s 128.

The South African position

A national minimum wage was introduced in South Africa when the National Minimum Wage Act (NMWA)[95] came into effect. The Act applies "to all workers and their employers" almost without exception.[96] For the purposes of the Act, a worker is "any person who works for another and who receives, or is entitled to receive, any payment for that work whether in money or in kind" and the word "wage" means "the amount of money paid or payable to a worker in respect of ordinary hours of work or, if they are shorter, the hours a worker ordinarily works in a day or a week".[97] In turn, the term "ordinary hours of work" means "the hours of work permitted in terms of section 9 of the Basic Conditions of Employment Act or in terms of any agreement in terms of section 11 or 12 of the Basic Conditions of Employment Act".[98] This cross-reference to the BCEA might appear to be problematical in the case of fishers because sections 9, 11 and 12 are within chapter 2 of the BCEA which, as already mentioned earlier, does not, in principle, apply to fishers. However, that issue has been addressed by the legislator through an amendment of section 3(3) of the BCEA resulting in chapter 2 applying also to persons employed on vessels at sea for purposes of the NMWA.

Regarding the settlement of wages and commissions, the NMWA and BCEA are silent on the matter. This matter is regulated in terms of the MSA-SA in the same way as in the MSA-NA.[99]

NORMATIVE MECHANISMS

The international position

The "right to freedom of association with others, including the right to form and join trade unions for the protection of [one's] interests" is recognised by the

---

95   9 of 2018.

96   s 3(1). The workers to whom the Act does not apply are the "members of the South African National Defence Force, the National Intelligence Agency and the South African Secret Service".

97   s 1.

98   ibid.

99   s 128 of the MSA-SA.

1966 International Covenant on Civil and Political Rights[100] as well as a number
of other international instruments, including the 1981 African Charter on Human
and Peoples' Rights[101] and three ILO conventions, among which is the WIFC.[102]
While the freedom of association ensures that workers and employers can associate
to negotiate work relations efficiently, sound collective bargaining practices assist
in creating a uniform industry standard regarding conditions of employment and
the right to collective bargaining is recognised in the WIFC by reference to the
1949 ILO Right to Organise and Collective Bargaining Convention (No 98).[103]

The Namibian position

In Namibia, the right to form or join trade unions is guaranteed by the
Constitution.[104] This right is expanded upon by the LA when it provides that
workers have the right to be members of a trade union and to participate in
lawful trade union activities.[105] In terms of the LA, a registered trade union
that represents the majority of the employees in an appropriate bargaining unit
is entitled to recognition as the exclusive bargaining agent of the employees in
that bargaining unit to negotiate a collective agreement on any matter of mutual
interest.[106] A trade union can seek recognition as the exclusive bargaining agent
of an appropriate bargaining unit by drafting a request in the prescribed form and
submitting it to the employer as well as the Labour Commissioner.[107] Within 30
days, the employer then has to notify the union, in the prescribed form, whether
the request was successful or not, if he or she does not want the matter to be dealt
with by the Labour Commissioner.[108]

---

100 999 *UNTS* 172. Adopted: 16-12-1966; EIF: 23-03-1976. See art 22(1).

101 (1982) 21 *ILM* 58. Adopted: 27-06-1981; EIF: 21-10-1986. See art 10.

102 See the fourth preambular par.

103 See n 10.

104 art 21(e).

105 s 6(1)(d)–(e).

106 s 64(1).

107 s 64(3).

108 s 64(6).

The LA does make provision for sectoral bargaining and sectoral agreements,[109] which were reached in a few economic sectors, such as the agricultural sector and the construction sector. This approach has allowed for the establishment of standards that apply across the sectors concerned. Unfortunately, no sectoral bargaining and sectoral agreement have been concluded for the fisheries sector to date.

The South African position

Institutional framework

Section 18 of the South African Constitution entrenches everyone's right to freedom of association.[110] This right provides the framework within which employees and their trade unions as well as employers and employers' organisations can collectively bargain to determine hours of work, wages, and other terms and conditions of employment.[111] As mentioned earlier, many provisions of the BCEA are not compatible with the fisheries sector due to the unique working conditions of fishers. South Africa established a Bargaining Council for the Fisheries Industry (BCFI), which now caters for six fisheries subsectors, and a Statutory Council for the Squid and Related Fisheries (SCS).[112] These structures were formed when employers and trade unions decided to cooperate towards their establishment in order to shift the bargaining power from the employers to a more equal footing between employers and the representatives of fishers. The establishment of the bargaining council and the statutory council were key milestones in the history of the South African fishing industry.

The BCFI negotiates the basic conditions of employment for fishers. For example, the Council: sets the hours of work and regulates rest and leave periods; sets the daily wages for each category of fisher; determines benefits such as protective clothing and those related to death and disability; regulates annual

---

109 s 71(2).

110 The right to freedom of association is regulated in a detailed fashion in ch II of the LRA.

111 Du Toit (n 58) 29.

112 For the variation of the BCFI main agreement that adds three subsectors to the original three, see GN R1007, R1008 and R1009 in *GG* 41131 of 22-09-2017.

leave, sick leave, maternity leave and family responsibility leave; decides how fishers are appointed and their employment terminated; and fixes the minimum age of employees. The BCFI also negotiates on behalf of fishers minimum social-welfare standards relating to medical care, health protection and social security. As a result, the BCFI main agreement[113] is the vehicle through which it is possible, when necessary, to make international standards and those of the BCEA applicable, by means of an extension of the agreement, to the whole subsector concerned as the minimum common denominator for all agreements at plant level.[114]

As indicated above, the SCS is also in place.[115] The Council is one of the statutory councils established in terms of the LRA in areas or sectors of an industry where no bargaining councils exist.[116] The functions of the statutory councils are to: perform dispute resolution functions; promote and establish training and education schemes; establish and administer pension, provident, medical aid, sick pay, holiday, unemployment schemes or funds and any similar schemes or funds for the benefit of one or more parties to the council; conclude collective agreements to give effect to any of the functions mentioned above.[117] In effect, a statutory council is similar to a bargaining council except that it has less power. For example, the SCS cannot currently negotiate wages for fishers within its jurisdiction. Those negotiations take place at plant level. However, the SCS can negotiate other conditions of employment just like the BCFI. In due course, once the SCS' parties represent the majority of fishers in the sector, the council will be replaced by a bargaining council, with the result that it will then be possible to negotiate wages potentially for the whole sector. That route has not been followed yet, but the SCS main agreement has nevertheless been extended to the whole subsector.[118]

Unfortunately, not all the fisheries subsectors are covered within the ambit of the BCFI and the SCS. The fishers who are not covered are in an unequal

---

113 GN R587 in GG 35549 of 27-07-2012.

114 GN R9 in GG 41371 of 05-01-2018.

115 See Statutory Council for Squid and Related Fisheries in South Africa "The Squid Council" (undated) https://www.squidcouncil.co.za/ (26-09-2018).

116 See ss 39(2) and 40.

117 s 43(1).

118 GN R1101 in GG 42658 of 23-08-2019.

bargaining position with prospective employers and, therefore, more vulnerable than the other employees.

Hours of work

The main agreement of the BCFI provides that an employer should not allow a fisher to work in excess of 14 hours per day.[119] In addition, the employer may not allow a fisher to work more than 5 hours continuously without a rest interval of at least 30 minutes.[120] The hours of rest must be in line with the occupational-health-and-safety legislation and the SAMSA regulations.[121]

The employer must, at the end of every voyage, grant a fisher 4 hours paid shore leave for every 24 hours that the fisher was at sea.[122] "Shore leave may be taken at the conclusion of a trip at the discretion of the employer[,] provided in the event of shore leave being granted away from the employee['s] homeport then the employer [is] responsible for the transport to the fishers' homeport".[123] The fisher and the employer can enter into any alternative written agreement dealing with shore leave.[124] This is in line with the international standards set in terms of the WIFC.

The main agreement of the SCS[125] does not cover matters relating to hours of work, probably due to the unpredictable nature of activities within the squid fishing industry. In the absence of any provision, fishers in that industry do not enjoy any more protection than the one afforded by regulation 93 which, as already indicated, conforms to the standard for hours of rest set by the WIFC.

---

119 clause 16.1.

120 clause 16.2.

121 clause 17.1. See s 17(7) of the Occupational Health and Safety Act (85 of 1993) as well as reg 93 of the Merchant Shipping (Safe Manning, Training and Certification) Regulations, 2013, discussed above.

122 clause 17.2.

123 clause 17.4. See also clause 17.3.

124 clause 17.5.

125 Collective Agreement on the Minimum Conditions of Employment of the Statutory Council for the Squid and Related Fisheries of South Africa of 11 April 2019 (GN R1101 in GG 42658 of 23-08-2019).

Regulation of remunerations

The MSA-SA provides that, when there is an agreement in place on board a fishing vessel with the employer covering wages agreed to under a registered bargaining council or statutory council in terms of the LRA, the terms of that agreement apply to the fisher.[126] In terms of the BCFI main agreement, industry minimum wages are set and periodically reviewed.[127] On that basis, each fishery sector constitutes a separate chamber and engages through collective bargaining in annual negotiations around salaries and conditions of employment. The main agreement of the BCFI appears to be consistent with article 23 of the WIFC when it provides that "the employer shall pay the employee all the remuneration due to him … at least once every 30 days".[128] By contrast, the agreement does not prescribe, as required by article 24 of the WIFC, that remittance by fishers of their wages to their families take place "at no cost".

As indicated above, the negotiation of wages is not within the SCS powers. It is possible that the Council's constitution[129] might be changed in such a way that it will in future serve as the forum for wage discussions or negotiations. Nonetheless, this does not prevent wage conditions from being negotiated between employers and trade unions.

CONCLUSION

Ensuring decent working conditions for fishers is essential to protect them from exploitation and being left in a vulnerable state. To this end, the ILO has taken the lead in improving the working conditions of fishers by facilitating the adoption of the WIFC. The latter is applicable to all types of commercial fishing and seeks to provide acceptable minimum standards that protect fishers in all aspects of their work. As a party to the WIFC, Namibia has a duty to implement the

---

126 s 102 (5)(b).

127 See the present rates in GN R9 in *GG* 41371 of 05-01-2018.

128 clause 10.3. In terms a 23, "[e]ach Member, after consultation, shall adopt laws, regulations or other measures providing that fishers who are paid a wage are ensured a monthly or regular payment".

129 Squid Council "The constitution of the Statutory Council for the Squid Industry" (undated) http://www.squidcouncil.co.za/wp-content/uploads/2014/06/Statutory_Council_Constitution.pdf (24-12-2018).

provisions of the Convention immediately, except in some cases where progressive implementation is allowed.[130]

The WIFC provides minimum standards on hours of work and wages. Namibia has taken progressive steps to align its legislation with the WIFC standards with the introduction of the 2016 variation notice that deals with hours of work.[131] The position with regard to wages is less easy to establish because the WIFC does not deal directly with that issue. The LA does ensure that employers provide fishers with a monthly or other regular payment.[132] At the same time, Namibia does not comply fully with article 24, which requires that fishers working on board fishing vessels "be given a means to transmit all or part of their payments received, including advances, to their families at no cost".

Though Namibia's legislative framework conforms to the minimum standards of the WIFC, except for article 24, there are lessons that Namibia can learn from South Africa's approach. In South Africa, a bargaining council and a statutory council have been established to regulate the minimum conditions of employment for the fishers employed in some subsectors of the fishing industry and the fishers concerned enjoy greater protection than the one enjoyed by fishers to whom the relevant agreements do not apply. There are provisions for similar structures in the LA and, therefore, there is no regulatory obstacle to the Namibian fishing industry making use of such structures to negotiate better conditions of employment than those required by the WIFC. Should those structures be established, it is hoped that the conditions of employment agreed under their auspices, including a minimum wage, would apply to all Namibian fishers.

130 See a 4.

131 See par 2.2 above.

CO-OPERATIVE GOVERNMENT IN MARINE SPATIAL PLANNING

RACHAEL CHASAKARA*

PATRICK VRANCKEN**

---

*   LLD candidate, Nelson Mandela University.

** Professor in Public Law and holder of the NRF Research Chair in the Law of the Sea and Development in a Africa, Nelson Mandela University.

INTRODUCTION

Oceans play a vital role for humankind because they are not only a major source of proteins, but they are also essential to trade while providing energy, employment and recreation. Marine ecosystems provide many goods and services on which all living organisms rely. The range of ecosystem goods and services include carbon sequestration, nutrient cycling, coastal protection through coral reefs or phanerogams, provision of food as well as grounds for tourism.[1] Yet, although the oceans are of paramount importance, their health is on a serious decline. Multiple stressors, such as overfishing and pollution, compromise the ability of the ocean and coastal ecosystems to support and sustain the goods and services people want and need.[2] Scientists have warned that "the loss of marine biodiversity is increasingly impairing the ocean's ability to produce seafood, resist diseases, filter pollutants, maintain water quality and recover from perturbations such as overfishing and climate change".[3]

Various studies have shown growth in existing and emerging human uses of the ocean. Once ostensibly empty, oceans are now subject to growing competition for finite space from a range of different sectors.[4] Globally, the increased pressure on the ocean space and the finite nature of resources have led to two types of conflict. The first involves conflicts between users competing for the same ocean space while their activities are not compatible and have adverse effects on each

---

1   Borja "Grand challenges in marine ecosystems ecology" 2014 1 *Frontiers in Marine Science* 1 3 and United Nations Environmental Programme World Conservation Monitoring Centre (UNEP-WCMC) *Marine and Coastal Ecosystem Services: Valuation Methods and their Practical Application* (2011) 3 and 8.

2   Foley, Halpern, Micheli, Armsby, Caldwell, Crain, Prahler, Rohr, Sivas, Beck, Carr, Crowder, Duffy, Hacker, McLeod, Palumbi, Peterson, Regan, Ruckelshaus, Sandifer and Steneck "Guiding ecological principles for marine spatial planning" 2010 *Marine Policy (MP)* 955.

3   Worm, Barbier, Beaumont, Duffy, Folke, Halpern, Jackson, Lotze, Micheli, Palumbi, Sala, Selkoe, Stachowicz and Watson "Impacts of biodiversity loss on ocean ecosystem services" 2006 *Science* 787.

4   White Paper on the National Environmental Management of Oceans GG 37692 of 29 May 2014 (NEMO) 1; Lu, Liu, Xiang, Song and McIlgorm "A comparison of marine spatial planning approaches in China: Marine functional zoning and the marine ecological red line" 2015 *MP* 94; Intergovernmental Oceanographic Commission (IOC) *Marine Spatial Planning: A Step-by-step Approach toward Ecosystem-based Management* (2009) 12; European Commission *Legal Aspects of Maritime Spatial Planning* (2008) 1; and Halpern, Frazier, Potapenko, Casey, Koeng, Longo, Lowndes, Rockwood, Selg, Selkoe and Walbridge "Spatial and temporal changes in cumulative human impacts on the world's ocean" 2015 *Nature Communications* 1.

other.[5] The second involves conflicts resulting from the fact that the increased level of human activities in the ocean space has resulted in a substantial and largely irreversible loss or damage to the diversity of natural life.[6] These conflicts jeopardise the ability of the ocean to provide the necessary ecosystem goods and services upon which humans depend.[7]

All those conflicts are caused largely by failures in the governance of the ocean space. Addressing them requires more effective governance systems.[8] Until now, ocean space has been regulated and allocated within individual economic sectors (sectoral zoning).[9] The problem with this approach is that regulation and management are done on a case-by-case basis without adequate consideration of the effects of the activities concerned on other human activities and the marine environment.[10]

It is now generally agreed that the future of the ocean requires the successful implementation of a comprehensive governance framework that replaces the sector-by-sector management approach with a proactive and holistic approach that accounts for all aspects and sectors of ocean governance.[11] The relatively new notion of marine spatial planning (MSP)[12] has emerged as a means to develop such a framework.[13] This chapter starts by providing a background to

5   Douvere and Ehler "New perspectives on sea-use management: initial findings from European experience with marine spatial planning" 2009 90 *Journal of Environmental Management* 77; Soininen "Planning the marine area spatially – A reconciliation of competing interests?" 2012 *International Environmental Law-making and Diplomacy Review* 85.

6   Intergovernmental Oceanographic Commission and the Man and the Biosphere Programme *Visions for a Sea Change* (2006) 8.

7   IOC (n 4) 19.

8   Crowder, Osherenko, Young, Airamè, Norse, Baron, Day, Douvere, Ehler, Halpern, Langdon, McLeod, Ogden, Peach, Rosenberg and Wilson "Sustainability. Resolving the mismatches in US ocean governance" 2006 *Science* 617; Hassan, Kuokkanen and Soininen "Marine spatial planning as an instrument of sustainable ocean governance" in Hassan, Kuokkanen and Soininen (eds) *Transboundary Marine Spatial Planning and International Law* (2015) 3; Couzens *et al* (n 5) 85.

9   Douvere "The importance of marine spatial planning in advancing ecosystem-based sea use management" 2008 *MP* 762 762.

10   ibid.

11   Foley *et al* (n 2) 956.

12   Note that there are differences in the terminologies used by different initiatives with regard to planning at sea. These include "maritime spatial planning", which is used by the European Union Commission, "marine planning" used in the United Kingdom and "coastal planning" used in the state of Victoria, Australia. The term "marine spatial planning" is used in this chapter because it is the terminology used in the South African legislation.

13   Kovacic, Zekic and Rukavina "Maritime spatial planning in Croatia - Necessity or opportunity for balanced development" 2016 *Scientific Journal of Maritime Research* 82 82.

the MSP framework. It then describes the constitutional co-operative governance framework before it explores the relationship between the two frameworks.

BACKGROUND

The key priorities of eliminating poverty while reducing unemployment and inequality, led South Africa to put forward a National Development Plan: Vision for 2030 (NDP).[14] The Plan calls for South Africa to develop strategic frameworks for environmental sustainability and inclusive economic growth.[15] One of the mechanisms put in place by the South African government to implement the NDP is Operation *Phakisa*,[16] a fast-track government initiative intended to provide solutions to the critical development issues.[17] One of the aspects of Operation *Phakisa* involves a unique initiative to address poverty, unemployment and inequality through the ocean economy.[18] That initiative is taking place with the policy framework set out in the White Paper on the National Environmental Management of Oceans (NEMO),[19] which recognises that various marine resources in South Africa's ocean space provide significant potential for the unlocking of further economic development opportunities.[20] For the purpose of seizing those opportunities, a well-implemented MSP process was identified as necessary to enable the maximisation of socio-economic benefits whilst providing adequate environmental protection.[21]

---

14 Republic of South Africa *White Paper on Reconstruction and Development* (GN 1954 in GG 16085 of 15-11-1994) 7; National Planning Commission *Diagnostic Report* (19 March 2015) 1; National Planning Commission *NDP: Vision for 2030* (2012) 14.

15 National Planning Commission *NDP: Vision for 2030* (2012) 47-48.

16 *Phakisa* means "hurry up" in Sesotho, and this initiative was designed to fast track the implementation of solutions on critical development issues that are highlighted in the NDP 2030 such as poverty, unemployment and inequality. Department of Planning, Monitoring and Evaluation "Operation Phakisa" (undated) http://www.operationphakisa. gov.za/Pages/Home.aspx (13-09-2019).

17 ibid.

18 ibid.

19 (n 4).

20 NEMO (n 4) i.

21 Republic of South Africa "*Operation Phakisa: Unlocking the Economic Potential of South Africa's Oceans*" (2014) 9 https://www.operationphakisa.gov.za/operations/oel/pmpg/Marine%20Protection%20and%20Govenance%20 Documents/Marine%20Protection%20and%20Govenance/OPOceans%20MPSG%20Executive%20Summary.pdf (13-09-2019).

The first step in the process was the drafting of a Marine Spatial Planning Bill (MSPB). Subsequent to the publication of the first draft of the Bill in 2016,[22] the Framework on Marine Spatial Planning in South Africa (MSPF) was published in 2017.[23] The MSPF contributed to the legislative drafting process by formulating goals, objectives and principles expected to facilitate the development, implementation and revision of marine area plans. When it comes into effect, the Marine Spatial Planning Act (MSPA)[24] will constitute the statutory basis for MSP by providing for the development of marine spatial plans as well as the institutional arrangements necessary for the implementation of those plans and the governance of ocean activities by users in multiple sectors.[25]

The decisions made on the basis of the MSPA will not only have direct implications for the country's maritime zones, which are almost exclusively under the jurisdiction of the national sphere of government,[26] but will also have indirect consequences for the coastal land areas over which the provincial and local spheres of government have jurisdiction. For that reason, it is imperative that those decisions "respect the constitutional status, institutions, powers and functions of government" in all the spheres and that, when taking or implementing those decisions, no organ exercises its powers or performs its functions in a manner that encroaches "on the geographical, functional or institutional integrity of government in another sphere".[27] To that end, Chapter 3 of the Constitution entrenches several principles of co-operative government and intergovernmental relations.

CO-OPERATIVE GOVERNANCE

Introduction

The principle of co-operative governance is nested in several provisions of the Constitution. Section 1 proclaims that the Republic of South Africa is "one

---

22 GN 347 in *GG* 39847 of 24-03-2016.
23 GN 451 in *GG* 40860 of 26-05-2017.
24 16 of 2018.
25 See long title.
26 Vrancken *South Africa and the Law of the Sea* (2011) 34-47.
27 s 41(1)(e) and (g) of the Constitution.

sovereign, democratic state". The unitarian weight this provision carries is balanced by the provisions of chapter 3 which emphasise that "governmental power is not located in national entities alone".[28] This is made clear in section 40(1), which explains that government is constituted as three "distinctive, interdependent and interrelated" spheres, namely the national, provincial and local spheres of government. The Constitutional Court in *Independent Electoral Commission v Langberg Municipality* explained that

> "[a]ll spheres are interdependent and interrelated in the sense that the functional areas allocated to each sphere cannot be seen in isolation of each other. They are all interrelated. None of these spheres of government ... have any independence from each other. Their interrelatedness and interdependence is such that they must ensure that, while they do not tread on each other's toes, they understand that all of them perform governmental functions for the benefit of the people of the country as a whole".[29]

In other words, the principle of cooperative governance requires that the three spheres of government cooperate with one another, consult one another, support one another and coordinate their actions and legislation with one another. The Intergovernmental Relations Framework Act (IRFA)[30] gives effect to chapter 3 by providing structures and institutions to promote and facilitate intergovernmental relations.[31]

The national sphere of government

In the national sphere of government, legislative authority vests in Parliament[32] and the executive authority vests in the President, who exercises that authority together with the other members of the Cabinet.[33]

The national sphere of government has legislative and executive jurisdiction over the whole national territory, which would appear to include

---

28 *Ex Parte President of RSA: In re constitutionality of the Liquor Bill* 2000 (1) SA 732 (CC) 39.

29 2001 (3) SA 925 (CC) 18.

30 13 of 2005.

31 See further section 4.3 below.

32 s 43(a) of the Constitution.

33 s 85(1)–(2) of the Constitution.

the South African internal waters and territorial waters.[34] The Constitution provides that Parliament may pass legislation on any matter, including a matter referred to in Schedule 4, but excluding a Schedule 5 matter unless it is a matter in which it may intervene.[35] Schedule 4 Part A of the Constitution contains a list of functional areas in which the national and provincial legislatures have concurrent competence. In other words, both the national and the provincial legislatures are empowered to pass legislation on any matter referred to in Schedule 4 Part A of the Constitution. In *Ex Parte President of RSA: In re Constitutionality of the Liquor Bill*,[36] the Constitutional Court held that one of the purposes of Schedule 4 of the Constitution is to enable the national government to regulate various issues inter-provincially. As far as it is concerned, Schedule 5 contains a list of functional areas of exclusive provincial legislative competence, in which Parliament may nevertheless legislate when "necessary" to maintain security, economic unity or national standards or to prevent a province harming others.[37] In all areas, such as water and minerals, in which the provincial legislatures do not have concurrent or exclusive competence Parliament has exclusive legislative competence.[38]

The Constitution provides a broad definition of the scope of the executive function in that it entails responsibility for the development, preparation and implementation of national policy and legislation as well as for the coordination of the functions of State departments and administrations.[39] This means that the executive is responsible for the execution and implementation of law, policy and administration. In that regard, it is important to note two general mechanisms – "assignment" and "delegation" – whereby legislation might be passed by one sphere

---

34 Vrancken (n 26) 34. Ss 3(2) and 4(2) of the Maritime Zones Act (15 of 1994) make it clear that national legislation applies in the two maritime zones.

35 s 44(1)(a)(ii) and (2) of the Constitution.

36 2000 (1) SA 732 (CC) 26.

37 s 44(2) of the Constitution.

38 Glazewski and Rumble "Administration and governance" in Glazewski (ed) *Environmental Law in South Africa* (2016) par 6.7.2 and s 44(1)(a)(ii) of the Constitution.

39 s 85(2)(a)–(d).

of government but be administered by another.[40] Assignment is the irrevocable transfer of authority, whilst delegation is the revocable transfer of authority.[41] These mechanisms involve legislation being passed by Parliament, but its administration being carried out by one or more provincial or local authorities.

Section 238(a) of the Constitution states that an executive organ in any sphere of government may delegate any power or function that is to be exercised in terms of legislation to any other organ of State, "provided the delegation is consistent with the legislation in terms of which the power is exercised or the function is performed". In addition, section 99 of the Constitution provides that a Cabinet member may assign any power or function that is to be exercised in terms of an Act of Parliament to a member of a provincial executive council or to a municipal council, subject to an agreement between these authorities and to certain conditions. In addition, section 44(1)(a)(iii) provides that Parliament may assign any of its legislative powers to any legislative body in another sphere of government. Finally, Schedule 6 provides that legislation governing a Schedule 4 or 5 matter which was administered by an authority within the national executive when the Constitution took effect, may be assigned by the President by proclamation to an authority within a provincial executive.[42]

The provincial sphere of government

South Africa has nine provinces, four of which are coastal provinces.[43] In the provincial sphere, the legislative authority vests in the provincial legislatures,[44] while the executive authority vests in the Premier, who acts together with other

---

40   In order for the local level of government to exercise a competence of the national or provincial government it has to be assigned such competence by the relevant governmental sphere. This is specifically in relation to environmental matters such as MSP, an issue which is a national and provincial government sphere competence. This competence needs to be assigned to the local government sphere in the relevant legislation so that the local sphere does not act *ultra vires*.

41   Glazewski and Rumble (n 38) par 6.9.

42   item 14(1) of Schedule 6. For example, the whole of the now repealed Sea-shore Act (21 of 1935) was assigned to coastal provinces by proclamation by the President, except s 2 which vested ownership of the sea and sea-shore in the President.

43   the Province of the Eastern Cape, the Province of KwaZulu-Natal, the Province of the Northern Cape and the Province of the Western Cape.

44   s 43(b) of the Constitution.

members of the Executive Council.[45] The provincial sphere of government has legislative and executive jurisdiction over the whole of the relevant provincial territory.[46]

The extent of the legislative competence of the nine provincial legislatures is provided for in section 104(1) of the Constitution, which empowers each provincial legislature to pass a constitution for its province,[47] to pass legislation on Schedules 4 and 5 matters, and to pass legislation on any matter outside those functional areas that is expressly assigned to the province by national legislation. Moreover, section 104(4) of the Constitution provides that provincial legislation that is reasonably necessary for, or incidental to, the effective exercise of power relating to any matter in Schedule 4 is "for all purposes" legislation with regard to that Schedule 4 matter. Over and above their concurrent legislative competences, the provinces enjoy exclusive competences in respect of matters listed in Schedule 5 Part A of the Constitution. As already pointed out, the fact that those competences are "exclusive" does not mean that national government is completely precluded from legislating in these areas.[48]

The above means that, unlike Parliament that has plenary legislative power, provincial legislatures have limited legislative powers. This was confirmed in *Premier: Limpopo Province v Speaker of the Limpopo Provincial Legislature* where the Constitutional Court held that the legislative powers of provinces are expressly restricted to the functional areas set out in Schedule 4 and 5 of the Constitution.[49] In *casu*, the Court decided that a provincial Bill that was enacted on a matter that did not fall within the provincial legislature's competence was unconstitutional and invalid.[50] This decision confirmed one of the principles that underpin co-operative governance, i.e. that no sphere should assume any powers or functions except those conferred on it in terms of the Constitution.[51]

---

45   s 125(1)-(2) of the Constitution.

46   Vrancken (n 26) 38-42.

47   The only provincial Constitution in force is the Constitution of the Western Cape (CWC).

48   Glazewski and Rumble (n 38) par 6.7.3.

49   2011 (11) BCLR 1181 (CC) 21-23.

50   60.

51   s 41(1)(f).

Section 125 of the Constitution sets out how the executive authority of provinces is conducted. This authority includes: the implementation of provincial legislation in the province;[52] the implementation of all national legislation within the functional areas listed in Schedule 4 of the Constitution, except where the Constitution or other legislation provides otherwise;[53] and the administration of national legislation outside the functional areas listed in Schedule 4 and 5 of the Constitution as assigned to the provincial executive in terms of an Act of Parliament.[54] Further relevant provisions are section 99(a) and (b) of the Constitution, which provide that "[a] Cabinet member may assign any power or function that is to be exercised or performed in terms of an Act of Parliament to a member of a provincial Executive Council or to a Municipal Council", subject to an agreement between these authorities and other conditions.

The local sphere of government

The local sphere of government has legislative and executive jurisdiction over the whole of the relevant municipal territory.[55] In that sphere, the legislative authority and the executive authority vest in the municipal councils.[56] The powers of local governments are more limited than the powers of the provinces because they are subject to both the national and provincial legislation.[57]

The Constitution establishes three categories of municipalities, all of which are present along the South African coast. Municipalities that have exclusive municipal executive and legislative authority in their area are classified as category A (metropolitan municipalities).[58] Examples of category A municipalities are the City of Cape Town Metropolitan Municipality, the Nelson Mandela Metropolitan Municipality and the eThekwini Metropolitan Municipality. A local municipality that shares municipal executive and legislative authority in its area with a district

---

52   s 125(2)(a).

53   s 125(2)(b).

54   s 125(2)(c).

55   Vrancken (n 26) 42.

56   ss 43(c) and 151(2) of the Constitution.

57   See s 151(3) of the Constitution. See further Simeon and Murray "Reforming multi-level government in South Africa" 2009 *Canadian Journal of African Studies* 536 544.

58   s 155(1)(a).

municipality (category C) falls within category B type of municipalities (local municipalities).[59] Examples of this category of municipalities are the Kou-Kamma Municipality, the Kouga Municipality, the Sunday's River Valley Municipality and the Ndlambe Municipality. A category C (district) municipality has executive and legislative authority in an area that includes more than one category B municipality.[60] An example is the Sarah Baartman District Municipality.[61]

The Constitution requires each provincial government to establish municipalities in its province in a manner consistent with the legislation that defines "the different types of municipality that may be established within each category",[62] i.e. the Municipal Structures Act ("the Structures Act").[63] Each provincial government must also "provide for the monitoring and support of local government in the province" and "promote the development of local government capacity to enable municipalities to perform their functions and manage their own affairs".[64] The Constitution enumerates the objects of the local government, which are: to provide democratic and accountable government for local communities; to ensure the provision of services to communities in a sustainable manner; to promote social and economic development; to promote a safe and healthy environment; and to encourage the involvement of communities and community organisations in the matters of local government.[65]

The municipal councils of the coastal municipalities have the power to make by-laws and to exercise executive authority for the effective administration of local tourism as well as "[p]ontoons, ferries, jetties, piers and harbours", with the exclusion of the regulation of international and national shipping and matters related thereto.[66] The municipal councils also have the power to make by-laws and to exercise executive authority for the effective administration of beaches, local

---

59   s 155(1)(b).

60   s 155(1)(c).

61   See further Vrancken (n 26) 43-44.

62   s 155(2).

63   117 of 1998.

64   s 155(6).

65   s 152(1).

66   s 156(1)(a) and (2) as well as Schedule 4 Part B of the Constitution.

sports facilities, municipal recreation and public places[67] as well as any other matter assigned to the municipality by national or provincial legislation.[68] Section 156(4) of the Constitution confirms this by requiring that the national and provincial governments assign the administration of any Part A matter listed in Schedule 4 and 5, if the matter would be most effectively administered locally and the municipality has the capacity to administer it.

CO-OPERATIVE GOVERNANCE IN THE MARINE SPATIAL PLANNING CONTEXT

Shared and related functional areas

MSP is not among the functional areas listed in Schedules 4 and 5 of the Constitution. As a result, there is little doubt that legislative authority and executive authority in this area vest solely in the national sphere of government. At the same time, because MSP is a "governance process of collaboratively assessing and managing the spatial and temporal distribution of human activities to achieve economic, social and ecological objectives",[69] it is influenced by, and has an impact on, a number of functional areas listed in Schedules 4 and 5 of the Constitution. These areas include, for instance: the environment, industrial promotion, regional planning and development, tourism, urban and rural development, local tourism, municipal planning, pontoons, ferries, jetties, piers and harbours, and provincial planning.[70] In other words, MSP is an area of exclusive national competence that has a complex relationship with various functional areas of concurrent national and provincial competence and various functional areas of exclusive provincial competence.

The nature of that relationship is affected by the extent of the overlap between the spatial area of jurisdiction of the organs in the national sphere of government, the spatial area of jurisdiction of the organs in the provincial sphere of government and the spatial area of jurisdiction of the organs in the local sphere of

---

67   s 156(1)(a) and (2) as well as Schedule 5 Part B of the Constitution.

68   s 156(1)(b) and (2) of the Constitution.

69   Department of Environment, Forestry and Fisheries *The Approach to Spatial Management System for South Africa's Marine Planning Areas* (2019) 1 (GN 1090 in GG 42657 of 28-08-2019, "the Approach Document").

70   Memorandum on the objects of the MSP Bill par 6.1.

government. However, even were the provincial and local spheres of government not to have any jurisdiction in the internal and territorial waters of the Republic, co-operative governance in MSP would still be required. It is true that there would be no scope for direct encroachment "on the geographical, functional or institutional integrity of government in another sphere"[71] because the spheres of government would not have overlapping areas of jurisdiction. However, there would still be room for a wide range of indirect encroachments, a state of affairs that resulted in the National Environmental Management: Integrated Coastal Management Act (NEMICMA),[72] having as one of its aims to provide, within the framework of the National Environmental Management Act (NEMA),[73] for "the co-ordinated and integrated management of the coastal zone by all spheres of government in accordance with the principles of co-operative governance".[74]

Probably the most obvious example is planning. In that regard, "[t]he Constitution confers different... responsibilities on each of the three spheres of government in accordance with what is appropriate for each sphere"[75] and the complex nature of the relationship between the three spheres of government in this area is acknowledged in the Spatial Planning and Land Use Management Act.[76] While the latter governs spatial planning on land, it is not difficult to envisage how a decision in that regard would have a negative impact on an adjacent marine area and vice-versa.

Another functional area is the environment which, it has been pointed out, "is an ideal example of an area of legislative and executive authority or power which had to reside in all three levels of Government and, therefore, could not be inserted in Parts B of Schedules 4 and 5 and was instead inserted in Part A of

---

71 s 41(1)(g) of the Constitution.

72 24 of 2008.

73 107 of 1998.

74 s 2(b).

75 *City of Johannesburg Metropolitan Municipality v Gauteng Development Tribunal* 2010 (6) SA 182 (CC) 55. The Constitutional Court explained that "[t]he Constitution confers 'planning' on all spheres of government by allocating 'regional planning and development' concurrently to the national and provincial spheres, 'provincial planning' exclusively to the provincial sphere, and executive authority over, and the right to administer 'municipal planning' to the local sphere" (at 56).

76 16 of 2013. See ss 9–11.

Schedule 4".[77] In other words, planning and the environment are two areas in which the drafters of the Constitution did not intend to allocate powers amongst the three spheres of government in "hermetically sealed, distinct and watertight compartments".[78] This rationale is even more compelling should, as seems to be the case, the territories of the coastal provinces and municipalities extend to the adjacent internal and territorial waters and, therefore, the spatial areas of jurisdiction of the three spheres of jurisdiction overlap each other not only on land, but in the South African waters up to the outer limit of the territorial sea.

Co-operative governance in the marine spatial planning instruments

One of the MSP principles proclaimed in the MSPF is the principle of collaboration and responsible ocean governance, which

"recognises that working in sectoral and institutional compartments is an inefficient way to manage marine space and other resources. Horizontal and vertical cooperation and integration within government as well as good administration will lead to stronger and more complementary decisions and actions".[79]

This principle is crucial if South Africa is to reach the MSP goal of contributing to good ocean governance, a goal that "requires a collaborative approach between organs of state relating to the ocean matters, through the establishment of formal and informal relations".[80] On that basis, the MSPF states that "[t]he implementation of the [m]arine [a]rea plans [will build] on the [c]onstitutional principle of cooperative governance"[81] and acknowledges that chapter 3 of the Constitution forms part of the legislative context within which MSP will be undertaken.[82] This means concretely that, during the process of development of the marine area plans,

"coastal management and land-use planning authorities must be informed and

---

77 *Le Sueur v Ethekwini Municipality* 2013 JDR 0178 (KZP) 21.

78 ibid 20. See also *City of Johannesburg Metropolitan Municipality v Gauteng Development Tribunal* 2010 (6) SA 182 (CC) 57.

79 par 28.

80 par 30.

81 par 32.

82 ibid.

properly consulted to ensure that harmonisation of plans is achieved... . Liaison and consultation between respective responsible authorities for terrestrial and marine planning, including plan development, implementation and review will help ensure, for example, that developments in the marine environment are supported by the appropriate infrastructure on land and reflected in terrestrial development plans".[83]

While co-operative governance is thus recognised as one of the main features of the process of development of the marine area plans, there is no mention of organs of State in the provincial and local spheres of government in section 5 of the MSPF - which describes in detail the marine spatial plans' development process - beyond the inclusion of "coastal authorities" among the stakeholders that "will be brought actively into the plan-making process".[84]

The MSPF approach is reflected in the MSPA. "[T]he promotion of collaboration and responsible use of the ocean through consultation and cooperation" is listed in the Act as one of the principles that should be applied and considered in MSP.[85] However, it would seem that, for the purposes of the Act, the principle has the meaning given to it in the MSPF and whether that is the case might well be confirmed in the new MSP framework that will be developed in terms of the Act.[86] In addition, the Act does not require more than that "affected organs of state" be "adequately consulted" during the process of development of the MSP framework and the marine area plans.[87] The manner and form of such consultation might in due course be determined by regulations[88] which, if the implementation of the Act is to be consistent with the Constitution, will possibly take the form of a reference to the relevant provisions of the NEMICMA and the IRFA.

---

83   par 34.

84   par 47.

85   s 5(1)(c).

86   in terms of s 6(a), 9(2)(a) and 12(1). The goal of contributing to good ocean governance is confirmed in the Approach Document (at 2).

87   s 8(1)(b).

88   s 13(c).

Intergovernmental relations frameworks

The IRFA is the Act of Parliament that section 41(2) of the Constitution required to be passed to: (a) "establish or provide for structures and institutions to promote and facilitate intergovernmental relations"; and (b) "provide for appropriate mechanisms and procedures to facilitate settlement of intergovernmental disputes". Accordingly, its stated object is "to provide within the principle of co-operative government set out in Chapter 3 of the Constitution a framework for the national government, provincial governments and local governments, and all organs of state within those governments, to facilitate co-ordination in the implementation of policy and legislation".[89]

IRFA provides for a President's Coordinating Council,[90] which is a consultative forum available to the President to, inter alia: (a) "raise matters of national interest with provincial governments and organised local government and to hear their views on those matters";[91] and (b) "to consult provincial governments and organised local government on … the co-ordination and alignment of priorities, objectives and strategies across national, provincial and local governments".[92] The President might make use of this forum after he or she has received the report on the implementation of MSP that the MSPA requires the Ministerial Committee established in terms of the Act[93] to submit to Cabinet at least every two years.[94] IRFA also provides for national intergovernmental fora, which may be established by any Cabinet member to promote and facilitate intergovernmental relations in the functional area for which that Cabinet member is responsible.[95] Those fora are one option for sector departments to fulfil their duty in terms of the MSPA to "ensure that their respective stakeholders are properly consulted".[96] In the provincial sphere of government, IRFA provides for "a Premier's intergovernmental forum

---

89   s 4.
90   s 6(1).
91   s 7(a).
92   s 7(b)(ii).
93   s 11(1).
94   s 11(7).
95   s 9(1).
96   s 8(2) of the MSPA.

to promote and facilitate intergovernmental relations between the province and local governments in the province".[97] The Premier may also establish a provincial intergovernmental forum for any specific functional area or any specific part in the province.[98] IRFA also empowers the Premiers of two or more provinces to "establish an interprovincial forum to promote and facilitate intergovernmental relations between those provinces".[99] The use of such fora might be seen in one or more of the coastal provinces as the most appropriate way to engage with local government or each other before being consulted by the National Working Group established in terms of the MSPA.[100] In the local sphere of government, IRFA provides for district intergovernmental fora "to promote and facilitate intergovernmental relations between the district municipality and the local municipalities in the district".[101] IRFA empowers two or more municipalities to "establish an intermunicipality forum to promote and facilitate intergovernmental relations between them".[102] Once again, the use of such fora might be seen in one or more municipalities as the most appropriate way to engage with each other before being consulted by the National Working Group.

In addition to the IRFA structures, the NEMICMA provides for the establishment of a National Coastal Committee (NSC),[103] which "must promote integrated coastal managemen t in [South Africa] and effective co-operative governance by co-ordinating the effective implementation of [NEMICMA] and of the national coastal management programme".[104] In view of the fact that the Committee is established by the same Minister who chairs the MSPA Ministerial Committee and that its composition is unlikely to result in its involvement adding value to the MSPA processes, the NSC will probably play no role in MSP matters

---

97   s 16.

98   s 21(1).

99   s 22(1).

100 s 9(1).

101 s 24.

102 s 28(1). See further Kotzé "Environmental governance" in Paterson and Kotzé (eds) *Environmental Compliance and Enforcement in South Africa. Legal Perspectives* (2009) 103-125.

103 s 35(1).

104 s 35(3). The national coastal management programme is "a policy directive on integrated coastal management" and provides for "an integrated, co-ordinated and uniform approach to coastal management by organs of state in all spheres of government, nongovernmental organisations, the private sector and local communities" (s 45(1)).

in the future. In the provincial sphere of government, the NEMICMA provides for the establishment of provincial coastal committees (PCCs),[105] which must "promote integrated coastal management in the province and the co-ordinated and effective implementation of [NEMICMA] and the provincial coastal management programme".[106] As in the case of the IRFA provincial structures, the use of PCCs might be seen in one or more of the coastal provinces as the most appropriate way to engage with stakeholders before being consulted by the MSPA National Working Group. The same applies, in the local sphere of government, with regard to the municipal coastal committees established in terms of section 42(2) of the NEMICMA.

CONCLUSION

To ensure good ocean governance, there is a need for a proper regulatory framework that outlines how the different government spheres will work together for the proper implementation of MSP. While the MSPA does not specifically mention co-operative governance, it requires collaboration and responsible ocean governance. The MSPF explains that cooperation and integration within government linked with good administration leads to stronger and more complementary decisions and actions.[107] These aspects can be viewed as forming part of co-operative governance.

In as much as the MSPA and the MSPF are lacking in detail regarding co-operative governance, there is nothing in these instruments that contradicts the principle of co-operative governance, hence they are in line with the Constitution. In order to ensure that the implementation of those instruments is consistent with the principle of co-operative governance, it is suggested that a reference be included in the regulations still to be made to the IRFA and the relevant provisions of the NEMICMA.

---

105 s 39(1).

106 s 39(2)(a). A provincial coastal management programme is "a provincial policy directive for the management of the coastal zone in the province" and provides for "an integrated, coordinated and uniform approach to coastal management in the province" (s 47(1)).

107 par 2.4.

PORT STATE JURISDICTION IN TERMS OF ARTICLE 218 OF THE UN CONVENTION ON THE LAW OF SEA: A SOUTH AFRICAN PERSPECTIVE

DENNING METUGE*

PATRICK VRANCKEN**

*   Postdoctoral fellow, NRF Research Chair in the Law of the Sea and Development in Africa, Nelson Mandela University.

**   Professor in Public Law and holder of the NRF Research Chair in the Law of the Sea and Development in Africa, Nelson Mandela University.

INTRODUCTION

For centuries, two basic principles have characterised legal practice in the law of the sea: the right of the Coastal State to control the waters adjacent to its coast and the freedoms of navigation and fishing beyond the waters under the Coastal State's control.[1] Though the subject of sporadic challenges for 300 years, the rules in respect of the freedoms of the high seas have long been accepted by all States as customary international law.[2] Centre stage at the Third United Nations Conference on the Law of the Sea (UNCLOS III) was the need to find a compromise between the claims of many Coastal States over ever wider breadths of waters adjacent to their coasts and the opposition of many States to such extensive exercise of jurisdiction at the expense of the freedoms of the high seas.[3] The result is the "new blue print for the partition of the seas"[4] contained in the 1982 United Nations Convention on the Law of the Sea (LOSC).[5] An innovation included in the LOSC is article 218,[6] which grants to the State in a port or off-shore terminal of which a vessel finds itself, enforcement powers with regard to specific infringements of international environmental standards.[7]

This chapter does not aim to discuss the various views with regard to the scope of Port State jurisdiction. The goal is more limited in that the chapter merely aims to establish whether South Africa has the legislative arsenal to exercise Port State jurisdiction on the basis of the provisions of article 218 and, where necessary, to provide recommendations to amend the relevant legislative provisions in such a way as to incorporate the innovative powers conferred upon Port States by article 218.

---

1   Sohn, Juras, Noyes and Franckx *Law of the Sea in a Nutshell* (2010) 1.

2   ibid 2.

3   Johnson *Coastal State Regulation of International Shipping* (2004) 2; Marten *Port State Jurisdiction and the Regulation of International Merchant* Shipping (2014) 1-2.

4   Gavouneli *Functional Jurisdiction in the Law of the Sea* (2007) 1.

5   1833 *UNTS* 3, (1982) 21 *ILM* 1261. Adopted: 10-12-1982; EIF: 16-11-1994.

6   König "Article 218" in Proelss (ed) *United Nations Convention on The Law of The Sea: A Commentary* (2017) 1489; Bang "Port State jurisdiction and article 218 of the UN Convention on the Law of Sea" 2009 *Journal of Maritime Law & Commerce (JMLC)* 291 291-298; Nordquist, Rosenne and Yankov (eds) *United Nations Convention on The Law of The Sea 1982: A Commentary* (1991) IV 260.

7   See below.

The following section provides a brief overview of State jurisdiction with regard to environmental matters at sea. Thereafter, the drafting history of article 218 will be explained and the content of the provision described. The extent to which South Africa has the legislative arsenal to exercise Port State jurisdiction on the basis of article 218 will then be established and recommendations aimed at filling existing gaps will be formulated.

STATE JURISDICTION WITH REGARD TO ENVIRONMENTAL MATTERS AT SEA

State jurisdiction is addressed in the LOSC under several categories: Flag State jurisdiction, Coastal State jurisdiction and Port State jurisdiction.[8] In a few cases, there is also reference to a fourth category of State jurisdiction: the jurisdiction of the State of nationality.[9] While the LOSC does not provide a definition of the terms "Flag State", "Coastal State" or "Port State",[10] it lays out the scope of State authority in environmental matters at sea within the broader legal regime of each maritime zone. As far as the Coastal State is concerned, the LOSC states that it exercises varying degrees of jurisdiction over its internal waters,[11] territorial sea,[12] contiguous zone,[13] exclusive economic zone (EEZ)[14] and continental shelf.[15] With regard to environmental regulation over its internal waters and territorial sea, the Coastal State may adopt laws and regulations for the preservation of its environment and "the prevention, reduction and control of pollution thereof".[16] Over its EEZ, the Coastal State has jurisdiction with regard to the "protection and preservation of the marine environment"[17] and may adopt laws and regulations that give effect to generally accepted rules and standards for the prevention, reduction

---

8   Gavouneli (n 4) 33.

9   See, for instance, art 97(1).

10   Gavouneli (n 4) 34.

11   Gavouneli (n 4) 34.

12   See art 2(1) and art 8(1).

13   art 2.

14   art 33.

15   art 56.

16   art 77.

17   art 21(1)(f). See also a 211(4) read with a 2(1).

and control of pollution from vessels.[18] Furthermore, in order to prevent pollution from vessels, the Coastal State may prevent a visiting foreign vessel within its port from sailing, where it has ascertained that the vessel is in violation of applicable international rules and standards relating to seaworthiness and, as a result, is a threat to the marine environment.[19] In addition, the Coastal State may exercise enforcement jurisdiction against a visiting foreign vessel that has violated either its national laws pertaining to the prevention, reduction and control of pollution from vessels or applicable international rules and standards, when such a violation has occurred within the Coastal State's territorial sea or EEZ.[20]

Save in exceptional cases,[21] the Flag State only has exclusive jurisdiction over the vessels flying its flag when they are on the high seas.[22] Flag States have an obligation to take measures to ensure that, with regard to the vessels flying their flags, "the master, officers and, to the extent appropriate, the crew are fully conversant with and required to observe the applicable international regulations concerning the ... prevention, reduction and control of marine pollution...".[23]

Moreover, the Flag State has an obligation to "cause an inquiry to be held by or before a suitably qualified person or persons into every marine casualty or incident of navigation on the high seas involving a ship flying its flag and causing ... serious damage to ... the marine environment".[24] In addition, the Flag States must ensure that vessels flying their flag or of their registry comply not only with applicable international rules and standards established through the competent international organisation or diplomatic conference, but also their national laws adopted in accordance with the LOSC for the prevention, reduction and control of pollution of the marine environment from vessels.[25] Furthermore, the Flag States

---

18   art 56(1)(b)(iii).

19   See art 211(5).

20   art 219.

21   art 220.

22   such as piracy. See art 100–107 and 110(1)(a).

23   art 92(1).

24   art 94(4)(c).

25   art 94(7).

are obligated to effectively enforce the applicable rules, standards and regulations irrespective of where violations are committed.[26]

The term "Port State", which is distinguished from the terms "Coastal State" and "Flag State" in the preamble to the 1995 Agreement for the Implementation of the Provisions of the 1982 United Nations Convention on the Law of the Sea Relating to the Conservation and Management of Straddling Fish Stocks and Highly Migratory Fish Stocks,[27] is only used in article 218 of the LOSC itself, where it refers to the State in a port or at an off-shore terminal of which a vessel finds itself.

DRAFTING HISTORY OF ARTICLE 218

Three factors in global maritime activity influenced the granting of jurisdiction to the Port State.[28] The first factor relates to the fact that the jurisdiction of the Flag State over the vessels flying its flag is, as already stated, exclusive on the high seas. This means that, when the Flag State does not comply with its duty to "effectively exercise its jurisdiction and control in administrative, technical and social matters over [the] ships flying its flag"[29] – which is often the case of the so-called "flags of convenience" –,[30] no action may be taken by other States while the vessels exercise the freedom of navigation. The second factor is the adoption by the IMO of instruments relating to safety and environmental protection, such as the 1974 International Convention for the Safety of Life at Sea, as amended (SOLAS),[31] the 1973 International Convention for the Prevention of Pollution from Ships (MARPOL)[32] and the 1978 International Convention on Standards of Training, Certification and Watchkeeping for Seafarers, as amended (STCW),[33] which allow Port States to inspect visiting

---

26   art 211(2) and 217(1).

27   art 217(1).

28   2167 *UNTS* 88, (1995) 34 *ILM* 1542, (1995) 29 *LOSB* 25. Adopted: 04-12-1995; EIF: 11-12-2001.

29   Marten (n 3) 42.

30   art 91(1) of the LOSC.

31   Gross "Safety in sea transport" 1994 *Journal of Transport Economics and Policy* 99 101.

32   1184 *UNTS* 1, (1975) 14 *ILM* 959. Adopted: 01-11-1974; EIF: 25-05-1980.

33   1340 *UNTS* 184, (1973) 12 *ILM* 1319. Adopted: 02-11-1973; EIF: 10-02-1983.

vessels.[34] The third factor is the increase in the number of significant oil spills such as that of the *Torrey Canyon* in 1967[35] and the *Amoco Cadiz* disaster in 1978, which prompted European States to convene in Paris and adopt the 1982 Paris Memorandum of Understanding on Port State Control (Paris MoU).[36] Under the latter, twenty-seven maritime authorities have agreed to undertake a harmonised set of Port State control (PSC) procedures in the North Atlantic basin from North America to Europe.[37]

As a matter of principle, Port States have always had the authority to deny or impose conditions for entry into their ports and other internal waters.[38] During the MARPOL negotiations, an attempt was made to not only increase the authority of the Port States by allowing them to exercise Port State control – that is to say the limited executive jurisdiction of the Port State to inspect documents evidencing compliance with generally accepted standards, to perform administrative duties such as the detention of ships until they are seaworthy and to order vessels to proceed to the nearest repair yard[39] – but also Port State jurisdiction, a wider authority that includes penalising and instituting proceedings regarding conduct by foreign vessels outside of the Port State's national jurisdiction.[40] That attempt failed and a

---

34   1361 *UNTS* 2. Adopted: 07-07-1978; EIF: 28-04-1984.

35   Bang "Is port State control an effective means to combat vessel-source pollution? An empirical survey of the practical exercise by port States of their powers of control" 2008 *International Journal of Marine and Coastal Law* 715 719. See also regs I/6 and 19 SOLAS; art X of STCW and art 5(2) of MARPOL.

36   See, for instance, Rares "Ships that changed the law: The *Torrey Canyon* disaster" 2018 *Lloyd's Maritime and Commercial Law Quarterly* 336 336-347.

37   See Paris MoU on Port State Control "A short history of the Paris Mou on PSC" (2019) https://www.parismou.org/about-us/history (07-05-2020).

38   See clause 9.2 Paris MoU. Since then, the IMO has facilitated the adoption of eight other regional memoranda on Port State control based on the Paris MOU model: the 1992 Viña del Mar Agreement between the maritime administrations of the Coastal States of South America http://www.marine-centre.org/Docs/MOU/LATIN_AMERICA_MOU.pdf (07-05-2020); the 1993 Tokyo Memorandum between the administrations of the Coastal States of the Asia-Pacific region http://www.tokyo-mou.org/organization/memorandum_of_understanding.php (07-05-2020]); the 1996 Caribbean Memorandum http://www.caribbeanmou.org/sites/default/files/Approved_MOU_Rev_7_Jan_2018.pdf (07-05-2020); the 1997 Mediterranean Memorandum https://iea.uoregon.edu/treaty-text/1997-mediterraneanmemorandumunderstandingportstatecontrolentxt (07-05-2020); the 1998 Indian Ocean Memorandum (available at http://www.iomou.org/moumain.htm (07-05-2020); the 1999 Memorandum for the Western and Central Regions of Africa http://www.abujamou.org/index.php?pid=5t77uyggfgdf6756 (07-05-2020); the 2000 Black Sea Memorandum http://www.marine-centre.org/Docs/MOU/BLACK_SEA_MOU.pdf (07-05-2020); and the 2004 Persian Gulf Memorandum https://www.riyadhmou.org/aboutmoutext.html (07-05-2020).

39   See, for instance, Bang (n 6) 293-294; Bodansky "Protecting the marine environment from vessel-source pollution: UNCLOS III and beyond" 1991 *Ecology Law Quarterly* 719 719–759 and Legatski "Port State jurisdiction over vessel-source marine pollution" 1977 *Harvard Environmental Law Review* 448 461.

40   Bang "Recommendations for policies on port State control and port State jurisdiction" 2013 *JMLC* 115 119.

decision as to whether and to what extent the jurisdiction of Flag States should be supplemented by Port State jurisdiction was left to be made during the negotiating process at UNCLOS III.[41]

> "In the early days of the negotiations, flag States, coastal States and some environmentally-friendly industrialised States pursued opposing interests with regard to port State jurisdiction. Whereas traditional flag States wanted to retain exclusive jurisdiction with limited inspection rights for port States and coastal States focussed on extensive enforcement rights in the EEZ, some industrialised States, such as Canada, the Netherlands and the United States, submitted proposals at the 1973 session of the Seabed Committee on far-reaching enforcement competencies for port States".[42]

The first version of the provisions that became article 218 appeared in the 1975 Informal Single Negotiating Text (ISNT)[43] as articles 27 and 28, provisions of which were merged in the 1976 Revised Single Negotiating Text (RSNT)[44] into article 28, which became article 219 of the 1977 Informal Composite Negotiating Text (ICNT)[45] and article 218 from the 1979 revised version of Informal Composite Negotiating Text (ICNT-Rev 1)[46] onwards. Initially, no distinction was made between Coastal States and Port States.[47] The term "Port State" was used for the first time in article 28(4) of the RSNT — where it became clear that the Port State is "the State that acts with regard to violations occurring outside the maritime zones under its own jurisdiction"[48] — and the term was later used in the titles of article 219 of the ICNT and article 218 thereafter. However, the geographical scope of the events concerned was only changed from "regardless of where the violation occurred"[49] to "outside the internal waters, territorial sea or exclusive economic zone of" the Port State in article 219 of the ICNT. By contrast, while article 27(3) of the ISNT limited the geographical scope of the events with regard

---

41   On the distinction between Port State control and Port State jurisdiction, see further Bang (n 39) 119-120.

42   König (n 6) 1490-1491.

43   ibid 1491.

44   Part III of UN Doc A/CONF.62/WP.8/Part III (1975).

45   UN Doc A/CONF.62/WP.8/REV.1/PART II (1976).

46   UN Doc A/CONF.62/WP.10 (1977).

47   UN Doc A/CONF.62/WP.10/Rev.1 (1979).

48   See art 27 of the ISNT.

49   König (n 6) 1491.

to which proceedings could be instituted, to the yet-to-be determined maritime domain of the Coastal State, that scope was already extended beyond the outer limit of the EEZ in article 28(1) of the RSNT.[50]

Initially, a distinction was only made between discharge violations and other infringements of international rules and standards with regard to the institution of proceedings.[51] In other words, the provisions relating to investigations applied for all infringements.[52] That power was quickly limited to discharges in article 28(1) of the RSNT, which also replaced the very general phrase "international rules and standards" with "international rules and standards established through the competent international organization or general diplomatic conference".[53] At the same time, the investigations which were initially mandatory[54] became optional.[55]

Neither article 27 nor article 28 of the ISNT took into account that the Port State requires the consent of another Coastal State in which the discharge took place, that of the Flag State or that of a State damaged or threatened by the discharge before instituting proceedings with regard to that discharge, unless the discharge caused, or is likely to cause, pollution in the waters of the Port State. Such a requirement was already confirmed in article 28(2) of the RSNT and is now stated in article 218(2) of the LOSC. By contrast, the ISNT already dealt with the records of investigations. Article 28(4) compelled the Port State to always forward the relevant reports to the Flag State. This provision was amended in article 28(4) of the RSNT in such a way that the transmission of those records was now optional and at the request of the Coastal State concerned. It became mandatory again and also at the request of the Flag State in article 219(4) of the ICNT. Similarly, the issue of requests by other States to investigate was already addressed in article 28(2) of the ISNT, which stated that it was not mandatory for the Port State to comply with such requests. Article 28(3) of the RSNT provided

50   See art 27(1) of the ISNT. The wording used in a 28(1) of the RSNT is "irrespective of the where the violation occurred".

51   Compare with art 27(3) of the ISNT.

52   Compare art 27(1) and (3) of the ISNT.

53   See art 27(1)(a) of the ISNT.

54   The word "applicable" was added at the beginning of the phrase in article 219 of the ICNT.

55   See art 27(1) of the ISNT.

that the Port State had to "endeavour to comply" and, since article 219(3) of the ICNT, the provision reads: "shall, as far as practicable comply".

Article 218 of the LOSC now reads as follows:

"1. When a vessel is voluntarily within a port or at an off-shore terminal of a State, that State may undertake investigations and, where the evidence so warrants, institute proceedings in respect of any discharge from that vessel outside the internal waters, territorial sea or exclusive economic zone of that State in violation of applicable international rules and standards established through the competent international organization or general diplomatic conference.

2. No proceedings pursuant to paragraph 1 shall be instituted in respect of a discharge violation in the internal waters, territorial sea or exclusive economic zone of another State unless requested by that State, the flag State, or a State damaged or threatened by the discharge violation, or unless the violation has caused or is likely to cause pollution in the internal waters, territorial sea or exclusive economic zone of the State instituting the proceedings.

3. When a vessel is voluntarily within a port or at an off-shore terminal of a State, that State shall, as far as practicable, comply with requests from any State for investigation of a discharge violation referred to in paragraph 1, believed to have occurred in, caused, or threatened damage to the internal waters, territorial sea or exclusive economic zone of the requesting State. It shall likewise, as far as practicable, comply with requests from the flag State for investigation of such a violation, irrespective of where the violation occurred.

4. The records of the investigation carried out by a port State pursuant to this article shall be transmitted upon request to the flag State or to the coastal State. Any proceedings instituted by the port State on the basis of such an investigation may, subject to section 7, be suspended at the request of the coastal State when the violation has occurred within its internal waters, territorial sea or exclusive economic zone. The evidence and records of the case, together with any bond or other financial security posted with the authorities of the port State, shall in that event be transmitted to the coastal State. Such transmittal shall preclude the continuation of proceedings in the port State".

INTERPRETATION OF ARTICLE 218

The scope of application of article 218 is clear in that it confers Port State jurisdiction over a vessel that is voluntarily within one of the State's ports or at one of its off-shore terminals "in respect of any discharge from that vessel outside the internal waters, territorial sea or exclusive economic zone of th[e] State in violation of applicable international rules and standards established through the competent international organization or general diplomatic conference".[56] The conferring of enforcement jurisdiction to Coastal States in such a case is not problematical.

Indeed, when a vessel is within a port or at an off-shore terminal of a Coastal State, that vessel is within the maritime territory of that State[57] and, therefore, under the latter's exclusive executive authority, an authority that may be used to enforce the provisions of the civil and criminal legislation of that State.[58] A confusion may arise in that the Coastal State exercises the same exclusive executive authority in the exercise of its Coastal State jurisdiction as it does in the exercise of its Port State jurisdiction. This explains why the term "Port State" is often employed to refer to a Coastal State both when it exercises its Coastal State jurisdiction and when it exercises its Port State jurisdiction.[59] However, as far as State ocean jurisdiction is concerned, "[a] port State is always a coastal State – although the reverse is not always true".[60] As indicated above, the drafters of the LOSC were clearly aware of this when the geographical scope of the events over which Port State jurisdiction may be exercised in terms of article 218 was changed from "regardless of where the violation occurred"[61] to "outside the internal waters, territorial sea or exclusive economic zone of" the Port State, that is to say outside the maritime zones over which the Coastal State exercises Coastal State jurisdiction.[62] It is in

---

56   See art 28(1) of the RSNT.

57   art 218(1).

58   See art 2, 8 and 12 of the LOSC.

59   See, for instance, Johnson (n 3) 44; Marten (n 3) 9; Molenaar "Port State jurisdiction: Towards mandatory and comprehensive use" in Freestone, Barnes and Ong (eds) *The Law of the Sea* (2006) 192 194.

60   See, for example, Molenaar (n 58) 193-194; Marten (n 3) 3; König "The enforcement of the international law of the sea by coastal and port States" 2002 *Zeitschrift für ausländisches öffentliches Recht und Völkerrecht* 5.

61   Gavouneli (n 4) 44.

62   See art 27(1) of the ISNT.

the exercise of the latter that the Coastal State has been conferred enforcement powers under the provisions of IMO instruments such as SOLAS and MARPOL. Indeed, those instruments only confer Coastal State jurisdiction to Coastal States over matters arising within their internal waters, territorial seas and EEZs. As far as SOLAS is concerned, a Coastal State may take corrective measures against a ship in its port if, subsequent to a survey, it is "determine[d] that the condition of the ship or its equipment does not correspond substantially with the particulars of the certificate or is such that the ship is not fit to proceed to sea without danger to the ship…".[63] Similarly, MARPOL specifically authorises a State party to prohibit and impose sanctions for the violations of its terms within the jurisdiction of the party in question.[64] The Port State, on the other hand, does not protect its own interests, but those of another State or, with regard to the high seas, the interest of all States. In this sense, the main distinction between the Coastal States' exercise of their Coastal State jurisdiction and their exercise of their Port State jurisdiction, is the functions they fulfil in the process.[65]

"[C]onsiderations of the rule of law suggest that a port State should not prosecute under Article 218 for discharge violations by foreign ships on the high seas unless it has first made such acts criminal offences under its own law".[66] However, article 218(1) makes reference to violations of "applicable international rules and standards", meaning that the Port State may not adopt domestic discharge standards applicable outside its maritime domain which are inconsistent with those internationally recognised rules and standards.[67] The main international instrument regulating discharge violations by vessels at sea is MARPOL.[68] While, as already indicated, the Coastal State may only apply MARPOL up to the outer limit of the EEZ when it exercises its Coastal State jurisdiction, article 218 is to the effect that the Coastal State may apply MARPOL with regard to discharges taking place

---

63 See art 219 of the ICNT.

64 See reg I/6(c) of SOLAS.

65 See art 4(2) of MARPOL. See further section 5 below.

66 See König (n 6) 1490.

67 Bang (n 6) 310.

68 McDorman "Port State enforcement: A comment on article 218 of the 1982 Law of the Sea Convention" 1997 *JMLC* 305 316. See also Bodansky (n 38) 762-763.

on the high seas when it exercises its Port State jurisdiction. This is in addition to the application of MARPOL by the Flag States, in the exercise of their Flag State jurisdiction, over discharges on the high seas by vessels flying their flags.[69]

State practice shows that some States have adopted domestic legislation giving effect to the provision of article 218, either in full or in part. For instance, article 1.10.07 of the Malagasy Maritime Code[70] is an example of a partial incorporation of article 218 when it provides that the "State may institute proceedings in respect of discharges outside its exclusive economic zone if such discharges give rise or may give rise to pollution of its own internal waters, its own territorial sea or its own exclusive economic zone". Indeed, the article incorporates article 218(1) to a limited extent because it does not empower the Malagasy State to institute proceedings in respect of discharges on the high seas that do not have an impact on the Malagasy maritime domain. In addition, article 218(4) is not incorporated at all. By contrast, article 1.10.07 incorporates fully article 218(3) when it provides that "[t]he Malagasy State shall make every possible attempt to accede to requests from any State for investigation concerning discharges that allegedly occurred within the maritime domain of the requesting State". Bulgaria has also adopted legislation giving effect to Port State jurisdiction, but only as far as article 218(3) is concerned.[71] In that regard, the ambit of article 218(3) is both limited – in that the State is expected to provide legal assistance on the basis of reciprocity when the Requesting State is not a EU member – and extended – in that legal assistance is to be provided irrespective of whether it is practicable to do so.

Because article 218(1) provides for Port State jurisdiction only as an optional measure rather than an obligation,[72] States do not violate the provision when they do not make use of their powers either because they do not have sufficient means to do so or because they elect not to act against foreign vessels for various reasons, such as gaining a competitive advantage or safeguarding port activities

---

69 Bodansky (n 38) 729.

70 See art 3(1) MARPOL.

71 See *Loi n°99–028 du 3 février 2000 portant refonte du Code maritime* http://www.droit-afrique.com/upload/doc/madagascar/Madagascar-Code-1999-maritime.pdf (07-05-2020) (own translation).

72 See art 55 of the Space, Inland Waterways and Ports Act of Bulgaria of 28 January 2000 http://www.conces.government.bg/save?fileId=3310&type=doc&fileName=Maritime_Space_Inland_Waterways.pdf (07-05-2020). For more examples, see also Bang (n 6) 303–309.

that are a source of economic growth for the State.[73] In other words, the optional character of Port State jurisdiction in terms of article 218(1)-(2) means that the latter does little to prevent States succumbing to the temptation of becoming "ports of convenience" in order to boost their economy or ensure the unimpeded entry of certain imported goods.

INCORPORATION OF ARTICLE 218 IN SOUTH AFRICAN LAW

Article 218 is the basis for Port State jurisdiction as a measure to regulate environment-related navigational standards. In accordance with that provision, South Africa may enact legislation to the effect that, when a vessel is voluntarily within one of its ports or off-shore terminals, it may exercise the executive and adjudicative Port State jurisdiction to investigate and,

> "where the evidence so warrants, institute proceedings in respect of any discharge from that vessel outside the internal waters, territorial sea or exclusive economic zone of [South Africa] in violation of applicable international rules and standards established through the competent international organization or general diplomatic conference".[74]

As indicated earlier, the "applicable international rules and standards" are contained in MARPOL which, as amended by its 1978 Protocol (MARPOL 1973/1978), came into force in South Africa in 1985.[75] The South African Maritime Safety Authority (SAMSA) is vested with the power to enforce the provisions of MARPOL, to which the Marine Pollution (Prevention of Pollution from Ships) Act (PPSA)[76] gives effect in relation to all South African vessels wherever they may be[77] as well as to any other vessels while they are in South African internal waters, territorial sea or EEZ.[78] To that extent and as a party to MARPOL, South Africa

---

73 Gavouneli (n 4) 45.

74 Molenaar (n 60) 193.

75 art 218(1).

76 South Africa acceded to Annex V in 1992, Annex III in 1997, Annex IV in 2015 and Annex VI in 2015 (see IMO *Status of IMO Instruments* (2020) 114).

77 2 of 1986. In terms of s 2(2)(b) read with s 1 of the PPSA, "[u]nless the context indicates otherwise, a reference in the Convention… to the Administration or Government shall, in relation to a South African ship or the Republic, be construed as, or as including, a reference to the [SAMSA] or any person acting on its authority".

78 s 2(1)(a).

has an obligation to implement its provisions and annexes to prevent the pollution of the marine environment by the discharge of harmful substances, or effluents containing such substances, in contravention of MARPOL.[79]

In contrast to article 218(1) that allows the Port State to institute proceedings where a discharge in violation of MARPOL has occurred outside the internal waters, territorial sea and EEZ of the State, MARPOL only requires South Africa to enact law prohibiting and sanctioning any violation of its standards within South Africa's maritime domain.[80] Indeed, with regard to foreign visiting vessels, the wording of section 2(1)(b) of the PPSA has the effect of limiting South Africa's application of MARPOL to the conduct of visiting vessels within the maritime zones that are subject to South Africa's jurisdiction.[81] In other words, the PPSA does not provide for the institution of proceedings in accordance with article 218(1) against visiting vessels that enter a South African port after committing a discharge violation on the high seas. For South Africa to be able to give effect to the provisions of article 218(1), the PPSA will have to be amended to include a provision that specifically extends its scope to visiting vessels that enter a South African port or offshore terminal after committing a discharge in violation of MARPOL on the high seas.[82]

As indicated earlier, South Africa is prohibited, in terms of article 218(2), from commencing any proceedings in terms of article 218(1) where the discharge violation occurred in

> "the internal waters, territorial sea or exclusive economic zone of another State unless requested by that State, the flag State, or a State damaged or threatened by the discharge violation, or unless the violation has caused or is likely to cause pollution in the internal waters, territorial sea or exclusive economic zone of [South Africa]".

---

79   s 2(1)(b). In terms of art 3(1) of MARPOL, the foreign vessels to which the provisions of the PPSA apply are those registered under the flag of a party to MARPOL or operating under the authority of such a party. See also Vrancken "South Africa" in Vrancken and Tsamenyi (eds) *The Law of the Sea: The African Union and its Member States* (2018) 696. In terms of a draft Marine Pollution (Prevention of Pollution from Ships) Amendment Bill, 2019, the PPSA would be amended in such a way as to give effect in South African law to Annex IV and Annex VI (GN 476 in *GG* 42688 of 06-09-2019).

80   s 2(2) of the PPSA read with a 1(1) of MARPOL.

81   See art 4(2)–(4) of MARPOL. See also Bang (n 6) 294.

82   Moreover, the wide wording of s 2(1)(b) conflicts with the limitation in art 3 of MARPOL. See further Vrancken *South Africa and the Law of the Sea* (2011) 369-370.

Once again, the PPSA does not provide for the institution of proceedings in accordance with article 218(2) against visiting vessels that enter a South African port after committing a discharge violation in the internal waters, territorial sea or EEZ of another State. For South Africa to be able to give effect to the provisions of article 218(2), the PPSA will have to be amended to include, in addition to a provision giving effect to article 218(1), a provision that stipulates that, when a visiting vessel enters a South African port or offshore terminal after committing a discharge violation in the maritime domain of another State, South Africa will not institute any proceedings unless: (a) requested to do so by the State in the maritime domain of which the discharge took place, the Flag State or a State damaged or threatened by the discharge violation; or (b) the violation has caused or is likely to cause pollution in the South African maritime domain.

Moreover, in terms of article 218(3),

> "[w]hen a vessel is voluntarily within a port or at an off-shore terminal of a State, that State shall, as far as practicable, comply with requests from any State for investigation of a discharge violation referred to in paragraph 1, believed to have occurred in, caused, or threatened damage to the internal waters, territorial sea or exclusive economic zone of the requesting State. It shall likewise, as far as practicable, comply with requests from the flag State for investigation of such a violation, irrespective of where the violation occurred".

MARPOL confirms that South Africa

> "may inspect a ship to which [MARPOL] applies when it enters the ports or offshore terminals under its jurisdiction, if a request for an investigation is received from any Party together with sufficient evidence that the ship has discharged harmful substances or effluents containing such substances in any place".[83]

However, in contrast to the mandatory character of article 218(3), compliance with a request for investigation in terms of MARPOL is optional. Moreover, article 218(3) does not require the Requesting State to provide "sufficient evidence" of a discharge violation by the vessel, but only requires that the Requesting State "believe" that a discharge violation as provided in article 218(1) has occurred. This

---

83   The amended provision will have to make it clear that the visiting vessels in question are only those flying the flag of a State party to MARPOL or operating under the authority of a party to MARPOL.

means that, for South Africa to be able to give effect to the provisions of article 218(3), the PPSA will have to be amended to include, in addition to provisions giving effect to article 218(1) and (2), a provision that stipulates that: (a) when South Africa receives a request for investigation of a discharge violation believed to have occurred in, caused, or threatened damage to the internal waters, territorial sea or EEZ of the Requesting State, that request must be investigated irrespective of whether sufficient evidence has been provided by the Requesting State; and (b) when South Africa receives a request from a Flag State for investigation of a discharge violation wherever it occurred, that request must, as far as practicable, be complied with.

As far as it is concerned, article 218(4) requires that any records of an investigation undertaken by the South African authorities pursuant to article 218 be transmitted upon request to the Flag or Coastal State. This requirement is mirrored in MARPOL when it provides that, where South Africa has elected to comply with the request for an investigation into a discharge violation, it must provide the report of its investigation to the Requesting State so that appropriate action can be taken in conformity with the Convention.[84] Article 218(4) also provides that proceedings instituted by South Africa on the basis of an investigation undertaken pursuant to article 218 may, subject to a number of safeguards,[85] be suspended at the request of a Coastal State when the violation has occurred within that State's internal waters, territorial sea or EEZ. Moreover, any "evidence and records of the case, together with any bond or other financial security posted with [SAMSA] shall in that event be transmitted to the coastal State", such a transmittal precluding the continuation of proceedings in South Africa. As earlier mentioned, the PPSA and MARPOL do not require that any proceedings to be undertaken in relation to a discharge violation that occurred outside South Africa's maritime domain. It is therefore not surprising that they do not contain any suspension-of-proceedings provisions that mirror those of in article 218(4), nor any provisions requiring that any bond or other financial security posted with SAMSA be transferred to the

---

84 See art 6(5) of MARPOL.

85 ibid.

Coastal State. Once again, the PPSA will have to be amended to give effect to the provisions of article 218(4).

CONCLUSION

Ports are within the territory of a Coastal State and, for that reason, that State may exercise, within its ports, both its Coastal State jurisdiction and its Port State jurisdiction. Coastal State jurisdiction, however, does not extend to discharge violations that occurred outside the State's internal waters, territorial sea or EEZ. The innovative character of Port State jurisdiction in terms of article 218 is that it provides a basis for the Coastal State to exercise its jurisdiction and institute proceedings against visiting vessels that are within one of its ports or offshore terminals with regard to discharge violations outside its internal waters, territorial sea or EEZ. However, in order for the relevant organs of the Coastal State to be able to exercise Port State jurisdiction, the provisions of article 218 need to be accurately and comprehensively incorporated into domestic law. The incorporation of MARPOL into South African domestic law by the PPSA does not do so because the Act as it stands only provides for the application of MARPOL by South Africa in the exercise of either its Coastal State jurisdiction or its Flag State jurisdiction. In order to address this issue and ensure that South Africa's ports are not safe havens for vessels from which illegal discharges have occurred outside the country's maritime domain, it is submitted, on the basis of the above discussion, that a suitable course of action would be to amend the PPSA as follows:

The insertion of the following definition in section 1:

"Convention on the Law of the Sea" means the United Nations Convention on the Law of the Sea adopted by the Third United Nations Conference on the Law of the Sea in Kingston on 10 December 1982.

The amendment of section 2(1) as follows:[86]

Subject to the provisions of this Act, the Convention shall have effect in relation to:

(a)   any South African ship, wherever it may be; **[and]**

(b)   any other ship while it is in the Republic or its territorial waters or exclusive economic zone: and

(c)   any other ship while it is outside the Republic or its territorial waters or exclusive economic zone in the cases where the Republic has jurisdiction in terms of section 2A.

The text in bold to be deleted and the underlined text to be inserted.

The insertion of a new section 2A, which reads as follows:

(1)   When a ship other than a South African ship and flying the flag of a State party to the Convention on the Law of the Sea is voluntarily within a port or at an off-shore terminal of the Republic, the Authority may undertake investigations and, where the evidence so warrants, proceedings may be instituted in respect of any discharge from that ship outside the internal waters, territorial sea or exclusive economic zone of the Republic in violation of applicable international rules and standards established through a competent international organization or general diplomatic conference, including those contained in the Convention.

(2)   No proceedings pursuant to subsection 1 shall be instituted in respect of a discharge violation in the internal waters, territorial sea or exclusive economic zone of another State unless –

(a)   requested by that State, the Flag State or a State damaged or threatened by the discharge violation; or

(b)   the violation has caused or is likely to cause pollution in the internal waters, territorial sea or exclusive economic zone of the Republic.

(3)   When a ship other than a South African ship and flying the flag of a State party to the Convention on the Law of the Sea is voluntarily within a port or at an off-shore terminal of the Republic, the Authority shall, as far as practicable, comply with requests from any State party to the Convention on the Law of the Sea for investigation of a discharge violation referred to in subsection 1, believed to have occurred in, caused, or

---

86   See art 223-233 of the LOSC.

threatened damage to the internal waters, territorial sea or exclusive economic zone of the Requesting State. It shall likewise, as far as practicable, comply with requests from a Flag State for investigation of such a violation, irrespective of where the violation occurred.

(4)   The records of the investigation carried out by the Authority pursuant to this section shall be transmitted upon request to the Flag State or to the Coastal State. Any proceedings instituted in the Republic on the basis of such an investigation may, subject to articles 223 to 233 of the Convention on the Law of the Sea, be suspended at the request of a Coastal State when the violation has occurred within its internal waters, territorial sea or exclusive economic zone. The evidence and records of the case, together with any bond or other financial security posted in the Republic, shall in that event be transmitted to the Coastal State. Such transmittal shall preclude the continuation of proceedings in the Republic.

THE PENALTY FOR PIRACY IN NIGERIAN LAW

OBINNA EMMANUEL NKOMADU*

PATRICK VRANCKEN**

---

*   Postdoctoral fellow, NRF Research Chair in the Law of the Sea and Development in Africa, Nelson Mandela University.

**   Professor in Public Law and holder of the NRF Research Chair in the Law of the Sea and Development in Africa, Nelson Mandela University.

INTRODUCTION

The Nigerian territorial sea and exclusive economic zone (EEZ) serve not only as a means of transportation for Nigeria, the region and the world at large,[1] but also as a source of food and employment. In addition, there are rich deposits of minerals, mineral oils and natural gas, which attract the attention of many actors,[2] including criminals who regularly attack the crew and passengers of passing vessels. The Council of the European Union has long acknowledged that the Gulf of Guinea has always been a hotspot for piracy[3] and, in March 2019, the European Parliament reiterated that the Gulf of Guinea, and the area off the coast of Nigeria in particular, remained the global epicentre for piracy.[4]

Indeed, since 2010, piracy has risen significantly in the area,[5] making the piracy problem in the region the most acute around the African continent.[6] In 2010, the International Maritime Organization (IMO) included the West African coast among the top six piracy hotspots in the world in its annual report.[7] In 2016, incidents of piracy in the Gulf of Guinea, and off the coast of Nigeria in particular, dominated the world scene, both in terms of number and severity. Two

---

1   Anyimadu *Maritime Security in the Gulf of Guinea: Lessons Learned from the Indian Ocean* (2013) 2.

2   Neethling "Piracy around Africa's West and East Coasts: A comparative political perspective" 2010 *Scientia Militaria – South African Journal of Military Studies* 89 100 (who points out that many members of the coastal communities "often claim to be fighting for a fairer distribution of Nigeria's vast oil wealth and [to] protest against the damage caused by oil production in the Delta").

3   Council of the European Union (EU) *EU Gulf of Guinea Action Plan 2015-2020* (2015) 6 http://data.consilium. europa.eu/doc/document/ST-7168-2015-INIT/en/pdf (22-05-2019). See also Council of the European Union *EU Strategy on the Gulf of Guinea* (2014) 4 https://eeas.europa.eu/sites/eeas/files/eu_strategy_on_the_gulf_of_guinea_7. pdf (21-05-2019).

4   European Parliament *Piracy and Armed Robbery off the Coast of Africa: EU and Global Impact* (2019) 7 http://www. europarl.europa.eu/RegData/etudes/IDAN/2019/635590/EPRS_IDA(2019)635590_EN.pdf (21-05-2019).

5   Report of the United Nations General Assembly (UNGA) Secretary-General on Oceans and the Law of the Sea (UN Doc A/66/70/Add.2 (29 Aug 2011)) par 71-72.

6   International Maritime Bureau (IMB) *Report of Piracy and Armed Robbery at Sea* (2017) 30. The area off the coast of Nigeria recorded 33 piracy attacks with 10 kidnapping incidents involving 65 crew members. This is far more than the 9 incidents recorded off the coast of Somalia in 2017. Similarly, in the first quarter of 2018, the Gulf of Guinea witnessed 29 piracy incidents, 22 of which occurred off the coast of Nigeria. This is to be compared to a single piracy incident off the coast of Somalia. See IMB *Report of Piracy and Armed Robbery at Sea* (2018) 23.

7   Report of the United Nations assessment mission on piracy in the Gulf of Guinea (7-24 Nov 2011) par 5 (UN Doc S/2012/45 of 19 Jan 2012). See also UNSC resolution 1816 (2008), UNSC resolution 1838 (2008), UNSC resolution 1844 (2008), UNSC resolution 1846 (2008), UNSC resolution 1851 (2008), UNSC resolution 1897 (2009), UNSC resolution 1918 (2010), UNSC resolution 1950 (2010), UNSC resolution 1976 (2011), UNSC resolution 2015 (2011), UNSC resolution 2020 (2011), UNSC resolution 2077 (2012), UNSC resolution 2125 (2013), UNSC resolution 2184 (2014), UNSC resolution 2246 (2015), UNSC resolution 2316 (2016), UNSC resolution 2383 (2017), UNSC resolution 2442 (2018) and UNSC resolution 2500 (2019).

out of three first-quarter hijackings occurred in the Gulf of Guinea.[8] For instance, in February 2017, "pirates damaged a ship's equipment, stole ship's property and crew's personal belongings and escaped before the naval teams boarded the vessel to rescue the crew".[9] In October 2017, Niger Delta pirates attacked a container ship and kidnapped six crewmembers, including the captain.[10] In March 2018, a Chinese vessel was attacked and hijacked by armed pirates, who forced the vessel into Benin waters and kidnapped two crewmembers before releasing the vessel.[11] In April 2019, nine pirates with AK-47 rifles and grenade launchers hijacked a merchant ship and robbed the crewmembers. The vessel was later freed with the help of a Spanish warship after the crew had been held hostage for four days.[12] That incident was followed by another attack during which six crew members of a Palau-flagged tanker were kidnapped and the remaining crew reportedly saved by a Nigerian warship.[13] More recently, in January 2020, off the coast of Nigeria pirates kidnapped 3 seafarers, injured 2 personnel on board and killed 4 Nigerian Naval Officers after a deadly exchange of gunfire.[14]

As a result of these attacks, the UN Security Council noted with concern "that the domestic law of a number of States lacks provisions criminalizing piracy and/or procedural provisions for effective criminal prosecution of suspected pirates"[15] and called upon "all States [including Nigeria] to criminalize piracy under their domestic law".[16] Section 2(4) of the Territorial Waters Act (TWA)[17] confirms that the Nigerian courts have "jurisdiction to try acts of piracy as defined by the law

8   IMB *Report of Piracy and Armed Robbery at Sea* (2016) 23.

9   IMB *Report of Piracy and Armed Robbery at Sea* (2017) 53.

10   Ships and Ports News "Niger Delta pirates attack containership, kidnap six crew" (24 Oct 2017) http://shipsandports.com.ng/niger-delta-pirates-attack-containership-kidnap-six/ (24-05-2019).

11   IMB *Report of Piracy and Armed Robbery at Sea* (2018) 24.

12   World Maritime News "Spanish warship frees ship hijacked by Nigerian pirates" (undated) https://worldmaritimenews.com/archives/275220/spanish-warship-frees-ship-hijacked-by-nigerian-pirates/ (21-05-2019).

13   World Maritime News "Pirates kidnapped six tanker crew off the coast of Nigeria" (undated) https://worldmaritimenews.com/archives/275645/pirates-kidnap-six-tanker-crew-off-nigeria/ (22-05-2019).

14   Ships and Ports News "Pirates kill naval officer; kidnap 5 sailors in Niger Delta" (14 Mar 2019) https://shipsandports.com.ng/pirates-kill-naval-officer-kidnap-5-sailors-niger-delta/ (16-01-2020).

15   UNSC resolution 1918 (2010) fourteenth preambular par.

16   UNSC resolution 1950 (2010) par 13. See also UNSC resolution 2018 (2011) par 2(a) and UNSC resolution 2039 (2012) par 5, which are addressed specifically at the States of the Gulf of Guinea.

17   5 of 1967.

of nations".[18] However, the Act neither defines "piracy" nor does it prescribe the penalty to be imposed upon the individuals who commit that offence.

The purpose of this chapter is to discuss the legislative provisions regarding the penalty to be imposed on persons found guilty of acts of piracy or attempts to commit such acts contained in the legislation recently passed by the Nigerian government and titled: "Suppression of Piracy and Other Maritime Offences Act, 2019" (SPOMO Act). This is done after having drawn from the experience of other African States and taking into account the Nigerian Criminal Code.[19]

PIRACY AS A CRIME IN NIGERIAN LAW

As indicated above, the TWA confers jurisdiction on the Nigerian courts to try piracy as defined by the law of nations. Piracy is defined in article 101 of the 1982 UN Convention on the Law of the Sea (LOSC)[20] as:

> "(a)   any illegal acts of violence or detention or any act of depredation, committed for private ends by the crew or the passengers of a private ship or private aircraft, and directed:
>
> i. on the high seas, against another ship or aircraft, or against persons or property on board such a ship or aircraft;
>
> ii. against a ship, aircraft, persons or property in a place outside the jurisdiction of any state;
>
> (b)   any act of voluntary participation in the operation of a ship or of an aircraft with knowledge of facts making it a pirate ship or aircraft;
>
> (c)   any act of inciting or of intentionally facilitating an act described in subparagraph (a) or (b)".

This definition is, for all material purposes, identical to the definition of piracy contained in article 15 of the 1958 Convention on the High Seas (HSC).[21] Both provisions make it clear that, for an act to constitute piracy, it must be: (1)

---

18   cap T5 Laws of the Federation of Nigeria 2004. See also s 3(3) TWA.

19   cap 77 Laws of the Federation of Nigeria 1990.

20   1833 *UNTS* 3, (1982) 21 *ILM* 1261. Adopted: 10-12-1982; EIF: 16-11-1994.

21   450 *UNTS* 82. Adopted: 29-04-1958; EIF: 30-09-1962.

an illegal act of violence or detention, or an act of depredation; (2) committed for private ends; (3) by the crew or passengers of a private ship or private aircraft; (4) directed against another ship or aircraft, or against persons or property on board such ship or aircraft; and (5) on the high seas or in a place outside the jurisdiction of any State; or (6) any act of voluntary participation in the operation of a ship or of an aircraft with knowledge of facts making it a pirate ship or aircraft; or (7) any act of inciting or of intentionally facilitating an act meeting requirements (1) to (5) or requirement (6). There is little doubt that an act meeting requirements (1) to (4) is also an act of piracy when it is committed in the EEZ of a Coastal State. Indeed, article 58(2) of the LOSC explains that articles 88 to 115 of the Convention apply also to the EEZ.[22] At the same time, there is no doubt that an act meeting requirements (1) to (4) is not an act of piracy when it is committed in the territorial sea of a Coastal State.[23] For that reason, section 2(1) of the TWA is of no assistance in the fight against piracy when it provides that any act or omission which

"is committed within the territorial waters in Nigeria, whether by a citizen of Nigeria or a foreigner; and … would, if committed in any part of Nigeria, constitute an offence under the law in force in that part, shall be an offence under that law and the person who committed it may, subject to section 3 of [the TWA], be arrested, tried and punished for it as if he had committed it in that part of Nigeria".

Section 3(1) does not assist either when it adds that a

"Nigerian court shall not try a person who is not a citizen of Nigeria for any offence

---

22 See *Republic of Seychelles vs Dahir and Others* 2010 SCSC 81 par 57 (the court held that the "acts alleged herein took place in the EEZ of Seychelles which therefore forms part of the high seas"). See also *Republic of Seychelles vs Liban Mohamed Dahir & 12 Others* Criminal Side No. 7 of 2012, judgment of 31 Jul 2012, par 7 read with par 44, https://sherloc.unodc.org/res/cld/case-law-doc/piracycrimetype/syc/2012/republic_vs__liban_mohamed_dahir_and_twelve_12_others_html/Seychelles_2012_Crim_No_7_2012_Judgement.pdf (accessed on 16-07-2020); *Republic of Seychelles vs Mohamed Aweys Sayid & 8 Others* Criminal Side No 19 of 2010, judgment of 15 Dec 2010, par 3 and 52 https://sherloc.unodc.org/res/cld/case-law-doc/piracycrimetype/syc/2010/the_republic_vs__mohamed_aweys_sayid_and_eight_8_others_html/Seychelles_2010_Crim_No_19_2010_Judgement.pdf (16-07-2020).

23 Rothwell and Stephens *The International Law of the Sea* (2016) 171-172, relying on DP O'Connell *The International Law of the Sea* (1982) II 979-983, explain that "[a] crucial element of th[e] definition of piracy is that piracy is an act which occurs on the high seas, and accordingly an equivalent act of violence which took place within the territorial sea would not be piracy for the purposes of international law … . [L]aws dealing with piracy can also be found in municipal law which may sometimes differ in important respects … with the effect that under municipal law acts of piracy may be committed within the territorial sea. However, in those instances, it will be the laws of the coastal state that will apply to any enforcement operations and unless exceptional arrangements have been put in place other states would have no jurisdiction over pirates within the territorial sea of a coastal State".

committed on the open sea within the territorial waters of Nigeria unless before the trial the Attorney-General of the Federation has issued a certificate signifying his consent to the trial of that person for that offence".

That is confirmed by section 3(3), which states that section 3(1) "shall not apply to the trial of any act of piracy as defined by the law of nations". While the TWA thus criminalises piracy indirectly by giving jurisdiction to the Nigerian courts to try acts of piracy, it does not prescribe the penalty for piracy. This lacuna made it impossible, until now, for a person who committed an act of piracy to be convicted by a Nigerian court for piracy because the Nigerian Constitution stresses that a person "shall not be convicted of a criminal offence unless [...] the penalty therefor is prescribed in a written law", the latter being defined as "an Act of the National Assembly or a Law of a State, any subsidiary legislation or instrument under the provisions of a law".[24]

In this regard, Nigerian law was at odds with the Defence Act[25] of South Africa (SADA), the Penal Law[26] of Liberia (LPL), the Merchant Shipping Act[27] of Kenya (MSA), the Penal Code[28] of Seychelles (SPC) and the SPOMO Act.

PENALTY FOR PIRACY IN OTHER JURISDICTIONS

South Africa

The SADA states that, for the purposes of the Act, piracy is

"(a)   any illegal act of violence or detention, or any act of depredation, committed for private ends by the crew, including the Master, or the passengers of a private ship or a private aircraft, and directed –

i. on the high seas, against another ship or aircraft, or against persons or property on board such a ship or aircraft;

ii. against a ship, aircraft, persons or property in a place outside the jurisdiction of any state;

---

24   s 36(12).

25   42 of 2002.

26   26 of 1976.

27   4 of 2009.

28   cap 158 as amended by Act 2 of 2010.

(b)   any act of voluntary participation in the operation of a ship or of an aircraft with knowledge of facts making it a pirate ship or aircraft contemplated in subsection (1); and

(c)   any act of inciting or of intentionally facilitating an act contemplated in subparagraph (a) or (b)".[29]

The SADA further provides that

"[a]ny person who commits an act of piracy is guilty of an offence, which may be tried in any court in the Republic designated by the Director of Public Prosecutions and, upon conviction, is liable to a fine or to imprisonment for any period, including life imprisonment".[30]

This provision allows a court to use its discretion to punish a person who is guilty of piracy along the full scale of gravity of acts associated with piracy, from a mere fine to the most severe punishment possible in the light of the unconstitutionality of the death penalty.[31] The SADA does not cover the case where a person attempts to commit an act of piracy. Instead, the case is covered by the Riotous Assemblies Act,[32] which provides that

"[a]ny person who attempts to commit any offence against a statute or a statutory regulation shall be guilty of an offence and, if no punishment is expressly provided thereby for such an attempt, be liable on conviction to the punishment to which a person convicted of actually committing that offence would be liable".[33]

In addition, the Criminal Procedure Act (CPA)[34] provides that

"[i]f the evidence in criminal proceedings does not prove the commission of the offence charged but proves an attempt to commit that offence or an attempt to commit any other offence of which an accused may be convicted on the offence charged, the accused may be found guilty of an attempt to commit that offence or, as the case may be, such other offence".[35]

---

29   s 24. On the differences between this provision and art 101 of the LOSC, see Vrancken and Hoctor "The contribution of the Defence Act to the fight against piracy" 2010 *Obiter* 428 430.

30   s 24(3).

31   *S v Makwanyane and Another* 1995 (3) SA 391 (CC), 1995 (6) BCLR 665 (CC).

32   17 of 1956.

33   s 18(1).

34   51 of 1977.

35   s 256.

The SADA does not spell out either how the South African courts may, in terms of article 105 of the LOSC, "determine the action to be taken with regard to the ships, aircraft or property [concerned], subject to the rights of third parties acting in good faith". These matters are also governed by the CPA, especially sections 20 to 23, with regard to seizures, and section 35, with regard to forfeiture.

Liberia

Piracy is defined in the LPL as

"any illegal act of violence or detention or any act of depredation committed for private ends by the crew or passengers of a private ship or private aircraft, or committed by the crew of a warship or government ship or government aircraft whose crew has mutinied and taken control of the ship or aircraft, and is directed:

a. On the high seas, against another ship or aircraft or against persons or property on board another ship or aircraft; or

b. Against a ship, aircraft, persons or property in a place outside the jurisdiction of any nation or government".[36]

This definition does not include an attempt to commit an act of piracy. The LPL provides that piracy is a felony of the first degree when the actor attempts to kill anyone, or purposely inflicts or attempts to inflict serious bodily injury[37] "in the course of committing the piracy", that is to say, when the act in question "occurs in an attempt to commit piracy, whether or not the piracy is successfully completed, or in immediate flight from the commission of, or an unsuccessful effort to commit piracy".[38] In that case, the penalty is "death or life imprisonment where such penalty is specified by statute, or where not so specified, to a definite

---

36 par 15.31(1).

37 In terms of par 1.7(c) and (p), the term "serious bodily injury" means "physical pain, illness or any impairment of physical function" that "creates a substantial risk of death or which causes serious permanent disfigurement, unconsciousness, extreme pain, or permanent or protracted loss or impairment of the function of any bodily member or organ".

38 par 15.31(3). In terms of par 10.1(1), "[a] person is guilty of criminal attempt if, acting with the kind of culpability otherwise required for commission of an offense, he purposely engages in conduct constituting a substantial step toward commission of the offense. A substantial step is any conduct, whether act, commission, or possession, which is strongly corroborative of the firmness of the actor's intent to complete the commission of the offense. Factual or legal impossibility of commission of the offense is not a defense if the offense could have been committed had the attendant circumstances been as the actor believed them to be".

term or imprisonment to be fixed by the court, the maximum of which shall be ten years".[39] In all other cases, piracy is a felony of the second degree,[40] the penalty for which is "a definite term of imprisonment to be fixed by the court, the maximum of which shall be five years".[41] The LPL provides that

> "[w]henever any vessel has been captured and brought into any port of the Republic under authority of paragraph 4, and has been condemned by trial in a court of admiralty, the vessel shall be adjudged to be sold and the proceeds of such sale distributed one half to the Republic and the other half to the captor. The court condemning such vessel shall decree such sale and distribution".[42]

Kenya

In Kenya, the MSA defines "piracy" as:

> "(a)   any act of violence or detention, or any act of depredation, committed for private ends by the crew or the passengers of a private ship or a private aircraft, and directed –
>
>> i. against another ship or aircraft, or against persons or property on board such a ship or aircraft;
>>
>> ii. against a ship, aircraft, persons or property in a place outside the jurisdiction of any state;
>
> (b)   any act of voluntary participation in the operation of a ship or of an aircraft with knowledge of facts making it a pirate ship or aircraft; or
>
> (c)   any act of inciting or of intentionally facilitating an act described in paragraph (a) or (b)".[43]

This definition does not, at the moment, include an attempt to commit an act of piracy. The United Nations Secretary-General has indicated that "UNODC, in cooperation with the Director of Public Prosecutions of Kenya, has proposed

39   par 50.5(1)(a).

40   par 15.31(3).

41   par 50.5(1)(b).

42   par 15.31(5).

43   s 369(1). It must be pointed out that the MSA "not only forbids *illegal* acts of violence or detention as the UNCLOS does, but it goes one step further and condemns *all* acts of violence or detention" (MB Kao "Against a uniform definition of maritime piracy" 2016 *Maritime Safety and Security Law Journal* 1 10).

amendments to the Merchant Shipping Act which would expand the law to include [attempts]. The proposed amendments are [still] under consideration by the Kenyan authorities".[44]

The MSA provides that any person who commits any act of piracy "shall be liable, upon conviction, to imprisonment for life".[45] However, this provision must not be interpreted as compelling the courts to impose a penalty of life imprisonment. Indeed, in *State v Musa Abdullahi Said and Six Others*, the presiding officer considered the

> "mitigation – very lengthy and passionate – by Mr. Magolo for all accused as well as the reply by Mr. Muteti. Whereas [he] agree[d] with Mr. Magolo that the accused persons [were] transformed in many ways and [he saw] the changes they ha[d] gone through since [the trial started], it [was] however not … lost on [him] that the accused persons intention was to forcefully take over the ship the SPESSART and the array of weapons in their possession attest[ed] to this. Their aggressiveness in their quest was demonstrated by their defiance of the first volley of shots fired at them. [He] however … also [took] cognizance of the fact that they did surrender without incident and did not offer any resistance on arrest".[46]

He added that

> "[n]o doubt [the] accused persons [were] young people but [he was] certain that even though they c[a]me from a country where there [was] no law and order, there [were] also very many young people like them, may be even poorer than them who would not engage in a crime such as piracy, or even any crime for that matter. They also exist[ed] in [Kenya] and it [was] to this youth that it [was] imperative that [he] sen[t] a loud message through the sentence [he] mete[d] that 'crime does not pay'. [He would] however take into consideration the appeal by counsel that the accused persons [were] reformed and recognize[d] the many rehabilitation programmes including schooling up to University level that ha[d] been opened up for offenders who [were] willing to transform their lives in Kenyan prison. Each accused person [was] therefore sentenced to serve (5) five years imprisonment".[47]

---

44   UNSC Report of the Secretary-General on specialized anti-piracy courts in Somalia and other States in the region (UN Doc S/2012/50) par 58.

45   s 371.

46   Criminal Case No 1184 of 2009, judgment of 6 Sep 2010, 24-25 http://www.piracylegalforum.org/wp-content/uploads/2014/09/Kenya_2010_Crim_No_1184_2009_Judgment-in-case.pdf (24-05-2019).

47   ibid 25.

On that basis, each accused person was sentenced to serve five years imprisonment.[48]

Likewise, in *Barre Ali Farah and Six Others vs Republic*, the court took note that the appellants had been sentenced to twenty years imprisonment and that

> "several piracy cases ha[d] been determined by the Courts in Mombasa with various imprisonment terms being meted out. In an attempt to harmonize sentencing and in appreciating that times have changed in Somalia, sentences have been reduced to a period of five (5) or seven (7) years and/or (10) years".[49]

The Court confirmed that the words "shall be liable" do not mean that it is mandatory for the courts to sentence to life imprisonment all those found guilty of the offence of piracy. In that case, the sentence of twenty years imprisonment was reduced to six years.[50]

The MSA does not provide for forfeiture and restitution.

Seychelles

In Seychelles, the SPC defines "piracy" as including:

> "(a)   any illegal act of violence or detention, or any act of depredation, committed for private ends by the crew or the passengers of a private ship or a private aircraft and directed–
>
>> i. on the high seas, against another ship or aircraft, or against persons or property on board such a ship or aircraft;
>>
>> ii. against a ship, an aircraft, a person or property in a place outside the jurisdiction of any state;
>
> (b)   any act of voluntary participation in the operation of a ship or an aircraft with knowledge of facts making it a pirate ship or a pirate aircraft; or
>
> (c)   any act described in paragraph (a) or (b) which, except for the fact that it was committed within a maritime zone of Seychelles, would have been an act of piracy under either of those paragraphs".[51]

---

48   ibid 26.

49   Criminal Appeal No 166 of 2012 consolidated with No. 167–172 of 2012, judgment of 14 Nov 2013, 4 https://www.unodc.org/res/cld/case-law-doc/piracycrimetype/ken/2013/criminal_appeal_166_of_2012_republic_vs_barre_ali_farah_and_6_others_html/Criminal_Appeal_166_167_-_172_of_2012_Consolidated.pdf (24-05-2019).

50   ibid.

51   s 65(4).

At the same time, the SPC provides that "[a]ny person who commits any act of piracy ... is guilty of an offence and liable to imprisonment for 30 years and fine of R1 million".[52] Once again, this provision must not be interpreted as compelling the courts to sentence a person convicted of piracy to imprisonment for 30 years and fine of R1 million. What the provision does is to indicate the maximum sentence for acts of piracy. In practice, the court sentenced the accused to terms of 10 and 11 years imprisonment in *Republic vs Mohamed Aweys Sayid and Eight Others*,[53] 18 and 24 years imprisonment in *Republic vs Abdukar Ahmed and Five Others*[54] as well as six and ten years imprisonment in *Republic vs Houssein Mohammed Osman and Ten Others*.[55]

The SPC provides that any person who attempts to commit an act of piracy is "liable to imprisonment for 30 years and a fine of R1 million".[56] The SPC also provides that the courts may "order the action to be taken as regards the ships, aircraft or property seized, according to the law".[57]

PENALTY FOR PIRACY IN THE SUPPRESSION OF PIRACY AND OTHER MARITIME OFFENCES ACT, 2019

The SPOMO Act provides that

"[p]iracy consists of any-

(a) illegal act of violence, detention or depredation committed for private ends by the crew or any passengers of a private ship or aircraft and directed –

i. in international waters against another ship or aircraft or against a person or property on board the ship or aircraft, or

---

52   s 65(1).

53   Criminal Side No 19 of 2010, judgment of 15 Dec 2010, 3 https://sherloc.unodc.org/res/cld/case-law-doc/piracycrimetype/syc/2010/the_republic_vs__mohamed_aweys_sayid_and_eight_8_others_html/Seychelles_2010_Crim_No_19_2010_Sentence.pdf (16-07-2020).

54   Criminal Side No 21 of 2011, judgment of 30 Jun 2011, par 6 https://www.unodc.org/res/cld/case-law-doc/piracycrimetype/syc/2011/the_republic_vs__abdukar_ahmed_five_5_others_html/SEY_1B.pdf (24-05-2019).

55   Criminal Side No 19 of 2011, judgment of 12 Oct 2011, par 8 https://sherloc.unodc.org/res/cld/case-lawdoc/piracycrimetype/syc/2011/the_republic_v_houssein_mohammed_osman_and_ten_10_others_html/SEY_6B.pdf (24-05-2019).

56   s 65(3).

57   s 65(7).

ii. against a ship, aircraft, person or property in a place outside the jurisdiction of any State;

(b) act of voluntary participation in the operation of a ship or of an aircraft with knowledge of facts making it a pirate ship or aircraft; and

(c) act of inciting or intentionally facilitating an act described in subparagraph (a) or (b)".[58]

It further states that

"[a] person who commits an act of piracy, [...] whether or not he was armed with a firearm or other weapon during the commission of the offence, is liable on conviction to life imprisonment and a fine of not more than N50,000,000, in addition to the restitution to the owner or forfeiture to the Federal Government of Nigeria whatever the person has obtained or gained from the commission of the crime".59

In addition, the Act does not only punish natural persons who commit piracy but punishes also corporate bodies engaged in the act of piracy. Indeed, the Act provides that "a body corporate or entity" that commits

"an offence of piracy, is liable on conviction to a fine of at least N500,000,000 and each of its directors or principal officers or any person responsible for its management and control, is liable to a fine of not less than N100,000,000 and imprisonment for at least 15 years each in addition to the restitution to the owner or forfeiture to the Federal Government of Nigeria whatever property or gains it has, or such officers have, obtained from the property".[60]

This is a welcome addition to the enforcement arsenal against piracy because, although a body corporate cannot itself commit an illegal act of violence or detention, or any act of depredation, it is possible for body corporates to finance, contribute and/or facilitate piratical activities.

As far as forfeiture is concerned, the Act is silent on the minimum period that must pass before property is forfeited to the State. This is a weakness of the Act because, as a matter of principle, the owner of stolen goods is entitled to lay

---

58   s 3.

59   s 12(1).

60   s 12(3).

claim to those goods for a reasonable time. In *Danladi*, a Supreme Court judge held that "the phrase 'reasonable time' implies that the time for the determination of the matter should not be too short or too long, depending on the nature and facts of the case".[61] Similarly, in *Ariori*, Obaseki JSC held that

> "[t]he meaning of "fair hearing" and "reasonable time" are not given in the 1963 Constitution nor in [the] new 1979 Constitution but they have however received judicial interpretation. In [his] view "fair hearing within a reasonable time" accords with the demands of justice and a waiver of this right amounts to a waiver of justice. Hearing has been defined in the Pocket Law Lexicon 8th Ed. By A.W. Motion as 'the trial of a suit'. Trial, on the other hand, is defined in the same pocket Law Lexicon as 'the hearing of a cause, civil or criminal, by a competent tribunal, the decision of the issues of law or fact in action. It may be by a judge or judges with or without jury or assessors'. Fair hearing, therefore, must mean a trial conducted according to all the legal rules formulated to ensure that justice is done to the parties to the cause. 'Reasonable time' must mean the period of time which, in the search for justice, does not wear out the parties and their witnesses and which is required to ensure that justice is not only done but appears to reasonable persons to be done".[62]

While the setting of a minimum period of at least 90 days appears to be required, one might also argue that no maximum period should be set. It was indeed made clear a century ago that

> "an owner of property who has been robbed by pirates has an absolute right to recover possession of the articles stolen from him, no matter where they may be. Even if the third party acquiring the goods has acted in good faith and is unaware that they were obtained by piratical means, his title to them must necessarily be illegal and precarious. That he can never become their owner follows from the absolute character of the principle *pirata non mutat dominium*".[63]

A middle path might consist in including in the Act a provision to the effect that "[c]laims for the recovery of property ... must be lodged by the lawful owners

61   *Danladi v Dangiri and Others* (2014) LPELR - 24020 (SC) 43–44 par D–A.

62   *R Ariori and Others v Muraino BO Elemo and Others* (1983) 1 SC 13 23.

63   Reply to the Report of the League of Nations' Committee of Experts in Rosenne *League of Nations: Committee of Experts for the Progressive Codification of International Law (1925–1928)* (1972) II 244–45.

with the authorities of the competent country within a period of … one year from the date on which the property was produced or found".[64]

CONCLUSION

The pieces of legislation discussed above stipulate penalties for acts of piracy. Each national legislation implicitly gives to the courts of the State concerned discretion to impose a sentence, provided that the courts do not exceed the maximum punishment prescribed in the legislation. The SADA provides that any person who commits an act of piracy is guilty of an offence and, upon conviction, is liable to a fine or to imprisonment for any period, including life imprisonment. By contrast, the Act does not deal with attempts, seizure and forfeiture. As a result, it is necessary to rely in this regard on other pieces of legislation that are of general application. The LPL distinguishes between piracy as a felony of the first degree and piracy as a felony of the second degree, with proportionate sentences. The position is the same as in South Africa with regard to attempts, seizure and forfeiture. In the case of Kenya, the courts have confirmed that the phrase "shall be liable" does not mean that it is mandatory to sentence a person to life imprisonment for the offence of piracy. In the same way, the SPC prescribes a maximum sentence that the courts may not exceed, but does not provide the minimum sentence for acts of piracy, thereby giving discretion to judicial officers. Only the SPC provides explicitly for the offence of attempting to commit an act of piracy.

As far as it is concerned the SPOMO Act follows the approach of the LPL by distinguishing between two categories of acts of piracy with regard to the maximum sentences. It prescribes minimum sentences and does not follow the approach adopted by all the pieces of legislation in the other States which do not provide for minimum sentences. While that former approach is probably the most suitable in view of the wide range of piratical acts and the threat that piracy poses to international navigation, maritime security and the economic development of States, failure to adequately punish pirates may contribute to related criminal

---

64   ibid 247.

activities such as gun running, drug trafficking, human trafficking and illegal fishing. While the pieces of legislation discussed do not provide for minimum sentences, it may be counter-productive for courts to impose sentences that are seen not to be adequate or commensurate to the offence. It was also indicated that, like the SPC, the SPOMO Act provides explicitly for the offence of attempting to commit an act of piracy, a crucial feature because it is important to punish all forms of participation in piracy. Following the same approach, the SPOMO Act contains the most detailed provisions governing seizures and forfeiture related to piracy among the legislation to which it has been compared. In addition, the SPOMO Act punishes also corporate bodies engaged in the act of piracy.

It was not possible, within the confines of this contribution, to compare the penalty-related provisions of the SPOMO Act to the relevant provisions in the legislation of all the other African Coastal States, let alone all the Coastal States in the world. However, what this study allows to submit is that the Nigerian courts have now at their disposal a set of provisions which have the benefit of combining different approaches followed in other African States and being sufficiently comprehensive to avoid having to rely on other (more generally applicable) pieces of legislation. In this way, Nigeria has made comparatively very significant progress in its ability to comply with its obligation, in terms of article 100 of the LOSC, to "cooperate to the fullest possible extent in the repression of piracy on the high seas or in any other place outside the jurisdiction of any State".

SANCTIONS, SHIPS, INTERNATIONAL SALES AND SECURITY OF PAYMENT

CHARL HUGO[*]

HENNIE STRYDOM[**]

[*] Professor of Banking Law and Director of the Centre for Banking Law, University of Johannesburg.

[**] Professor in Public International Law and holder of the NRF Research Chair in International Law, University of Johannesburg.

INTRODUCTION

In furtherance of real (or perhaps perceived) world and national security, sanctions – in more recent times, especially targeted financial sanctions – have emerged as a powerful weapon to combat international crime. As an enforcement measure under article 41 of the United Nations (UN) Charter, targeted financial sanctions are a result of the suffering to which the Iraqi population was subjected under the UN's conventional economic sanctions regime imposed on Iraq following Saddam Hussein's unlawful military invasion and occupation of Kuwait in 1990. This blunt measure made no distinction between the guilty and the innocent or between the delinquent leaders and the general population. To mitigate against such consequences, targeted or smart sanctions against specific individuals and entities became the preferred enforcement measure since 1999 with the adoption of United Nations Security Council (UNSC) resolution 1267.[1] This practice, which has become even more pronounced with the adoption of counter-terrorism measures after 9/11,[2] is currently also employed by individual States acting on their own against delinquent members of the international community.

Today, such sanctions may, in the first place, take the form of international sanctions arising from decisions of the UNSC in terms of which Member States are required to enact legislation or to adopt other measures to implement these sanctions. For this reason, the chapter starts with an overview of the UN sanctions regime applicable to the subject-matter of the chapter to which States are required to give effect by means of domestic laws and policies.

In South Africa, this is done, inter alia, through the Protection of Constitutional Democracy against Terrorist and Related Activities Act (POCDATARA)[3] and the Financial Intelligence Centre Act (FICA).[4] The POCDATARA[5] sanctions, which

---

1   See also White and Abass "Countermeasures and sanctions" in Evans (ed) *International Law* (2018) 521 542, 543; Shaw *International Law* (2017) 957.

2   See, inter alia, Strydom "Counter-terrorism measures and human rights" in Maluwa, Du Plessis, and Tladi (eds) *The Pursuit of a Brave New World: Essays in Honour of John Dugard* (2017) 395.

3   33 of 2004.

4   38 of 2001.

5   See Hugo and Spruyt "Money laundering, terrorist financing and financial sanctions: South Africa's response by means of the Financial Intelligence Centre Amendment Act" 2018 *TSAR* 227 249 et seq.

are restricted to the domain of terrorism, prohibit any person from dealing with property that is associated with terrorism or persons or organisations that carry out such acts.[6] The wider-ranging relevant provisions of FICA were introduced by the Financial Intelligence Centre Amendment Act and eventually came into force on 1 April 2019, somewhat later than the other provisions of the amending legislation, apparently because it took time to develop and put into place the mechanisms required for their implementation.[7] South Africa also adopted the Application of Resolutions of the Security Council of the United Nations Act,[8] which provides, in section 1, for the domestic application of UNSC resolutions by way of proclamation in the Government Gazette. However, the Act has never been put into force and effect.

In the second place, as indicated above, sanctions may be imposed independently of the UN by means of national legislation of a particular country. In this respect, we restrict ourselves to the sanctions imposed by the United States of America (US), which are probably the most important for purposes of this contribution. The prominence of US sanctions increased dramatically in the wake of the terrorist attacks of 9/11.[9] We refer here to the sanctions administered by the Office of Foreign Assets Control (OFAC) of the US Treasury, the official website of which states its role as follows:

> "The Office of Foreign Assets Control ('OFAC') of the US Department of the Treasury administers and enforces economic and trade sanctions based on US foreign policy and national security goals against targeted foreign countries and regimes, terrorists, international narcotics traffickers, those engaged in activities related to the

---

6   See ss 3 and 4.

7   See the Financial Intelligence Centre Amendment Act 1 of 2017, and, on the implementation of the sanctions provisions, Financial Intelligence Centre Notice by the Director in terms of Section 26A(3) of the Financial Intelligence Centre Act, 2001 https://www.fic.gov.za/Documents/Website%20Notice%20by%20the%20 Director%20-%201%201%20April%202019.pdf (28-8-2020). See further Financial Intelligence Centre Roadmap for the Short Term Implementation of the Financial Intelligence Centre Amendment Act, 2017 par 1.8. It was, however, initially envisaged that the provisions would have come into operation towards the end of 2018. See also Spruyt "The Financial Intelligence Centre Amendment Act and the application of a risk-based approach" in Hugo and Du Toit (eds) *Annual Banking Law Update* (2017) 19 n 8.

8   172 of 1993.

9   See Carter and Farha "Overview and operation of the evolving US financial sanctions, including the example of Iran" *Proceedings of the Annual Meeting (American Society of International Law)* Vol 107 (2013) 315 n 2 citing Uniting and Strengthening America by Providing Appropriate Tools Required to Intercept and Obstruct Terrorism (USA Patriot Act) 2001.

proliferation of weapons of mass destruction, and other threats to the national security, foreign policy or economy of the United States".[10]

To give effect to these sanctions, OFAC published and regularly updates a list of "specially designated nationals" (SDNs) who are targeted.[11] In this respect, the OFAC website states:

"As part of its enforcement efforts, OFAC publishes a list of individuals and companies owned or controlled by, or acting for or on behalf of, targeted countries. It also lists individuals, groups, and entities, such as terrorists and narcotics traffickers designated under programs that are not country-specific. Collectively, such individuals and companies are called 'Specially Designated Nationals' or 'SDNs.' *Their assets are blocked and U.S. persons are generally prohibited from dealing with them*"[12].

The SDNs include a large number of natural persons and companies (including import and export companies, shipping companies and banks) tied to, inter alia, Iran, Syria, North Korea and, closer to our borders, Zimbabwe.[13] A later addition to the list, and especially relevant for the purposes of this contribution, is a large number of vessels (ships and aircraft).[14]

All "U.S. persons" must comply with the OFAC regulations. "U.S. persons" include:

"all U.S. citizens and permanent resident aliens regardless of where they are located, all persons and entities within the United States, all U.S. incorporated entities and their

---

10 https://www.treasury.gov/resource-center/sanctions/Pages/default.aspx (19-3-2019).

11 https://www.treasury.gov/ofac/downloads/sdnlist.pdf (26-2-2019). The list is updated regularly – the one referred to is dated 19 March 2019. There is much activity in relation to the imposition and relaxation of OFAC sanctions. See, for example, the overview by Boscariol, Briscoe, Goodale, Harwig, Meyer, Stagg and Ward "Export controls and economic sanctions" in *The Year in Review* An Annual Publication of the ABA/Section of International Law (Spring 2016) 27 34-39.

12 https://www.treasury.gov/resource-center/sanctions/SDN-List/Pages/default.aspx (19-3-2019). The italics are ours.

13 See, for one example that has received attention in South African courts (refer to n 16 below in this regard), the OFAC SDN List (n 11) which, on page 271, contains the following inscription: "BREDENKAMP, John (a.k.a. BREDENKAMP, John A.; a.k.a. BREDENKAMP, John Arnold), Thetford Farm, P.O. Box HP86, Mount Pleasant, Harare, Zimbabwe; 10 Montpelier Square, London SW7 1JU, United Kingdom; Hurst Grove, Sanford Lane, Hurst, Reading, Berkshire RG10 0SQ, United Kingdom; Middleton House, Titlarks Hill Road, Sunningdale, Ascot, Berkshire SL5 0JB, United Kingdom; New Boundary House, London Road, Sunningdale, Ascot, Berkshire SL5 0DJ, United Kingdom; Mapstone House, Mapstone Hill, Lustleigh, Newton Abbot, Devon TQ13 9SE, United Kingdom; Dennerlei 30, Schoten, Belgium; 62 Chester Square, London, United Kingdom; DOB 11 Aug 1940; citizen Netherlands; alt. citizen Zimbabwe; alt. citizen Suriname; Passport ND1285143 (Netherlands); alt. Passport Z01024064 (Netherlands); alt. Passport Z153612 (Netherlands); alt. Passport 367537C (Suriname) (individual) [ZIMBABWE]".

14 https://www.treasury.gov/resource-center/sanctions/SDN-List/Pages/default.aspx (19-3-2019) 1238 et seq.

> foreign branches [as well as in the case of certain sanctions] ... foreign subsidiaries owned or controlled by U.S. companies ... [and] foreign persons in possession of U.S.-origin goods ... ".[15]

Targeted sanctions relating to ships impact upon international sales mainly in two manners. First, they may affect directly the free movement of ships by denying them access to particular harbours, being refuelled or from offloading or transhipping goods on board as well as subjecting the ship and its cargo to seizure and asset freezes. Secondly, they may impact indirectly by preventing financial institutions from processing payment in respect of transactions involving a targeted ship. We deal with this aspect in more detail below. In the case of US sanctions, banks in other countries, which, as a cold legal fact, may not technically be bound by the US legislation in this regard, will mostly also refuse to process or make a payment on the basis of strong business and reputational considerations.[16] The impact of sanctions on the ability of banks to make payment in international sale transactions is particularly evident in letter-of-credit practice – the dominant method of payment when security of payment becomes a real concern. The letter of credit has developed over the past century[17] into a remarkably secure instrument ensuring not only that the seller is paid, but also that the buyer receives the goods contracted for.[18]

Targeted financial sanctions and security of payment in international sales – to put it mildly – experience a very difficult co-existence. Against the background of this general introduction, we deal first with sanctions affecting the movement

---

15 https://www.treasury.gov/resource-center/faqs/Sanctions/Pages/faq_general.aspx (19-3-2019).

16 See, for example, the litigation in South Africa between Bredenkamp (the SDN referred to in note 13 above) and Standard Bank in which the bank went to great lengths to close the account of Bredenkamp for business and reputational reasons arising from his status as listed individual: *Bredenkamp v Standard Bank of South Africa Ltd* 2009 5 SA 304 (GSJ); *Bredenkamp v Standard Bank of South Africa Ltd* 2009 6 SA 277 (GSH); and *Bredenkamp v Standard Bank of South Africa Ltd* 2010 4 SA 468 (SCA).

17 Much has been written on the historical development of letters of credit. See in this regard Hugo "The development of documentary letters of credit as reflected in the Uniform Customs and Practice of Documentary Credits" 1993 *SA Merc LJ* 44 et seq. Ground-breaking early work includes that of Biro "Das Akkreditivgeschäft der Merchant Bankers" 1959 *Oestereichische Bank Archiv* 408 et seq; Ritter "Vom Akkreditiv" 1921 *Hanseatische Rechts-Zeitschrift* 609; Hershey "Letters of Credit" 1918-1919 *Harvard LR* 1; McCurdy "Commercial Letters of Credit" 1921-1922 *Harvard LR* 539 et seq, 715 et seq; Kozolchyk "The legal nature of the irrevocable commercial letter of credit" 1965-1966 *American Journal of Comparative Law* 395; and Ellinger *Documentary Letters of Credit* (1970) 26 et seq.

18 Sharrock (ed) *The Law of Banking and Payment in South Africa* 403-404.

of ships (and related issues). We then deal with their impact on payment (especially in the letter-of-credit context) before formulating some conclusions.

SELECT UN SANCTIONS LINKED TO TRANSACTIONS INVOLVING TARGETED SHIPS AND THEIR CARGO

The UN sanctions regime against the Democratic People's Republic of Korea (DPRK) was adopted in response to the country's decision, in 1993, to withdraw from the 1968 Treaty on the Non-proliferation of Nuclear Weapons[19] and its subsequent nuclear weapon tests coupled with the test-launching of inter-continental ballistic missiles in blatant disregard for UNSC resolutions demanding the suspension of all such activities.[20] Between 2006 and 2017, a pattern of adjustment and expansion of sanctions developed, prompted by the DPRK regime's obstinate determination to develop and test nuclear weapons and ballistic missiles in clear violation of UNSC resolutions that considered such conduct a threat to international peace and security.

As the sanctions regime expanded and became more stringent over time, the DPRK shipping industry became a prime target. This was necessary in view of ensuing sanction-evasion practices in the form of the re-designation of vessels, the changing of their identity numbers and names, and transhipments of cargo containing listed items. With 240 merchant ships under its jurisdiction, the opportunities for sanctions evasion by the DPRK regime and its targeted officials were manifold. Over time, the evasion practices also attracted the attention of the Panel of Experts established by UNSC resolution 1874 (2009) to assist the Security Council Sanctions Committee to carry out its mandate as specified in resolution 1718 (2006) in respect of the supply, sale or transfer by the DPRK of certain listed materials, goods or equipment and the export thereof by UN Member States to the DPRK. In its 2018 report, the Panel concluded as follows:

> "In addition to ongoing violations and increasingly sophisticated evasion practices, the Panel's latest investigations show that the Democratic People's Republic of Korea is already flouting the most recent resolutions by exploiting global oil supply chains,

---

19   729 *UNTS* 161, (1968) 7 *ILM* 889. Adopted: 01-07-1968; EIF: 05-03-1070.

20   See inter alia UNSC resolution 1695 (2006) par 2.

complicit foreign nationals, offshore company registries and the international banking system. The Panel investigated illicit ship-to-ship transfers of petroleum comprising a multi-million-dollar business that is driving an international network of brokers and ship charterers as well as unwitting global commodity trading companies and oil suppliers. In tandem, the Democratic People's Republic of Korea continued to export almost all the commodities prohibited in the resolutions, generating nearly $200 million in revenue between January and September 2017. In continuing its illicit coal exports, the country combined deceptive navigation patterns, signals manipulation, trans-shipment and fraudulent documentation to obscure the origin of the coal".[21]

The salient features of the UN's sanction regime as they relate to the subject-matter of this contribution fall into two categories, namely restrictions on the movement of ships and restrictions on certain financial transactions. Both are aimed at preventing the supply, sale or transfer of certain materials, equipment, goods, technology or weapons which could contribute to the DPRK's nuclear-related, ballistic missile-related or other weapons-of-mass-destruction-related programme.

Restrictions on the movement of ships take, in the first instance, the form of a duty on Territorial States to inspect all cargo to and from the DPRK when there are reasonable grounds to believe that the cargo contains items prohibited by the UNSC's sanctions regime.[22] This also applies to vessels on the high seas, which must be inspected with the consent of the Flag State or which, when the Flag State does not give its consent, must be directed by the Flag State to proceed to a convenient port for inspection by the Territorial State.[23] Prohibited items identified during inspections are subject to seizure and disposal by the Inspecting State.[24] On the same grounds, the UN Member States and their nationals are prohibited from providing bunkering services, such as the provision of fuel or supplies or other services, to DPRK vessels.[25]

Following another nuclear test by the DPRK on 6 January 2016, the measures imposed by resolution 1718 (2006) and 1874 (2009) were to apply

---

21 UN Doc S/2018/171 (5 March 2018).

22 UNSC resolution 1874 (2009) par 11.

23 par 13.

24 par 14.

25 par 17.

also to the shipment of items to or from the DPRK for repair, servicing, testing, reverse-engineering and marketing, regardless of whether ownership or control is transferred, and to any individual travelling for the purposes of carrying out these activities.[26] Resolution 2270 prohibits the leasing or chartering of vessels or aircraft by nationals of, or residents in, Member States, or by any other designated person or entity, to the DPRK. It also calls upon Member States to de-register any vessel that is owned, operated or crewed by the DPRK and not to register any such vessel that is de-registered by another Member State pursuant to this resolution.[27] Member States are also prohibited from allowing into their ports any vessel in respect of which the Member State has information that provides reasonable grounds to believe that the vessel is owned or controlled by a designated individual, or contains cargo the supply, sale, transport or export of which is prohibited.[28] In this regard, Annex III to the resolution contains a list of 31 vessels that are considered "economic assets" subject to the asset-freeze obligation under the PDRK sanctions regime.

Another nuclear test in September 2016 caused the UNSC to further tighten and expand on the sanctions already imposed. For instance, the chartering and leasing prohibition in paragraph 19 of resolution 2270 was made applicable to "all leasing, chartering or provision of crew services to the DPRK without exception" unless approved by the Security Council Committee in advance.[29] Moreover, when the Committee has reasonable grounds to believe that vessels are or have been related to the DPRK's prohibited weapons programmes, it may require the following steps to be taken against designated vessels: (a) that the Flag State de-flags the vessel; (b) that the Flag State instructs the vessel to proceed to a port identified by the Committee, in coordination with the Port State; (c) that all UN Member States prohibit a designated vessel from entering their ports unless for emergency reasons or under direction of the Committee; and (d) that the vessel becomes subject to asset freeze measures.[30] Further adjustments followed in

---

26   SC resolution 2270 (2016) par 7.
27   par 19, 20.
28   par 22.
29   SC resolution 2321 (2016) par 8.
30   par 12.

2017, in response to yet another nuclear test on 2 September 2017, determining that failure by a Flag State to cooperate with the inspection of its vessels on the high seas would result in the Committee designating the vessel in question for the measures imposed by the UNSC in resolutions 1718 (2006) and 2321 (2016). In such instances, the Flag State is under an obligation to de-register the vessel immediately.[31] Under this resolution, UN Member States must also prohibit their nationals or persons or entities under their jurisdiction, as well as vessels flying their flag, from facilitating or engaging in ship-to-ship transfers to or from DPRK-flagged vessels of any prohibited goods or items that are being supplied, sold or transferred to or from the DPRK.[32]

As indicated above, restrictions on financial transactions are another salient feature of the sanctions regime against the DPRK. Targeted in this regard is the provision of financial services through or from Member States' territories, or to or by their nationals or entities, that could contribute to the DPRK's prohibited weapons programmes. In addition, financial or other assets or resources that are associated with such programmes fall under the Member State's freezing of assets obligations.[33] The resolution also extends the imposition of financial sanctions to international financial and credit institutions by interdicting the entering by such institutions into new commitments for grants, financial assistance or concessional loans to the DPRK.[34] Also affected is public financial support for trade with the DPRK, including the granting of export credits, guarantees or insurance to Member States' nationals or entities involved in such trade.[35]

In its March 2013 resolution,[36] following another nuclear test by the DPRK on 12 February 2013, the UNSC more fully addressed the violation of the DPRK sanctions regime. Already in the preamble the resolution urged Member States to apply the Financial Action Task Force's (FATF) new interpretative note on recommendation 7 on customer due diligence and record keeping regarding

---

31   UNSC resolution 2375 (2017) par 8.
32   par 11.
33   UNSC resolution 1874 (2009) par 18.
34   par 19.
35   par 20.
36   UNSC resolution 2094 (2013).

targeted financial sanctions in relation to non-proliferation.[37] Furthermore, the resolution included brokering or other intermediate services,[38] bulk cash payments[39] or any other financial or other assets or resources that could contribute to the DPRK's prohibited weapons programmes as activities that will fall under the DPRK sanctions regimes. For the same reason, the resolution prohibits the opening of new branches, subsidiaries or representative offices of DPRK banks in the territories of Member States, as well as the establishing of new joint ventures or correspondent relationships with banks in their jurisdiction if they have information or have reasonable grounds to believe that such financial services could contribute to the DPRK's nuclear or ballistic-missile programme.[40] Further obligations were imposed in 2016 to the effect that UN Member States were to interdict their nationals, and persons and entities under their jurisdiction from providing insurance or re-insurance services to vessels owned, controlled or operated by the DPRK unless a vessel is used exclusively for humanitarian purposes and exempted in advance by the Security Council's Sanctions Committee.[41]

THE IMPACT OF SANCTIONS ON PAYMENT (ESPECIALLY BY LETTER OF CREDIT)

The letter of credit as payment method

A letter of credit (also known as a documentary credit) is essentially an undertaking by a bank to pay the beneficiary of the letter of credit provided certain conditions are met.[42] The underlying contract is normally an international contract of sale in which the buyer and seller have agreed to payment by letter of credit. The buyer, to give effect to the payment clause of the contract of sale, requests (mandates) a bank (typically the buyer's own bank – *the issuing bank*) to issue a letter of credit in favour of the seller (the beneficiary of the letter of

37 available at https://eurasiangroup.org/Methodology/eng/note/7/ (27-6-2018).
38 UNSC Resolution 2094 par 7.
39 par 11.
40 par 12.
41 UNSC resolution 2321 (2016) par 22.
42 Sharrock (n 18) 403.

credit).[43] The mandate given by the buyer also contains the conditions that need to be met by the seller in order to be paid by the bank. These conditions are invariably documentary. In other words, in order to be paid by the bank, the seller will have to provide certain stipulated documents.[44] These documents must comply strictly with the terms of the letter of credit issued by the bank (which in turn should reflect exactly the instructions of the buyer in the mandate). If the seller, accordingly, presents conforming documents, it will be entitled to payment in terms of the letter of credit and, if the bank has paid against conforming documents, it will be entitled to reimbursement in terms of the contract of mandate.[45]

It is important to take note of the fact that letters of credit are almost always issued and dealt with in accordance with rules drafted under the auspices of the Banking Commission of the International Chamber of Commerce (ICC), namely the *Uniform Rules and Practice for Documentary Credits (UCP)*.[46] It is important to realise that these rules have no higher status than contractually incorporated terms of contract. The Banking Commission of the ICC, moreover, provides continuous guidance relating to letter-of-credit practice in the form of opinions (written and published answers to questions mostly from banks) and formal guidance notes (which are also published).[47]

The presentation of many different documents can be required by the letter of credit. Amongst those most often encountered are the commercial invoice, the transport document (for example a marine bill of lading or a combined transport document), the insurance document and any of a number of certificates, such as a

---

43   Sharrock (n 18) 404-405, 407.

44   408-409.

45   409.

46   For a more detailed analysis of the history and role of the ICC and the *UCP 600*, see Hugo "Letters of credit and demand guarantees: a tale of two sets of rules of the International Chamber of Commerce" 2017 *TSAR* 1.

47   Hugo (n 46) 13. One such guidance paper dating back to 2014, which is especially relevant in this context and is considered in more detail below, is the "Guidance Paper on the Use of Sanctions Clauses in Trade Finance-related Instruments subject to ICC Rules" Document 470/1238 (https://cdn.iccwbo.org/content/uploads/sites/3/2014/08/Guidance-Paper-on-The-Use-Of-Sanctions-Clauses-In-Trade-Finance-Related-Instruments-Subject-To-ICC-Rules.pdf).

certificate of inspection, a certificate of quality and a certificate of origin.[48] These documents contain much information. Apart from an accurate description of the goods and the price, the commercial invoice may well indicate who the consignor or exporter is, who the consignee is (and the buyer if it is someone other than the consignee), the country of origin of the goods, the country of destination of the goods, the ports of loading and discharge of the goods and the names of contact persons of the buyer and the consignor. Much of this information may also be replicated on the bill of lading which, in addition, will also indicate the name of the carrier and – of particular importance for the purpose of this contribution – the name and IMO registration number of the vessel.[49] The insurance document will, furthermore, indicate who the insurer is and, likewise, the certificates will identify their issuers as well as the information certified (such as the quality or origin of the goods) and the date and place where this was done.

The bank's undertaking in a letter of credit has a very special legal status: it is independent or autonomous. This means that the question whether or not the bank is obliged to pay the beneficiary is determined solely with reference to the letter of credit and not with reference to the contract of sale (the underlying contract)[50] or the mandate (from which the bank's right to reimbursement

---

48   These are the most common documents encountered in documentary sales (see Sharrock (n 18) 395). The UCP 600 contains provisions relating only to commercial invoices (a 18), transport documents (aa 19-27) and insurance documents (a 28). However, the parties are free to contract for any document they may wish to have. See also, specifically in relation to the different documents encountered in the sanctions context, Strong and Herd "Letter of credit payment & sanctions" http://www.strongandherd.co.uk/international-trade-articles/article-letters-of-credit-sanctions/ (21-3-2019).

49   The background and role of the IMO number is stated as follows on the webpages of More Than Shipping ("Lloyd's and IMO numbers for shipping vessels" https://www.morethanshipping.com/lloyds-imo-number-vessels/ (21-3-2019)): "The International Maritime Organization (IMO) number is a unique reference for ships and for registered ship owners and management companies. IMO numbers were introduced under the SOLAS Convention to improve maritime safety and security and to reduce maritime fraud. The ship number consists of the three letters 'IMO,' followed by a unique seven-digit number assigned to sea-going merchant ships under the International Convention for the Safety of Life at Sea (SOLAS). In 1987, the IMO adopted Resolution A.600(15), 'aimed at enhancing maritime safety, and pollution prevention and to facilitate the prevention of maritime fraud' by assigning to each ship a permanent identification number which would continue despite any subsequent change in the vessel's name, ownership or flag". (The italics are ours.)

50   *Phillips v Standard Bank of South Africa Ltd* 1985 3 SA 301 (WLD) 303; *Loomcraft Fabrics CC v Nedbank Ltd* 1996 1 SA 812 (A) 815. For analyses of the independence principle in general in letter-of-credit practice, see Sharrock (n 18) 422 et seq (condensed) and Enonchong *The Independence Principle of Letters of Credit and Demand Guarantees* (2011) (comprehensive). See also art 4 of the *UCP 600*.

arises).[51] This is a very strong rule of letter-of-credit law. There are exceptions to the rule, the best-established being fraud by the beneficiary. However, reliance on the exceptions is seldom successful.[52] Certainty of payment is regarded as a dominant policy consideration in international trade. This has led courts to invoke the vivid imagery of the flowing of "lifeblood" and the avoidance of "thrombosis" by interfering with the passage of money.[53]

The above explanation of the operation of payment by letter of credit takes account only of the minimum number of parties involved in the transaction, namely the buyer, the seller and the *issuing bank*. Normally, however, more banks are involved. It is necessary to deal briefly with their respective roles.[54]

Typically, the issuing bank will not communicate the letter of credit directly to the beneficiary. It will instruct another bank in the seller's country to do so. This bank is known as the *advising bank*. The advising bank acts as a mere messenger on the instructions of the issuing bank which, almost invariably today, it will receive by means of SWIFT communication.[55] The advising bank accordingly does not make any payment undertaking.

Moreover, the beneficiary will not normally be required to deliver the documents to the issuing bank, which is typically in another country. The letter of credit communicated (advised) to the beneficiary will nominate a bank in the beneficiary's country that will receive the documents and effect payment on

---

51 art 4 of the *UCP 600*. See also Sharrock (n 18) 422; Hugo *The Law relating to Documentary Credits from a South African Perspective with Special Reference to the Position of the Legal Position of the Issuing and Confirming Banks* (1996 thesis Stell) par 6.2.4 and 6.5.2.

52 See the *Phillips* case (n 50) 303 and the *Loomcraft* case (n 50) 817. In the latter case, Scott AJA stated that, although the onus of proving fraud was the "ordinary civil one", he stressed that it "will not lightly be inferred" (817G). For a South African case in which fraud was successfully raised, see *Group Five Construction (Pty) Ltd) v Member of the Executive Council Public Transport Roads and Works Gauteng* 2015 (5) SA 26 (GJ).

53 *RD Harbottle (Mercantile) Ltd v National Westminster Bank Ltd* 1977 2 All ER 862 (QB) 870b-d ("lifeblood") and *Intraco Ltd v Notis Shipping Corporation (The Bhoja Trader)* 1981 2 Lloyd's Rep 256 (CA) 257 (both "lifeblood" and "thrombosis").

54 For a more detailed overview of the role of the different banks, see Sharrock (n 18) 404-414 and 430-433. See also art 2, 7-9, 12, 13 and 38 of the *UCP 600*.

55 The acronym stands for the "Society for Worldwide Interbank Financial Telecommunications" based in Belgium. See Carter and Farha (n 9) 316, who explain that it provides "just a communication system" (that is to say that it has no direct settlement function) but, by providing a "common language" for payment instructions for financial institutions around the world" it is "vital to the settlement of international payments".

behalf of the issuing bank.[56] This *nominated bank*, too, acts as mandatary of the issuing bank and does not itself make any payment undertaking. Hence, when it pays, it discharges only the issuing bank's obligation to pay. Once it has paid, the nominated bank is entitled to be reimbursed by the issuing bank provided, of course, the documents presented to it by the beneficiary were conforming (in other words in strict compliance with the requirements of the letter of credit).

In certain instances, especially when either the issuing bank or the country in which the issuing bank is located is not trusted by the beneficiary, the latter may require that the letter of credit be confirmed by a bank in its own country or in another reputable country. In this case, another bank, the *confirming bank*, will become involved. A confirming bank may play the role of both advising and nominated bank (thereby replacing them), but this is not necessarily the case. Its main purpose, however, is to confirm the letter of credit, that is to add its own independent undertaking to that of the issuing bank. Hence, the beneficiary of a confirmed letter of credit has an independent claim against both the issuing bank and the confirming bank under the letter of credit. Provided the beneficiary tenders conforming documents, it can therefore enforce payment against either of these banks.

In the event of the beneficiary being a middleman, that is the beneficiary itself is purchasing the goods from a supplier or manufacturer in order to resell them, a transferable letter of credit may be used. A transferable letter of credit enables the beneficiary to pay its supplier by utilising the letter of credit issued in its favour. In order to be transferable, the letter of credit must state that it is transferable. In this case, the beneficiary may request the nominated bank, now renamed the *transferring bank*, to make part of the credit available to a second beneficiary (the manufacturer or supplier). The nominated or transferring bank will then, against conforming documents, pay the supplier its price, pay the beneficiary its profit, and then recover the full purchase price from the issuing bank.

---

56 The effecting of payment can take many forms in different permutations. It may be simply to pay on delivery of conforming documents (sight payment). It can also be to pay some time after the delivery of conforming documents (deferred payment). It may further be to accept a term bill of exchange against delivery of conforming documents and to pay the bill of exchange (the banker's acceptance) when it matures. Finally, it may be to "negotiate" the conforming documents. The awkward term "negotiate" means to purchase the conforming documents from the beneficiary (of course at a discount) and then to present them for payment to the issuing bank.

The letter of credit may, finally, provide for reimbursement of the nominated bank by a bank other than the issuing bank known as the *reimbursing bank*. Such reimbursement may or may not be covered by special rules emanating from the ICC. A failure by the reimbursing bank to reimburse the nominated bank, however, does not relieve the issuing bank from reimbursing the nominated bank (in this context – the *claiming bank*).[57]

Payment in a letter of credit transaction is often deferred. This can be done by making use of a so-called deferred payment credit in which the bank's undertaking is to pay, not on acceptance of conforming documents, but at a specified time thereafter (for example "90 days after the date of the bill of lading"). Deferment can also be done by making use of an acceptance credit (as opposed to the payment credit described above). In this case, the bank's undertaking is to accept a term bill of exchange against delivery of conforming documents and to pay it on maturity. This type of arrangement may enable the extension of credit to the buyer. Moreover, since the seller who has delivered conforming documents acquires an unconditional right against the bank to be paid on a specific future date, and banks are normally reliable debtors, the seller is typically able to be paid much earlier by discounting his right to payment to a forfaiter or factor.

The OFAC sanctions (linked to ships) affecting payment by letter of credit

Towards the end of the SDN list, there is a separate section relating to vessels (ships and aircraft), which first appeared in 2008, now comprising some 21 pages, introduced as follows:

> "Blocked vessels have been segregated into a separate section of the SDN List, below. Except in limited circumstances, *financial institutions are instructed to reject any funds transfer referencing a blocked vessel and must notify OFAC, preferably via facsimile with a copy of the payment instructions that funds have been returned to the remitter due to the possible involvement of a blocked vessel in the underlying transaction. See 31 C.F.R. §* 501.604(b)(1). Financial institutions should contact OFAC's Compliance Outreach and Implementation Division for further instructions should the name of a blocked vessel appear in shipping documents presented under a letter of credit or if noticed

---

57   See art 13 of the *UCP 600*.

in a documentary collection. Blocked vessels must themselves be physically blocked should they enter U.S. jurisdiction. Freight forwarders and shippers may not charter, book cargo on, or otherwise deal with blocked vessels".[58]

The list contains more than 500 vessels[59] carrying flags of, inter alia, the DPRK, Iran, Syria, Cuba, Mongolia, Malta, Panama, Trinidad and Tobago, Russia, Comoros, Cyprus, Liberia, Sierra Leone and Tanzania. One inscription on the list, selected randomly, reads, for example:

"IRAN YOUSHAT Bunkering Tanker Iran flag; Additional Sanctions Information - Subject to Secondary Sanctions; Vessel Registration Identification IMO 8319952 (vessel) [IRAN] (Linked To: ISLAMIC REPUBLIC OF IRAN SHIPPING LINES)".[60]

As is clear from this example, the listing contains not only the name of the ship (*Iran Youshat*), but also the permanent non-variable IMO registration number (8319952) in order to address the problem of ship-owners changing the names of their vessels to circumvent sanctions.[61] For this reason, a letter of credit may require that the bill of lading should contain the IMO number. Bills of lading, however, often do not and shippers sometimes refuse to state this number on the bill of lading.[62] In this respect, it would accordingly appear that maritime practice and sanctions may not be well-synchronised as yet.[63]

The practical implication of this is, inter alia, that no US bank, whether involved in a letter of credit transaction as issuing bank, nominated bank, confirming bank, transferring bank or reimbursing bank, will process payment of a letter of credit should any of the vast array of documents presented in terms of

---

58 https://www.treasury.gov/ofac/downloads/sdnlist.pdf (19-3-2019). This list is updated almost daily. The listed vessels appeared on pages 1238-1259 of the list as it was when accessed. The italics are ours.

59 It is of interest to note, moreover, that certain logistics companies have lists of their own naming additional ships that are not on the OFAC list. See, in this regard, the list of Expeditors at https://www.expeditors.com/vessels-of-concern which contains a further 33 ships.

60 https://www.treasury.gov/ofac/downloads/sdnlist.pdf (19-3-2019) 1248.

61 Strong and Herd (n 48). See also n 49 above in relation to the IMO number.

62 See "Requirement of IMO Number in Bill of Lading" https://shippingandfreightresource.com/requirement-imo-number-bill-lading/ (21-3-2019).

63 See in general on this non-alignment, Stewart and Osborne "Discussion paper: UN maritime sanctions and the International Maritime Organisation" Project Alpha, Centre for Science and Security Studies, King's College London (15 November 2018) https://projectalpha.eu/discussion-paper-un-maritime-sanctions-and-the-international-organisation/ (21-3-2019).

the credit contain a reference to a so-called blocked vessel. For it to do so would be unlawful under US law. Translated into the language of the South African law of contract, performance by a US bank of its obligations in terms of the letter of credit transaction is legally impossible. The permutations are many. We restrict ourselves to a few examples.

(i)   A letter of credit is issued by a US bank in favour of a South African beneficiary. The letter of credit is confirmed by a South African bank. The beneficiary presents conforming documents to the South African bank. The documents, however, indicate that, in the final leg of the voyage, the goods were carried on an OFAC-listed vessel. If the South African bank pays the beneficiary, it will not be reimbursed by the US bank. If it does not pay the beneficiary, however, it will be in breach of its contractual obligations towards the beneficiary in terms of its confirmation of the letter of credit because the performance of its obligations is not unlawful in South African law. Hence, it should be possible for the beneficiary to enforce payment against the South African confirming bank.

(ii)   A letter of credit is issued by a US bank in favour of a South African beneficiary. The beneficiary presents conforming documents to a South African nominated bank. The documents, however, indicate that, in the final leg of the voyage, the goods were carried on an OFAC-listed vessel. If the South African bank pays the beneficiary, it will not be reimbursed by the US bank. Since the nominated bank has made no payment undertaking towards the beneficiary, there is no reason why it should pay the beneficiary.

(iii)   An acceptance letter of credit is issued by a US bank in favour of a South African beneficiary. The beneficiary presents conforming documents to the South African nominated bank together with a bill of exchange drawn on the nominated bank payable 90 days after acceptance. The documents, however, indicate that, in the final leg of the voyage, the goods were carried on an OFAC-listed vessel. If the South African nominated bank pays the beneficiary in accordance with its obligations under the bill of exchange (accepted by the nominated bank), it will not be reimbursed by the US bank. However, in accordance with South African law it will be contractually bound to pay the beneficiary, or any subsequent holder (who may have purchased it in a discounting transaction) on maturity of the bill of exchange.

(iv)   A South African bank issues a letter of credit in favour of a Ghanaian beneficiary. The letter of credit, however, is payable in US dollars and, accordingly, requires the services of a US correspondent bank. The documents indicate that the goods were carried on an OFAC-listed vessel. The US bank will be legally unable to process the transaction. Performance will accordingly be impossible irrespective of the fact that the sale may well be perfectly legal both in South African and in Ghanaian law.

Against this background, it is clear that banks involved in letter-of-credit transactions in various capacities may find themselves in a precarious position. In an article focusing on the risks relating to traditional trade financing instruments (the main one of which is the letter of credit) in the context of sanctions and the fight against international financial crime, Marxen identifies certain "unintended consequences of increased and stricter compliance rules". He states, inter alia:

> "The compliance matrix is ... expanded by extraterritorial application of laws and regulations by some countries, most notably the United States of America (also referred to as long-reach or long-arm approach or legislation) in matters of, inter alia, sanctions. By treating transactions that are nominated in US-Dollars, in some cases irrespective of where contract formation takes place, where goods or services are exchanged or delivered, and where parties are domiciled, to be subject to US-American law, the United States of America, effectively, imposes its own compliance expectations onto the global financial network and international banking and trade".[64]

One of the "unintended consequences", it is submitted, has been the emergence of so-called "sanctions clauses" being included in letters of credit.[65]

---

64 Marxen "Traditional trade finance instruments a high risk? A critical view on current international initiatives and regulatory measures to curb financial crime" in Hugo (ed) *Annual Banking Law Update* (2018) 161 177-178 (footnotes omitted). See also Stanton "North Korea: The myth of maxed-out sanctions" 2 *Fletcher Sec Rev* (2015) 20 23, who refers to "the Treasury Department's global reach". At 24, he puts it thus: "Treasury has harnessed its regulatory power of the dollar system to ferret out money laundering and terrorist financing within the millions of transactions flowing through the system. By availing themselves of the dollar system, banks subject themselves to Treasury's regulatory authorities, and undertake obligations to know their customers, report large cash transactions, and report suspicious activity. Treasury's authorities allow it to gather financial intelligence, to block assets involved in illicit activity, and even to restrict or even block a foreign bank's access to the dollar system".

65 According to the ICC Banking Commission (n 47) par 2.1, sanction clauses flow from a concern of banks "about the implications of sanctions for their own obligations" and in order to "notify their counterparties, whether correspondent banks or beneficiaries" of these implications.

In a recently released guidance paper, the ICC Banking Commission quotes the following three clauses:[66]

(a)   "Presentation of document(s) that are not in compliance with the applicable anti-boycott, anti-money laundering, anti-terrorism, anti-drug trafficking and economic sanctions laws and regulations is not acceptable. Applicable laws vary depending on the transaction and may include United Nations, United States and/or local laws".[67]

(b)   "[Bank] complies with the international sanction laws and regulations issued by the United States of America, the European Union and the United Nations (as well as local laws and regulations applicable to the issuing branch) and in furtherance of those laws and regulations, *[Bank] has adopted policies which in some cases go beyond the requirement of applicable laws and regulations.* Therefore [Bank] undertakes no obligation to make any payment under, or otherwise to implement, this letter of credit (including but not limited to processing documents or advising the letter of credit), if there is involvement by any person (natural, corporate or governmental) listed in the USA, EU, UN or local sanctions lists, or any involvement by or nexus with Cuba, Sudan, Iran or Myanmar, or any of their governmental agencies".[68]

(c)   "Trade and economic sanctions ('sanctions') imposed by governments, government agencies or departments, regulators, central banks and/or transnational organizations (including the United Nations and European Union) impact upon transactions involving countries, or persons resident within countries currently including [long list of countries follows]...... . Issuing bank and all of its related bodies corporate might be subject to and affected by, sanctions, with which it will comply. Please contact issuing bank for clarification before presenting documents to issuing bank ... or undertaking any dealings regarding this credit involving countries or persons affected by sanctions. Issuing bank is not and will not be liable for any loss or damage whatsoever associated directly or indirectly with the application of sanctions to a transaction or financial service involving issuing bank. *Issuing bank is not required to perform any obligation under this credit which it determines in its discretion will, or would be likely to, contravene or breach any sanction. This clause applies notwithstanding any inconsistency with the current edition of the ... [UCP]".*[69]

---

66   See n 47 above. These three types of clauses are also considered in Reed Smith "Sanctions clauses – safeguarding payment under letters of credit" (11 January 2012) https://www.reedsmith.com/en/perspectives/2012/01/sanctions-clauses--safeguarding-payment-under-letters-of-credit (19-8-2018).

67   par 3.1 (a).

68   par 3.1 (b) (our italics).

69   par 3.1 (c) (our italics).

A sanctions clause that effectively states simply that the issuing bank is bound by the laws to which it is subject, is uncontroversial but also meaningless. In addition, such laws will necessarily apply irrespective of whether they, or one or some of them, may be in conflict with provisions of the *UCP 600*. As pointed out above, the UCP constitutes no more than terms of contract and cannot trump prescriptive law. Hence, sanctions clause (a) quoted above is unproblematic, but it also serves no purpose, except perhaps of drawing attention to the existence of sanctions laws.

As pointed out in the Guidance Paper, however, sanctions clause (b) quoted above is more problematic. This clause draws attention to the fact that the bank has adopted (internal) policies relating to sanctions which may go further than the applicable laws and regulations. Although not stating so explicitly, the logical interpretation of the clause must be that the bank may also decline to pay or process the transaction if it would be inconsistent with its own internal policies, irrespective of the law. The beneficiary is not privy to these internal policies and is therefore unable to assess the strength of the bank's undertaking. Moreover, the nominated and/or confirming bank similarly have no knowledge of these internal policies and, accordingly, cannot assess accurately whether they will be reimbursed. It is suggested, furthermore, that the mandate given by the issuing bank to the nominated bank relating to a letter of credit containing such a clause may indeed fail to meet the requirements of a valid contract. This is a complex question, the answer to which may well differ from jurisdiction to jurisdiction. A detailed consideration of it falls outside the scope of this paper. We limit ourselves to stating that, in our view, true consensus may be a problem[70] and so may lack of certainty.[71] Moreover, the issuing bank's obligation could conceivably be seen as subject to a potestative condition ("I will perform if I want to"), in which case there is no valid contract in South African law.[72]

All that is said above in relation to clause (b) is applicable mutatis mutandis to clause (c), which allows the issuing bank not to pay or process payment on the

---

70   See Van Huyssteen, Lubbe and Reinecke *Contract General Principles* (2016) par 2.21.

71   Van Huyssteen et al (n 70) par 8.2–8.2.

72   Van Huyssteen et al (n 70) par 9.151; De Wet and Van Wyk *De Wet en Yeats Die Suid-Afrikaanse Kontraktereg en Handelsreg* (1978) 135.

basis of a determination "in its discretion" that such payment would contravene or would be likely to contravene sanctions. Against this background, the Guidance Paper concludes by recommending "that banks should refrain from issuing trade-finance-related instruments that include sanctions clauses that purport to impose restrictions beyond, or conflict with, the applicable statutory or regulatory requirements".[73] It also advises parties involved in letter-of-credit transactions to "refrain from bringing into question the irrevocable, independent nature of the credit …, the certainty of payment or the intent to honour obligations".[74]

Despite the afore-mentioned ICC Guidance Paper which dates back to 2014, however, sanctions clauses akin to (b) and (c) quoted above are still encountered often. The Banking Commission of the ICC is, for example, currently in the process of drafting an official opinion to a query from a bank lamenting "a very unfortunate trend"[75] of rejections of documents by issuing banks in terms such as the following:

> "Note the documents have been rejected and returned to you by courier because of local and international laws and regulations *and internal policy* for AML/CTF and foreign sanctions in accordance with our L/C terms".[76]

This "trend" is diametrically opposed to conventional letter-of-credit law, in terms of which documents can only be returned if they are in fact not in conformity with the requirements of the letter of credit.[77] In the case on which the opinion was sought, it was well established that the documents were not rejected for being non-conforming. The requester for the opinion puts it thus:

> "When questioned the issuing bank confirmed that its refusals were not caused by the presentations being non-compliant with the terms and conditions of any credit. Rather, follow up responses from the bank appear to indicate that the refusals were due

---

73   ICC Banking Commission (n 47) par 4.1.

74   ICC Banking Commission (n 47) par 4.2.

75   See ICC Banking Commission Document 470/1280 (09-09-2018) 2.

76   ibid (the italics are ours). The sanctions clause concerned reads as follows: "Our bank process [sic] transactions in accordance with local and international laws and regulations, and reserve [sic] the right to comply with foreign sanctions as well. Consequently documents issued by or showing any involvement of parties sanctioned by any competent authority or contained any information thereon [sic] might not be processed by our bank at our [sic] sole discretion and without any liability on our [sic] part".

77   See art 15 of the UCP 600 read with art 7, 14 and 16.

> to regulatory concerns, which were then subsequently clarified to relate to internal policy and risk concerns, rather than regulatory".

At the time of the drafting of this contribution, the opinion sought had not yet been released by the ICC Banking Commission but, in light of its Guidance Paper, it is likely to be highly critical of this approach (or trend).

It is clear, however, that the once highly secure letter-of-credit business has become significantly riskier in these times of targeted financial sanctions. Beneficiaries are less certain of being paid and banks which have paid or have committed themselves to pay, may not be able to recover the money paid. A US bank that refuses to pay or reimburse due to the fact that the documents disclose that the goods were carried on a listed vessel will be able to rely on the fact that it would be illegal for it to pay or reimburse. Non-US banks, outside of the United States, however, will not be able to rely on such a defence. Hence, such banks which have bound themselves contractually to pay (for example, by confirming a letter of credit or by accepting a term bill of exchange against delivery of conforming documents) can conceivably be sued by beneficiaries should they refuse to pay. The legal risk of non-compliance with sanctions has clearly become significant in the context of the document-rich letter-of-credit trade. Moreover, even where no American bank is involved, non-compliance with OFAC sanctions holds, for the banks involved, enormous reputational risks which can lead to a prohibition of maintaining correspondent accounts within US financial institutions, thereby cutting off access to the US dollar payment systems as well as business in the United States generally.[78]

This has led to "the value of the documentary letter of credit ... as an instrument of trade being reduced"[79] and to an increase in clean (that is non-documentary) trading terms which, ironically, may be counterproductive. Marxen puts it thus:

---

78 Carter and Farha (n 9) 319; Stanton (n 64) 24.

79 Newsletter Clyde&Co "Trade sanctions – Clyde & Co seminar tests market impact" (May 2012) https://www.clydeco.com/uploads/Files/Publications/2012/CC001134_SanctionsUpdate_Trade_Sanctions_Seminar_03.05.12.pdf (31-3-2019), which quotes the following comment by an attendee: "Banks are wary. That's the reality of doing international business. Often you could trade legally but are constrained operationally because the bank won't take the risk".

"Changing and expanding financial crime legislation makes it increasingly difficult and cumbersome for banks and other parties involved in international trade and international trade finance to comply with applicable laws… In many cases, banks have responded by limiting their risk exposure … Significant de-risking decisions have been reported in international banking and trade finance which, in turn, have contributed to the emergence of clean payment trading terms in international contracts. Clean payment transactions, regrettably, deprive banks of transactional oversight and therefore limit their capabilities of identifying and reporting financial crime. The unintended consequences of de-risking and clean payment terms run counter to the initial aim of increasing customer and transactional monitoring and insight to scrutinise data for signs of financial crime".[80]

CONCLUSION

A benign and non-cynical view of the sanctions reflected on above may be that they have been designed and implemented in furtherance of world peace. In this context, it is of interest to note that both the League of Nations and the ICC arose from the grim aftermath of the devastation of World War 1, with express desires by the two bodies to further world peace. For the League of Nations, this was its "principal mission"[81] – and one could probably say that the same is true of the UN, although the preamble of its Charter goes significantly wider.[82] Their

---

80   (n 64) 183.

81   https://en.wikipedia.org/wiki/League_of_Nations (7-5-2019).

82   See https://www.un.org/en/sections/un-charter/preamble/index.html. It reads as follows: "WE THE PEOPLES OF THE UNITED NATIONS DETERMINED to save succeeding generations from the scourge of war, which twice in our lifetime has brought untold sorrow to mankind, and to reaffirm faith in fundamental human rights, in the dignity and worth of the human person, in the equal rights of men and women and of nations large and small, and to establish conditions under which justice and respect for the obligations arising from treaties and other sources of international law can be maintained, and to promote social progress and better standards of life in larger freedom, AND FOR THESE ENDS to practice tolerance and live together in peace with one another as good neighbours, and to unite our strength to maintain international peace and security, and to ensure, by the acceptance of principles and the institution of methods, that armed force shall not be used, save in the common interest, and to employ international machinery for the promotion of the economic and social advancement of all peoples, HAVE RESOLVED TO COMBINE OUR EFFORTS TO ACCOMPLISH THESE AIMS. Accordingly, our respective Governments, through representatives assembled in the city of San Francisco, who have exhibited their full powers found to be in good and due form, have agreed to the present Charter of the United Nations and do hereby establish an international organization to be known as the United Nations".

success in this regard has not been unmitigated.[83] The introductory phrase of the preamble to the ICC's constitution, on the other hand, states that its fundamental objective "is to further the development of an open world economy with the firm conviction that international commercial exchanges are conducive to both greater global prosperity and peace amongst nations".[84] Its focus, accordingly, was to facilitate international trade in the belief that this would, indirectly, contribute towards world peace. Its trade facilitation work has been successful in many respects, especially in the harmonisation of trade practices and law[85] as well as dispute resolution. This gives rise to the profound irony that trade facilitation and sanctions stand in direct contrast to one another. Especially in relation to wide-reaching national sanctions imposed by powerful States such as the US, we suggest that it is important continually to interrogate whether those sanctions are indeed contributing towards world peace.[86]

The wide reach of current targeted financial sanctions also poses the question whether they still serve the purpose of targeting guilty leaders without disastrous consequences for innocent citizens. We are inclined to the view that the nature and multitude of the actors involved (even the ship carrying the goods) cannot but lead to significant collateral consequences resulting in suffering for millions of innocent people. It should be noted in this regard that international human-

---

83   as emerges movingly from the final verse of the lyrics of the Irish folk song Green Fields of France which, by occasion, has been described as "probably the finest anti-war song ever written" (http://www.irish-folk-songs.com/the-green-fields-of-france-lyrics-and-chords.html (7-5-2019): "Well Will Mc Bride I can't help wonder why - Do those that lie here know why did they die - And did they believe when they answered the call - Did they really believe that this war would end war - Well the sorrow the suffering the glory the pain - The killing the dying was all done in vain - For young Willy Mc Bride it all happened again - And again, and again, and again, and again" (the hyphens are ours).

84   http://www.iccwbo.org/constitution/Article1 (7-5-2019). On its official web page, under the heading "Who we are" the following is stated: "ICC is the world business organization, enabling business to secure peace, prosperity and opportunity for all" (https://iccwbo.org/about-us/ (7-5-2019)). This focus on peace is also evident from the title of the PhD thesis of Tomasot Selling Peace: The History of the International Chamber of Commerce, 1919-1925 (2015) Georgia State University (full text accessible at https://scholarworks.gsu.edu/cgi/viewcontent.cgi?article=1045&context=history_diss). See also Hugo "Non-governmental initiatives towards the harmonisation of international trade law" 2003 Journal of Juridical Science 142 149.

85   For reflections on some of its successes specifically in relation to the harmonisation of international trade law, see Hugo (n 46) 1-20.

86   There appears to be mounting pressure internationally against specific US sanctions. INSTEX (for "Instrument for Supporting Trade Exchanges"), a special purpose vehicle registered in France with Germany, France, and the UK as initial shareholders, aimed at countering recent US sanctions against Iran, was set up recently after a joint announcement in November 2018 "affirming the EU's commitment to maintaining financial channels with Iran". See, in this regard, https://www.gtreview.com/news/mena/analysis-will-europes-new-iran-payment-mechanism-work/ (9-5-2019).

rights–based litigation flowing from sanctions aimed at terrorists is growing.[87] This development requires serious reflection.

On the financial side, one inevitable consequence is the rising costs of banking and trade financing due to the massive burden on banks which have to scrutinise documents in order to comply with sanctions emerging from the UNSC and individual countries and which may differ in important respects. Moreover, there is a growing expectation that banks should go even further (with further cost implications) by embarking on "vessel tracking" before processing payment.[88]

This tension between trade facilitation and the intended or unintended consequences of sanctions is reminiscent of the conflict between two imperatives that followed in the wake of the 9/11 terrorist attacks and the ensuing counter-terrorism sanctions regime. At the occasion of receiving an honorary degree from the University of Tilburg in 2002, Kofi Annan, the then UN Secretary-General of the United Nations, cautioned that we are facing a nearly unsolvable conflict between protecting the traditional civil liberties of citizens and ensuring their safety from catastrophic terrorist attacks.[89] Soon after the first UN sanctions-based counter-terrorism measures were adopted, it became clear that the swift and universal condemnation of the methods and practices of terrorism incited an over-zealous response by some States which threatens the very civil liberties they are supposed to protect. As indicated above, this invited corrective action to restore the balance. The question is whether we have reached the same point with sanctions impacting on international sales and the processing of payments in respect of transactions involving targeted ships.

---

87   See for instance the *Sayadi v Belgium* communication before the UN Human Rights Committee, CCPR/
       C/94/D/1472/2006 (29 December 2008); *Kadi & Al Barakaat International Foundation v Council of the European
       Union and Commission of the European Communities*, European Court of Human Rights, Grand Chamber, C-401/05
       P and C-415/05 (2008); *Al Jedda v United Kingdom*, European Court of Human Rights, Grand Chamber, Appl no
       27021/08 (7 July 2011); *Nada v Switzerland* European Court of Human Rights, Grand Chamber ditto Appl no
       10593/08 (12 September 2012); *European Commission and Others v Yassin Abdullah Kadi*, European Court of Human
       Rights, joined cases C-584/10 P and C-593/10 (18 July 2013).

88   See Updates "Tracking vessel voyages" Jan 2018 *Documentary Credit World* 4.

89   Available at www.un.or/press/en/2002/SGSM8515.doc.htm (28-05-2019).

ASPECTS OF THE BILL OF LADING AS A DOCUMENT OF TITLE IN THE ERAS OF THE THIRD AND FOURTH INDUSTRIAL REVOLUTIONS

SAREL F DU TOIT[*]

[*] Professor, Department of Mercantile Law, University of Johannesburg.

INTRODUCTION

South African mercantile law, with its roots in the *lex mercatoria* and forming part of a partially uncodified mixed jurisdiction, has always been inherently flexible and adaptable to new circumstances.[1] Usually, the law has to adapt to new technology and would be able to do so without legislative intervention, but the story of the electronic bill of lading is a rare case where the law had been kept waiting by technology. In 2001, the author concluded:

> "It seems that the only way in which a bill of lading can be replicated is by way of a registry. There is no unique electronic document that can live a life of its own. ... The fact that uniqueness in a digital world is achieved by way of a registry is not due to any legal shortcoming, but today at least is a characteristic of the available technology".[2]

Thus, a truly free electronic bill of lading, as easy to issue and use as a paper bill of lading, without the participants having to form part of a closed registry, was not possible in the not too distant past. In the years since the correct – though perhaps unfortunate – statement quoted above, Bitcoin emerged from the shadows and, more importantly, led to the widespread acceptance of blockchain technology.

This chapter will provide a recent historical overview of attempts to dematerialise the bill of lading during the Third Industrial Revolution – "the shift from mechanical and analogue electronic technology to digital electronics"[3] – from the 1970s to the 1990s. But an electronic bill of lading could only advance so far during the computer age. For electronic bills of lading, technology has at last caught up and, in the Fourth Industrial Revolution,[4] the age of artificial intelligence

---

1   For but one example see *London and South African Bank v Donald Currie & Co* (1875) 5 Buch 29 34: "The enormous development of commerce in recent times [the case was reported in 1875] requires a corresponding development of the mercantile law so that it becomes impossible to rigidly apply the rules which obtained in Holland in the beginning of the present century [the nineteenth century] to questions which arise out of customs of later growth". The Constitution of the Republic of South Africa, 1996 further determines that a court must, if necessary, develop the common law in order to give effect to a right in the Bill of Rights (s 8(3)(a)) and the Constitutional Court, the Supreme Court of Appeal and the High Court each has the inherent power to develop the common law, taking into account the interests of justice (s 173).

2   Du Toit "Towards electronic bills of lading: a South African perspective" in Weerasooria (ed) *Financial Regulation and Payment Systems* (2001) 121 153. A heading in an article by Herd ("'Blocks of lading' Distributed ledger technology and the disruption of sea carriage regulation" (2018) 18 *QUT Law Review* 306 308) states aptly: "The Internet: Not Quite the Technology to Dematerialise the Bill of Lading".

3   "Digital revolution" https://en.wikipedia.org/wiki/Digital_Revolution#1970s (11-05-2019). The terms Third and Fourth Industrial Revolution are not used consistently by any stretch of the imagination.

4   "Industry 4.0" https://en.wikipedia.org/wiki/Industry_4.0 (11-05-2019).

and so much more, blockchain made a negotiable electronic bill of lading possible. Blockchain is inevitably mentioned as one of the disruptive technologies of the Fourth Industrial Revolution (Industry 4.0), being inextricably linked with, and anchoring, the current Revolution.[5] The chapter will further consider whether the law recognises such a blockchain bill of lading and, if it does, will consider whether the bill can effect delivery of the goods in terms of South African law. As such, the focus will be specifically on aspects of the bill of lading as a document of title.[6] The characteristics of a bill of lading as a document of title in South African law are: a document of title is transferable; the holder of the document is (usually) in possession of the goods; the transfer of the document will (usually) transfer possession of the goods; the transfer of the document can (but will not necessarily) lead to a transfer of the ownership in the goods; and the holder of the document (usually) has a right to delivery of the goods against the carrier.[7] The focus will be on whether these functions can be replicated by recognising an electronic bill of lading as a bill of lading, and whether the property-law consequences in respect of the underlying goods will remain undisturbed.

Throughout this chapter, the assumption will be that South African law applies to both the bill of lading and to any consequences in terms of the law of property in respect of the transported goods.[8]

---

5   A rudimentary Internet search will unearth titles such as "The Fourth Industrial Revolution built on blockchain and advanced with AI" (Pollock https://www.forbes.com/sites/darrynpollock/2018/11/30/the-fourth-industrial-revolution-built-on-blockchain-and-advanced-with-ai/#6917401b4242 (11-05-2019)); the author will abstain from further references. AI will likely play an important role in the use of blockchain bills of lading, *eg* in the detection of fraud and money laundering, and "Internet of Things technology could provide real-time information about the location, temperature and condition of the goods and update the blockchain with this information" – Herd (n 2) 309, 310. For a clear explanation of blockchain technology, using an example from the island Yap, see Spruyt "An assessment of the emergent functions of virtual currencies" 2018 *TSAR* 707 709-710.

6   Contractual rights and obligations fall outside the scope of this chapter: see Du Toit *The Bill of Lading in South African Law* (2000 thesis RAU) ch 6.

7   For the reason of these qualifications and a more comprehensive explanation of the characteristics, see Du Toit (n 6) 129-131, and for an explanation of how the holder of the bill of lading can be said to be in possession of the goods, see 103-104. For the functions of a bill of lading, see Du Toit ch 5 and for the practical problems created by using a paper bill of lading, see ch 8.

8   According to s 2(1)(a)-(b) of the Sea Transport Documents Act 65 of 2000, the Act applies "to any sea transport documents [including a bill of lading – s 1 *sv* "sea transport document" (a)-(c)] issued in the Republic" and – rather strangely – "to goods consigned to a destination in the Republic, or … landed, delivered or discharged in the Republic". For criticism, see Du Toit "Comments on the Sea Transport Documents Act 65 of 2000" 2003 *TSAR* 731 732. The Act does not deal at all with many legal aspects regarding either the bills of lading or the goods in question. As far as these matters are concerned, the assumption is that South African law will apply (see s 6(1) of the Admiralty Jurisdiction Regulation Act 105 of 1993, in respect of what the South African law to be applied will look like, and Du Toit (n 6) ch 3, for an analysis). Regarding *res in transitu* and the law governing the validity of a transfer

THIRD INDUSTRIAL REVOLUTION

Before the registries[9]

The only workable solution to replicating negotiable electronic bills of lading were registries such as SeaDocs[10] and Bolero,[11] among others. This was the only way in which the unique characteristics of a bill of lading could be preserved. These registries will not be discussed here. However, preceding the registries some innovative solutions, given the available technology, emerged which provided a roadmap towards the eventual adoption of blockchain bills of lading. These solutions also provided a legal framework enabling such bills of lading and identified some of the legal intricacies that may still hinder any future evolution of electronic bills of lading.

Grönfors' Cargo Key Receipt[12]

The Cargo Key Receipt (CKR) developed by Grönfors can be seen as a precursor to the negotiable electronic bills of lading. It was based on the Datafreight Receipt System (DRS) of the Atlantic Container Line (ACL), which has been in operation since 1971. The DRS was introduced because of the congestion caused by the late arrival of bills of lading. The system was built around the concept of the waybill and not the bill of lading. When writing in 1982, Grönfors felt that customers were not prepared to accept more sophisticated methods that, unlike in the case of a waybill, make provision for the negotiation of the transport document as does the bill of lading.[13] Therefore, there is no negotiability or transferability. Nevertheless, the method is instructive because it illustrates how a paper document such as a waybill

---

of ownership, see Neels "Die *lex causae* vir eiendomsoordrag van *res in transitu*" 1991 *TSAR* 309. *Cf* UNCITRAL Model Law on Electronic Transferable Records (2017) art 1 and 19.

9   See Ong "Blockchain bills of lading" NUS Centre for Maritime Law Working Paper 18/07 Aug 2018 https://law.nus.edu.sg/cml/pdfs/wps/CML-WPS-1807.pdf (12-05-2019) 4-6.

10   See Bury "Electronic bills of lading: a never-ending story?" 2016 *Tulane Maritime Law Journal* 197 213-214; Du Toit (n 6) 272-276.

11   See Bury (n 10) 218-224 and 224 *et seq* for more recent developments; Du Toit (n 6) 309-317.

12   For an account of the history of the project, see Henriksen *The Legal Aspect of Paper-less International Trade and Transport* (1982) 97-99. The descriptions of the systems in par 2.2-2.5 are based on Du Toit (n 6) 254-261, 268-272, 278-281.

13   Grönfors *Cargo Key Receipt and Transport Document Replacement* (1982) 43.

can be replaced. The DRS operates in the following way. The necessary information is entered into a computer at the port of shipment, the shipper gets a receipt for the cargo and the information is transmitted to the port of destination. Before the ship arrives at its destination, the computer issues a notice of arrival informing the receiver of the date and time when she can collect her goods, and containing the other information originally entered into the computer. The notice is then mailed to the receiver.[14] Although this system was a huge step forward, it did not make provision for parties other than the shipper, carrier and receiver to be involved, thus excluding a bank financing the transaction and demanding security.[15] To remedy this shortcoming, Grönfors proposed Project NODISP. This system requires some further explanation before returning to the role of a bank.

While the shipper is in possession of the duplicate waybill (first copy of the waybill), she can change her instructions to the carrier by, for example, changing the port of destination.[16] After handing this duplicate waybill over to the consignee or to a bank, the shipper cannot intervene anymore. To regulate this situation in a paperless environment, Grönfors proposed Project NODISP. The shipper makes the following declaration: "The shipper has irrevocably declared that he has assigned his right to control the goods during transport to the receiver of the goods".[17] This declaration is entered into the computer, shown on the receipt given to the shipper and also reproduced in the documentation at the port of destination. Rather than using the full declaration, the declaration is shortened to the word "nodisp" that is reproduced on all relevant documentation.[18] There is no need for the shipper to physically transfer a duplicate waybill to the consignee, nor is there a need for the consignee to be in possession of a duplicate waybill to

---

14   Grönfors (n 13) 15-16, 35.

15   A consignee also does not know that the shipper will not "resell or reroute the goods in transit" (see Kozolchyk "Evolution and present state of the ocean bill of lading from a banking law perspectice" 1992 *Journal of Maritime Law and Commerce* 161 220; Kozolchyk "The paperless letter of credit and related documents of title" 1992 *Law and Contemporary Problems* 39 86).

16   See Grönfors *Towards Sea Waybills and Electronic Documents* (1991) 27-28. Regarding the duplicate waybill, Grönfors states that it is "only used as an easy way to prove who has the right to control but not as a necessary condition for having such right" (51). A further advancement is that a duplicate sea waybill is seldom issued, and thus an express declaration similar to "nodisp" discussed below is used to facilitate transfer of the right of control to the consignee. The idea was taken from the Cargo Key Receipt pattern (55-56). *Cf* rule 6 of the CMI Uniform Rules for Sea Waybills (dealing with the right of control).

17   Also see Grönfors (n 13) 77-79.

18   Grönfors (n 13) 27-28.

ensure nobody interferes with the delivery of the goods.[19] The only unavoidable printout is the receipt given to the shipper in exchange for the goods so that he can check whether the information is correct.[20]

Holding a waybill does not give the holder any right to delivery of the goods because the goods are simply delivered to the receiver indicated on the waybill – the waybill is not presented in exchange of the goods. Therefore, even though a financing bank is in possession of the waybill, it is usually indicated as the receiver on the waybill as well, and the real receiver of the goods is indicated by way of a notify address only: "By this legal 'trick' the non-negotiable character of the document is, so to speak circumvented and the bank's grip on the goods when they have arrived at the place of final destination remains firm".[21] Under the computerised system, a bank will be satisfied when it sees the receipt with a "nodisp" clause indicating that it is the receiver of the goods.[22] The bank now knows that nobody can interfere with the delivery of the goods to it (if necessary). It is in the same position as being in possession of the duplicate (paper) waybill indicating that it is the receiver of the goods. A bank will further not accept a claused waybill (for example showing that the goods are defective in some way) as security. For that reason, the code word "clean" must be added together with "nodisp" in order to satisfy a bank.[23]

The CKR system as adopted by ACL works in the following way when used in conjunction with a letter of credit.[24] A letter of credit is opened in favour of the seller, payable against presentation of a CKR. After the shipment of the goods, the shipper (seller) gets the first printout of the CKR, which is marked "nodisp", "clean"

19   According to Grönfors (n 13) 36, "the basic idea was to 'translate' the function of the duplicate waybill by the express NODISP declaration by the carrier, thus using the computer as bearer of the same function".

20   Grönfors (n 13) 33, 37-38.

21   Grönfors (n 13) 27, 43-44.

22   Grönfors (n 13) 31-32. See also at 38 where the author wrote: "The delivery of this receipt to the bank means, that the bank can rely upon the fact that these data were in fact stored into the record of the carrier's computer and that their correctness at that very moment was checked by the carrier against the real goods taken in charge". (Italics omitted.)

23   Grönfors (n 13) 39, 77-79. See also at 86-87, where the author points out that a further code word, "security", was later added because of objections by banks wanting more security. The code word means that the carrier undertakes to hold the goods as specified in the receipt as security and collateral for the bank named as consignee. See further Grönfors (n 16) 76.

24   For a full description, see Grönfors (n 13) 96-98, 101, 36-37.

and "security" and indicates the name of the buyer's bank (who opened the letter of credit) as consignee. The information is transmitted to the port of destination. The seller is paid by her bank against surrender of the CKR. The seller's bank transmits the necessary information to the buyer's bank, informing it that it has debited the account of the buyer's bank. The latter in turn debits the buyer's account. Before the ship's arrival, the buyer's bank gets the notice of arrival, which includes a CKR attached to it and states that "the goods will be delivered against the enclosed Cargo Key Receipt duly assigned by the bank as consignee". The buyer is also notified as the notify addressee. When the buyer's bank obtains payment from the buyer, it assigns the CKR to the buyer, who then demands delivery of the goods from the carrier.

The system can be further refined by issuing the receipt to the shipper and the notice of arrival at the port of destination electronically, and transmitting the information to the bank electronically, but this will not change the basic functions of the system.[25]

The system[26] "has been successfully tried out in full scale [in the 1980s] but is not yet regularly used".[27] The main disadvantage is that the system is an initiative of one carrier and is therefore limited to the ports that the carrier visits.[28] Traders who are not regular customers of the carrier might view the system with suspicion and financing banks (especially the exporter's bank) might not be interested in the system.[29] An odd feature of the system, when a bank is involved, is the delivery of the goods against presentation of the CKR, usually assigned (that is indorsed) by the bank to the buyer. As Toh See Kiat[30] wrote, "[p]erhaps this physicality was

---

25   Grönfors (n 13) 40.

26   See Grönfors (n 13) 80-95 for objections raised by Swedish and American banks to the system, and his response to those objections.

27   Grönfors (n 16) 76; Grönfors (n 13) 95, 96. It seems that the system was "mothballed": see Kozolchyk "Evolution" (n 15) 222-223.

28   Toh See Kiat *Paperless International Trade: Law of Telematic Data Interchange* (1992) 184; Urbach "The electronic presentation and transfer of shipping documents" in Goode (ed) *Electronic Banking: The Legal Implications* (1985) 115.

29   Toh See Kiat (n 28) 217 n 168 wrote that the exporter's financier "has no means of protecting himself should his principal (the importer's financier) fail to reimburse the payment or become insolvent. All he has is a worthless CKR – he cannot sell it, he cannot claim the goods on it, he cannot eat it. This is perhaps another reason for the unpopularity of the CKR idea – the financiers likely to be involved are financiers with such close, established relationships that there cannot be many of them in world-wide context". See Kiat 185, 216-217 n 166, who correctly rejected the argument of Grönfors (n 13) 58, 91 that the consignor (seller) can resume the right of disposal if the buyer, for example, refuses to pay or to receive the goods.

30   (n 28) 184. Also see Goode *Proprietary Rights and Insolvency in Sales Transactions* (1989) 81.

permitted to raise the enthusiasm of the financiers in the project". This does not really cause a problem because the CKR is not posted at the port of shipment to the port of discharge, and both the buyer and the buyer's bank are physically situated at, or near, the port of discharge. There is nevertheless no need to deliver against a CKR: the carrier knows that the bank is the consignee and it will deliver the goods to the bank unless the bank instructs the carrier otherwise in whatever way. There is no need for the carrier to see the CKR.

Toh See Kiat[31] wrote that the CKR system "is nothing more than a sea waybill with a 'NODISP' handicap" and it can therefore not be attractive to an exporter. It is nevertheless submitted that this system was a sound way to replace the waybill at the time. The electronic transmission of information is an improvement over a paper waybill. The limitation of this system – and this is not a criticism as the system was never designed to replace the bill of lading – is that the goods cannot be traded *en route*.[32]

Reinskou's Notification-Confirmation System

The system proposed by Reinskou seems clear and simple at first glance. This may largely be because of the fact that it contains none of the details of the CMI Rules for Electronic Bills of Lading or the even more comprehensive rules of functioning registries. Reinskou followed a functional approach, leaving him free from the shackles of the traditional bill of lading: "the problem is not how to construct a system to which the law on negotiability is applicable. The problem is how to make a system that will lead to the same legal consequences

---

31   (n 28) 185.

32   See, however, Grönfors (n 13) 67 and the criticism of Toh See Kiat (n 28) 184-185. Grönfors (n 16) 59-60 proposed that the waybill pattern can be elaborated to get closer to the bill of lading pattern, by allowing the consignee to assign his right to control and right to obtain delivery to another party (apart from the bank assigning its right to claim delivery to the real buyer). The consignee must also expressly notify the carrier of the assignment. It is submitted, however, that, if a bill of lading is needed, a bill of lading or an electronic equivalent of the bill of lading should be used. The bill of lading developed precisely because of the uncertainty and chaos that might develop in a long chain of assignments without embodying the right that is assigned in a paper document, which also tells the carrier to whom delivery must be made. Toh See Kiat 185 indicated why such an assignment is not possible in English law. Even if it were, it should be avoided.

as those which today follow from the law on negotiability".[33] The system works in the following way:[34]

> "The fundamental idea is the conception of a notification-confirmation system. Whenever a right in the goods is created or assigned, the transferor notifies the carrier of the transaction. The carrier registers the change and sends the transferee [the "lawful receiver"] a confirmation of his acquired right. If e.g. the goods are sold while at sea, the seller who is registered as the owner, will notify the carrier of the sale. The carrier registers the buyer as the new owner and confirms to him that he is now the owner of the goods".

The first confirmation is issued by the carrier[35] to the shipper after the shipment of the goods, unless the carrier is already notified of a sale of the goods, in which case the confirmation will be sent to the buyer and a "duplicate" to the shipper as a receipt.[36] The confirmation sent by the carrier will include the contract of carriage as well as a description of the goods as in a regular bill of lading.[37] Reinskou stressed that "the legally significant events for the creation of legal rights and obligations are the messages themselves. The carrier's registration of the notifications and the information stored in his computer are of no legal consequence in this process".[38] The electronic process is used for speed and efficiency in the delivery of the messages. Negotiability and other essential characteristics of the traditional bill of lading are created by contractual means. The original contract of carriage will state that the carrier will issue confirmations to transferees after being notified by a transferor and every confirmation will contain the same clause binding the carrier to take part in the system. According to Reinskou, the confirmation "is formulated as an independent [unilateral]

---

33 Reinskou "Bills of lading and ADP: description of a computerized system for carriage of goods by sea" 1981 *Journal of Media Law and Practice* 161. Reinskou wrote at 160 that "[t]he conclusion to draw [...] is that there is no serious legal or technical obstacle to computerization, or to put it into Latin: Navigare necesse est, Documenta non sunt necessaria".

34 Reinskou (n 33) 162.

35 There is, of course, no need for the computer equipment to be physically located on the ship. See Reinskou (n 33) 179.

36 Reinskou (n 33) 172-173. The original information (such as a description of the goods) may be transmitted directly from the shipper to the carrier. The carrier then checks the information and adds to it, if necessary, before issuing the confirmation.

37 Reinskou (n 33) 162.

38 Reinskou (n 33) 163.

promise" that "will govern the contractual relationship between the carrier and the buyer".[39] The promise irrevocably binds the promisor. In South African terms, it would perhaps be clearer to state that an offer is made by the carrier to carry the goods on the terms set out in the confirmation, which is of course the same as the original contract of carriage.[40] The contract of carriage and confirmations will further stipulate that the carrier is discharged if it delivers the goods in good faith to the party to whom it transmitted the last confirmation (normally the carrier is discharged when delivering to the holder of a bill of lading without any notice or knowledge of irregularities).[41] When a letter of credit is used, the seller notifies the carrier of a transfer to the nominated bank and the carrier confirms to the nominated bank. The latter pays the seller if there are no irregularities. The nominated bank in turn notifies the carrier of a transfer to the issuing bank and the carrier confirms to the issuing bank. The transfer from the issuing bank to the buyer will take place in the same way, usually when the buyer pays the bank.[42] Security will be achieved by way of public-key cryptography.[43]

The most obvious deterrent of the system is that it imposes a burden on the carrier that it did not have to bear previously.[44] This is admitted by Reinskou[45] but, of course, the carrier will recoup its expenses by way of higher freight.[46] The further problem with such a system is that it will be available only to participants. Reinskou[47] indicated that, when goods are sold to an outsider, the carrier can issue a normal bill of lading after the notification and at the request of the seller. Further negotiation within the system is then suspended. In the extract on how the system works that was quoted above, Reinskou indicated that a party will be registered as the owner of the goods. This approach should not be followed. Instead, a party

---

39 Reinskou (n 33) 166.

40 Reinskou wrote against the background of Scandinavian law.

41 Reinskou (n 33) 167. See also at 170 for a summary of other contractual clauses.

42 Reinskou (n 33) 177-178, 184-185.

43 See Reinskou (n 33) 179-182.

44 See Basedow "Dokumentelose Wertbewegungen im Gütertransport" in Kreuzer (ed) *Abschied vom Wertpapier? Dokumentelose Wertbewegungen Effekten-, Gütertransport- und Zahlungsverkehr* (1988) 96-97.

45 (n 33) 186.

46 Traders might not be so willing to pay for the additional costs of communications. See Toh See Kiat (n 28) 186.

47 (n 33) 185.

should be registered as the holder of the bill of lading and questions of ownership should be left to the law that governs the transaction. There is no definite link between being the holder of a bill of lading and being the owner of the goods. Another difficulty is getting all the parties to agree on the very detailed contract that is required.[48] It should also not be forgotten that the system is of course essentially a registry kept by the carrier.

Toh See Kiat[49] wrote that Reinskou's system appears at first glance to be very similar to the CMI Rules on Electronic Bills of Lading. Toh See Kiat nevertheless stated that the fundamental difference between the systems is that "Reinskou aims to reproduce the effects of the bill of lading by means of a contractual arrangement (a legal technique) [while the CMI Rules] uses a technical technique (supported by a contract) to do the same". It is not clear why this should make any difference, and whether there even is such a fundamental difference between the two systems to warrant the one being classified as a functional approach and the other as a technical approach. It is submitted that both these systems are based on the functional approach. A multitude of aspects has not been considered in Reinskou's system, compared to, for example, the CMI Rules on Electronic Bills of Lading. This is not so much a criticism of Reinskou's theoretical system as an indication that, in practice, the statutory or contractual framework will need to be extremely comprehensive.

Henriksen's Special Technical Method

Henriksen devised a special technical method to provide for negotiability. The system was developed in response to Grönfors' CKR and Reinskou's

---

48   Toh See Kiat (n 28) 186. The liability of the carrier in the case of miscommunication or system failure should be extensively governed in the contract. Toh See Kiat also indicated that there are privity-of-contract issues and problems regarding consideration in English law if the carrier does not send a confirmation to a transferee, because the latter is then not a party to the contract. The contract of carriage between the shipper and the carrier, in which the carrier undertakes to send confirmations to subsequent transferees, can be regarded as a *stipulatio alteri* in South African terms. A delictual claim might also provide some degree of relief to such a transferee. The problem of consideration does not arise in South African law. On the other hand, Toh See Kiat indicated that, while the carrier might be exonerated by the contract of carriage against wrongful delivery, the carrier is still not protected from a suit in tort instituted by a non-participant. In South African terms, it will at least be necessary to prove that the carrier was negligent before a delictual claim will succeed and, as in the case of the traditional bill of lading, the carrier is unlikely to be negligent when he delivered to the last confirmed transferee without notice of any irregularities.

49   (n 28) 186.

Notification-Confirmation System. As Henriksen emphatically stated, he was not criticising the juristic work of Grönfors or Reinskou, but rather the functional approach adopted for these two projects whereby the technique of possession and surrender of a physical paper document is replaced by another technique with the same legal consequences.[50] Henriksen preferred a technical approach because then a completely new legal technique does not need to be developed and a new technique with many different legal consequences in different countries is avoided.[51] Probably the most important consideration for Henriksen is that a technical approach will not lead to widespread legal uncertainty. The rules relating to the traditional paper system were clarified over a long period through use and interpretation by the courts and, therefore, parties bound by these rules do not generally run into unforeseen complications. The clear rules relating to the existing paper system can be applied to a large extent when researching a technical approach.[52] Taking the technical approach as a starting point, Henriksen described his approach in the following way:[53]

> "A document consists of a piece of paper (or something similar) to which various forms of data are committed. We wish to eliminate the paper, not the necessary data. Today legal consequences attach to possession and surrender of the actual paper document. The first thing that suggests itself is to attach these legal effects to what remains after the paper is eliminated – i.e. the data. Thus the idea is that the present-day document shall be replaced by 'original data contents' – something tangible – and that possession and surrender of these original data contents, such as the data contents of a B/L, shall be endowed with exactly the same legal effects in all respects as possession and surrender of the original paper document (e.g. B/L) has today. ... In the event this idea is realized, the symbolic function of the document will be linked with possession of the original data contents, not with the original document as in today's system".

The wording of a document indicates whether it is a bill of exchange, promissory note or bill of lading. Similarly, the particular formulation of the data contents will identify the type of document.

---

50   Henriksen (n 12) 119.

51   This stems from the fact that even the legal consequences of traditional paper routines differ from country to country. See Henriksen (n 12) 120.

52   Henriksen (n 12) 120.

53   Henriksen (n 12) 121.

When dealing with concepts such as originality and uniqueness, which are essential for a paper document such as a bill of exchange, the drawback of public-key cryptography is that the transferor of a message can transmit the same message to different parties, as he always retains a copy of the message.[54] Henriksen wrote that "[t]he recipient will therefore be in the same position as if the data sender holds an unlimited (indefinite) number of original documents and transmits one of them to the recipient".[55] Effross[56] concluded that, "[a]lthough PKI [public key infrastructure] would practically resolve many issues associated with negotiability, until the threat of cloned 'couriers without luggage' can be technologically eliminated the electronic negotiable instrument may well remain only a digital dream". Henriksen attempted to provide a solution to circumvent this problem.

The system makes use of public-key cryptography (the double encryption system) to confirm the identity of the sender of the message and ensure that only the transferee can read the message. As a point of departure, the computers used in the system are programmed to have three specific characteristics.[57] First, the computer of the transferor erases the message when receipt of the message is confirmed by the transferee. Secondly, when X uses his secret key to encrypt a message entered into the computer by himself (that is not a message received from another party), the computer will add the phrase "generated by X" to the message. Of course, the computer must be programmed in such a way that X cannot prevent this from happening. The original message plus the additional phrase will then be encrypted to provide the digital signature of X. Thirdly, if X adds to a message that he received from another party (that is not a message entered by himself) the computer adds the phrase "added by X" when X uses his secret key to encrypt the message. The message will then contain the original message that X received, the phrase added by

---

54   Apart from the fact that there will not be a single original, public-key cryptography can be used to transfer a message between more than two parties successively, adding additional information such as an indorsement where necessary. See Henriksen (n 12) 63-64; Effross "Notes on PKI and digital negotiability: would the cybercourier carry luggage?" (1998) 38 *Jurimetrics: The Journal of Law, Science and Technology* 385 390-391 for a description. According to Henriksen, he was the first person to describe this use of public-key cryptography whereby the transferee further transfers the message to a third party. The system is similar to the one described here, but without the three special characteristics of the computer (see below).

55   Henriksen (n 12) 122. Also see Perritt "Contract, evidence and agency issues" in Baum and Perritt *Electronic Contracting, Publishing and EDI Law* (1991) 365-366.

56   (n 54) 395.

57   Henriksen (n 12) 123-124.

the computer and the additional information (such as an indorsement) added by X. All of this will be encrypted to provide the digital signature of X.

The system then works in the following way.[58] A sends a message to B (message A).[59] Message A contains "generated by A" (inserted by the computer just before encryption took place when A signed the message using his secret key) and the original message. B "indorses" the message to C (message B). Message B contains "generated by A", the original message of A, "added by B" (inserted by the computer just before encryption took place when B signed the message using his secret key) and B's indorsement. When C is satisfied, C acknowledges receipt of the message to B and B's computer automatically erases the messages and signatures stored on it.[60] B sent the digital signature of A and the digital signature of B to C. C therefore has the digital signature of A, message A (arrived at by using the public key of A on the digital signature of A), the digital signature of B and message B (arrived at by using the public key of B on the digital signature of B).[61]

By comparing message A and message B, C can see that they were generated by A and an indorsement was added by B. Suppose that B wanted to commit fraud. B made a printout of A's digital signature before the message on his computer was erased by C confirming receipt of the message. B enters the digital signature from the printout into his computer and arrives at message A by using A's public key. B also adds an indorsement to D. When B signs the message, the phrase added will be "generated by B" because this message was not received from another party. The phrase "added by B" will not be included in the message because B did not add anything to a message that he received from another party. When D receives the messages, he will see that message A correctly states "generated by A", but message B states "generated by B" instead of the correct "generated by A". Presentment of the messages to A will similarly warn A of the irregularity. According to Henriksen,

---

58   Henriksen (n 12) 124-127.

59   What is actually sent is the digital signature of A, ie message A encrypted with A's secret key. A can eg be a "drawer" creating a payment order. See Toh See Kiat (n 28) 170.

60   The acknowledgement of receipt should happen virtually instantaneously because B must not have time to transmit a second copy of the message before the acknowledgement destroys the message on his computer. See Toh See Kiat (n 28) 203 n 64. Alternatively, it is submitted that B's computer should prevent sending the same message before a specified period of time lapses. The problem is not addressed by Henriksen.

61   Before C could have access to any of the signatures listed here, he had to decrypt all the information he received with his secret key as B encrypted all the information he sent to C by using C's public key.

"[o]n the face of it" the system is compatible with concepts such as "good faith" and "holder in due course". Printouts of messages or information have no similar legal effect in the system as that of the originals.[62]

It is submitted that the greatest weakness in the system is the fact that each party controls his own computer and may manipulate the computer program. This is admitted by Henriksen,[63] but he submitted that near-perfect forgery of paper documents can also occur, although only a small number of documents are in fact falsified. It is submitted that one possible solution can be for the parties to log onto a computer system maintained by a trusted independent third party. In such a case, the parties do not have access to the programs running on the system.[64] Apart from this flaw, the greatest advantage of the system is probably, and ironically, the high level of security. Indeed, only the specific transferor can create the message using his secret key and only the transferee can read the message using his secret key. The messages can be relied on with confidence except if a party reprograms his computer.

Toh See Kiat[65] identified a further problem. When the final holder transfers the message to the "drawee", the message on that holder's computer is destroyed. If the holder is not paid, how does he prove the fact that the instrument is "dishonoured"? Toh See Kiat submitted that "a presentment for payment in such a system should best be made through a third party, such as a clearing house, which would keep records of the message and corresponding payment credit, if any". Toh See Kiat[66] also criticised the system for being closed because a central body would have to supply the computer programs and issue the public keys. This is somewhat harsh: no electronic system prior to blockchain would ever be completely open, especially if public-key cryptography is used. It is nevertheless admitted that, without the necessary computer programs, a party would be unable to participate. Toh See Kiat then strangely (as he is usually very positive about the recognition of electronic routines) went on to criticise the system because "a relay of electrons or photons will never be viewed by judges and lawyers as equivalent to the far

---

62   Henriksen (n 12) 128.

63   (n 12) 128.

64   The problem with this approach, however, is that one is then basically dealing with a registry.

65   (n 28) 172.

66   (n 28) 180.

more permanent structure of ink and celluloid molecules that constitutes paper". Of course, there must be a legal framework in which to implement and recognise the system but, thereafter, a delivery is achieved by transferring the message and the whole point of the system is to ensure that there is only one original.[67] Toh See Kiat[68] concluded:

> "It is difficult to expect conservative, cautious lawyers to adopt concepts associated with paper in a totally alien environment. Old dogs definitely do not learn new tricks, especially the mental gymnastics required for such technical devices. Far better to start with a clean slate, or at least a slate with very few leftovers from the old".

There is no doubt that a functional approach will often be better, but this system developed by Henriksen deserves considerable recognition, even though it will probably never be used extensively in practice. Many other so-called functional approaches relating to the bill of lading are merely electronic variations on registries. Henriksen's system created an electronic negotiable instrument that, to a large extent, lives an independent life similar to its paper sibling. That said, a registry would probably have been a more effective way of designing an alternative to the bill of lading at the time.

Reed's Standalone Dematerialised Instrument

Reed described what he called a standalone dematerialised instrument. Such a dematerialised instrument must exhibit the same characteristics as a paper instrument: "1. Uniqueness. 2. It evidences the obligation represented by the instrument, e.g., the debt in the case of a bond. 3. It evidences the chain of transfers to the current holder".[69] Reed wrote that the first and third requirements are linked because, as "it is possible to make an infinite number of copies of an electronic record, each indistinguishable from the original, it is only the chain of transfers which is capable of distinguishing the original from a copy". This is not

---

67 Toh See Kiat (n 28) 214 n 126 asked: "Where is the document 'issued'? How would you 'deliver' it? Can the message received at the destination be an 'original' since in reality it is a totally different set of electrons from those that began the journey?" Toh See Kiat 180 also questioned whether a bill of lading can be regarded as "clean" in the system. The answer is simply that one looks at the wording of the message, just as one looks at the wording of the traditional bill of lading to determine whether it is clean.

68 (n 28) 180.

69 Reed *Electronic Finance Law* (1991) 118.

correct. Without any further special methods as described by Henriksen, once the same message is sent to two different transferees, both chains will look as if they contain a valid chain of transfers. Public-key cryptography is used to ensure the second and third characteristics.

The system will work in the following way.[70] A wants to send a message[71] to B. A encrypts the message with his private key and transmits the encrypted message to B. If B wants to transfer the message to C, he adds an indorsement to the encrypted message that he received, encrypts the result with his private key and transmits it to C. C decrypts what he received with B's public key, thus showing him the indorsement, and then uses A's public key to show the text of the original message. Up to here, the system is basically the same as that of Henriksen without the three special characteristics. Reed, however, deals with the possibility of C transmitting the same message to more than one party (that is the issue of uniqueness) in a different way. Reed submitted that A "will presumably be liable to repay only the first recipient of the message, subsequent recipients being limited to an action against [C] for breach of contract or deceit". This, however, showed that one is not dealing here with a standalone instrument yet. Reed therefore proposed that a third party needs to authenticate the transfer and the appropriate third party is simply A.[72] If A authenticates more than one transfer from one specific party, he will be liable to more than one party for payment. So, if C in this example transfers the message to D, C will request authentication from A and A will send authentication of C's ownership directly to D. Reed wrote:

> "This procedure obviously requires [A] to maintain detailed records, if only for his own protection. Although it might be argued that [A] is for all practical purposes maintaining a register of ownership, this is not in fact so. [A's] records are for his own use only, i.e., so as to avoid authenticating multiple transfers of the same bond; the evidence that the bond is unique and has been validly transferred is contained in the dematerialised instrument itself, and can be checked by successfully decrypting the various messages contained in it".

---

70   Reed (n 69) 118-119.

71   The example used by Reed (n 69) 118 is that A issues a bond to B.

72   Reed (n 69) 120. See also the figure on p 121.

Reed[73] concluded:

> "The advantages of a stand-alone instrument are that there is no need to invest in the substantial infrastructure of a registry and dedicated telecommunications network. ... If stand-alone instruments are created, they are likely to be used for low-volume, high-value applications where the trading partners are unlikely to be members of a common electronic trading community".

It is indeed unlikely that such a system will ever be used in practice. It is further submitted that, whatever Reed might say, the system is perilously close to being a registry.

FOURTH INDUSTRIAL REVOLUTION

Blockchain and bills of lading

An Internet search will turn up numerous blockchain bill-of-lading initiatives[74] but, for an outsider, there is little information to be found as detailed as the description of the systems proposed by pioneers such as Grönfors, Reinskou, Henriksen and Reed. It is thus not possible to comment in the same manner as has been done above, but at the same time, that is probably not needed. The legal framework that will be examined below is much more technology-neutral than earlier suggested solutions and likely to be capable of adapting to both blockchain and whatever the future may hold.

Blockchain technology made it possible for an electronic bill of lading to be circulated as a token on a blockchain ledger.[75] Unlike a registry with membership,

---

73   Reed (n 69) 121.

74   See Bury (n 10) 236 and Chetrit, Danor, Shavit, Yona and Greenbaum "Not just for illicit trade in contraband anymore: using blockchain to solve a millennial-long problem with bills of lading" 2018 *Virginia Journal of Law & Technology* 56, 82-83, 92 *et seq* in respect of Wave: "Wave is a blockchain-based software platform that connects all members of the international trade supply chain to a decentralised network and enables them to directly exchange documents, including bills of lading" (93). The website (wavebl.com (12-05-2019)) does not contain information that would enable further analysis. See Dentons "Blockchain in the energy sector: evolving business models and the law" 2018 *International Energy Law Review* 233 247-248 and cargox.io (12-05-2019) regarding CargoX; again little information is publicly available. The problems of the traditional bill of lading have often been discussed: see *eg* Du Toit (n 6) ch 8.

75   See Takahashi "Blockchain technology and electronic bills of lading" 2016 *Journal of International Maritime Law* 202.

the ledger may be an open, decentralised platform.[76] Such blockchain bills of lading will be unique.[77] Ong[78] explains:

> "A blockchain bill of lading system collects all announced transfers of a number of bills of lading into a block at regular intervals through its ledger, which displays the addresses at which the tokens are kept. The ledger operates as a timestamp server … Blockchain bills of lading can, using timestamping and cryptographic techniques, single out the earliest transfer of a blockchain bill of lading as the authorised transfer and void later unauthorised transfers in the process, enabling blockchain bills of lading to be unique".

The question is whether South African law is able to regulate such blockchain bills of lading effectively.

Recognition of electronic bills of lading

Electronic Communications and Transactions Act 25 of 2002 ("ECT Act")

As a point of departure, the ECT Act provides that "[i]nformation is not without legal force and effect merely on the grounds that it is wholly or partly in the form of a data message".[79] The definitions of "data" and "data message" are wide enough to include the information contained in a bill of lading.[80] This conclusion is reinforced by the need specifically to exclude bills of exchange from the operation of the Act.[81] Of further importance is the recognition of the requirements of writing and signature in an electronic domain[82] and, particularly with reference to a negotiable bill of lading, that of originality.[83] It is submitted that the section on originality is sufficiently wide – "the integrity of the [data

---

76 Takahashi (n 75) 202, 205-206.

77 Takahashi (n 75) 204-205.

78 (n 9) 11-12.

79 s 11(1).

80 See *eg* s 1, where the term "data message" is defined as "data generated, sent, received or stored by electronic means".

81 s 4(3)-(4), sch 1 item 3 and sch 2 item 4.

82 s 12-13.

83 s 14.

message] must be assessed … having regard to all other relevant circumstances"[84] – to recognise only electronic bills of lading that can be regarded as original and unique to the same extent as paper counterparts.[85] Although the ECT Act seeks to promote technology neutrality, only technology capable of rendering an original and unique bill of lading should underlie the recognition of an electronic bill of lading. Currently, it is submitted, the only technology capable of doing that is blockchain technology.

The Act also states:[86]

> "An expression in a law, whether used as a noun or verb, including the terms 'document' … 'submit', 'lodge', 'deliver', 'issue' … or words or expressions of similar effect, must be interpreted so as to include or permit such form, format or action in relation to a data message unless otherwise provided for in this Act".

It is submitted that these terms already provide for an electronic bill of lading being issued, delivered and presented, and one can add to this the "transfer" or "negotiation"[87] of a bill of lading, with "indorsement" if necessary, even stretching to the "holder" of the bill of lading (the list in the section is not exhaustive). It is submitted therefore that the ECT Act provides the necessary legal framework for the recognition of a *unique* electronic bill of lading.[88]

Sea Transport Documents Act 65 of 2000[89]

According to section 9(1)(a) of the Act, the minister may make regulations

> "prescribing the circumstances in which and the conditions subject to which a record or document produced by a telecommunication system or an electronic or other information technology system, and effecting transactions such as those effected by any sea transport document, is to be regarded as a sea transport document".

---

84   s 14(2)(c). See also s 14(2)(a)-(b).

85   s 2(f).

86   s 19(2).

87   Although a bill of lading is not a negotiable instrument, it can be transferred or negotiated. See Du Toit (n 6) 68-72.

88   See also Hare *Shipping Law and Admiralty Jurisdiction in South Africa* (2009) 725-726. New documents of title can be created by custom (*Kum v Wah Tat Bank Ltd* 1971 1 Lloyd's Rep 439 443, 444). Even in the absence of a legislative framework such as the ECT Act, it is suggested that a court should recognise a custom as to electronic bills of lading displaying the characteristics of a document of title or develop the common law if necessary.

89   See Du Toit (n 8) 731-737; Hare (n 88) 669-673.

No regulations have been made to date. Section 3(1) states that

> "A sea transport document may be transferred by the holder, either— (a) by delivery of the document, endorsed as may be necessary◻ or (b) subject to section 9(1)(a), through the use of a telecommunication system or an electronic or other information technology system".[90]

It is submitted that, even though there are no regulations in terms of section 9(1)(a), section 3(1)(b) allows the negotiation of an electronic bill of lading. It is further submitted, in the absence of regulations and in accordance with the provisions in the ECT Act relating to originality, that only an original and unique electronic bill of lading should be recognised and thus allowed to be negotiated.

UNCITRAL Model Law on Electronic Transferable Records ("Model Law")[91]

Underscored by technology neutrality, and following an approach of functional equivalence, the Model Law does not prescribe the underlying technology that is used – "whether based on registry, token, distributed ledger or other technology" – for the electronic transferable record.[92] As such, the Model Law provides a framework for the use of blockchain technology, but also for any future technology not currently considered or known that may still be used for the transfer of bills of lading. The Model Law also does not change the substantive law underlying a transferable electronic record.[93] For example,

---

90 According to s 3(2)(c) of the Sea Transport Documents Act, the holder is *inter alia* (see s 3(2)(a)-(b)) the person to whom the document has been transferred in accordance with subsection (1), thus including s 3(1)(b), which mentions an electronic or other information technology system. See Du Toit (n 8) 732-733 for criticism of the section.

91 The Model Law was adopted by the United Nations Commission on International Trade Law (UNCITRAL) on 13 July 2017, with a recommendation that States consider the Model Law favourably when revising or adopting legislation relevant to electronic transferable records. Preceding the Model Law, a number of international instruments could have an influence on electronic bills of lading, including the following: UNCITRAL Model Law on Electronic Commerce (1996 – see Du Toit (n 6) 302-306 for an analysis) art 16 and 17; United Nations Convention on Contracts for the International Carriage of Goods Wholly or Partly by Sea ("Rotterdam Rules") art 1 par 18 and 19 and ch 3; CMI Rules for Electronic Bills of Lading (1990 – see Du Toit (n 6) 281-298 for an analysis). As these instruments precede blockchain bills of lading, further discussion falls beyond the scope of this chapter. For the implementation of the Model Law in Bahrain, see Herd (n 2) 316-317. Generally see Šafranko "The notion of electronic transferable records" 2016 *InterEULawEast: J Int'l & Eur L, Econ & Market Integrations* 1; Ong (n 9) 12 *et seq*.

92 *Explanatory Note to the UNCITRAL Model Law on Electronic Transferable Records* ("*Explanatory Note*") par 18. See the description of an "electronic transferable record" in terms of art 10 quoted below. The term "electronic record" is defined in art 2.

93 Model Law art 2; *Explanatory Note* par 22.

"The Model Law focuses on the transferability of the record and not on its negotiability on the understanding that negotiability relates to the underlying rights of the holder of the instrument, which fall under substantive law".[94]

Article 7(1) provides the usual principle of non-discrimination that is found in international instruments and statutes dealing with electronic commerce: "An electronic transferable record shall not be denied legal effect, validity or enforceability on the sole ground that it is in electronic form". A comprehensive analysis of the Model Law is not undertaken in this contribution, but sections that may be significant for blockchain bills of lading are examined below, with the aim to express a view on their suitability in South African law.

Chapter II of the Model Law deals with functional equivalence, starting with the usual sections on writing and signature in articles 8 and 9.[95] Article 10 considers transferable documents and instruments:

"1. Where the law requires a transferable document or instrument, that requirement is met by an electronic record if:

(a) The electronic record contains the information that would be required to be contained in a transferable document or instrument; and

(b) A reliable method is used:

(i) To identify that electronic record as the electronic transferable record;

(ii) To render that electronic record capable of being subject to control from its creation until it ceases to have any effect or validity; and

(iii) To retain the integrity of that electronic record.

2. The criterion for assessing integrity shall be whether information contained in the electronic transferable record, including any authorized change that arises from its creation until it ceases to have any effect or validity, has remained complete and unaltered apart from any change which arises in the normal course of communication, storage and display".

---

94   *Explanatory Note* par 20.

95   See the discussion in *Explanatory Note* par 68-79. In the case of distributed ledgers, pseudonyms rather than real names may be used to identify the signatory: "That identification, and the possibility of linking pseudonym and real name, including based on factual elements to be found outside distributed ledger systems, could satisfy the requirement to identify the signatory" (par 78; see also par 117 in respect of article 11).

According to the *Explanatory Note*,[96] article 10 reflects the outcome of discussions regarding the "uniqueness" of a transferable instrument – a "peculiar challenge" in an electronic environment, as has already been intimated in the introduction to this chapter. Multiple claims for the performance of the same obligation are avoided by notions of "singularity" (the basis of article 10) and "control"[97] as set out in article 11. The Model Law steered away from using the term "original"[98] as a "static notion" in favour of these terms due to the dynamic nature of electronic transferable records – they circulate and may only be in a final form upon presentation.[99] Article 11 provides:

> "1. Where the law requires or permits the possession of a transferable document or instrument, that requirement is met with respect to an electronic transferable record if a reliable method is used:
>
> -2. Where the law requires or permits transfer of possession of a transferable document or instrument, that requirement is met with respect to an electronic transferable record through the transfer of control over the electronic transferable record".

It was suggested above that the control of an electronic bill of lading may be covered by the provisions of the ECT Act and the Sea Transport Documents Act, but an express provision such as article 11 is to be preferred. Referring to "exclusive" control may be superfluous in terms of South African law, but such a reference can be included for clarity in an electronic environment.[100] Of course, in accordance with the underlying substantive law, control or possession[101] does not equate to lawful control. Flowing from article 11(2), article 15 deals more specifically with the indorsement of a transferable electronic record:

> "Where the law requires or permits the endorsement in any form of a transferable document or instrument, that requirement is met with respect to an electronic

---

96   par 81.

97   *Explanatory Note* par 81-85. The notions of "singularity" and "control" are different and should be distinguished: see par 112.

98   Multiple "originals" (even on different media) may still be issued in terms of the Model Law: see *Explanatory Note* par 191-195 and Du Toit (n 6) 110-111.

99   *Explanatory Note* par 189-190.

100   *Explanatory Note* par 111.

101   The terms "possession" and "control" are used interchangeably and in accordance with the use in an international instrument such as the Model Law. See Du Toit (n 6) 103 n 146.

> transferable record if the information required for the endorsement is included in the electronic transferable record and that information is compliant with the requirements set forth in articles 8 [writing] and 9 [signature]".

As before, the aim of the section is functional equivalence without changing the substantive law.[102] The Model Law also provides for the amendment of an electronic transferable record,[103] thus, it is submitted, catering for an instance such as the substitution of the name of the consignee. Lastly, the Model Law deals with the replacement of a paper instrument[104] with an electronic transferable record (article 17) and the replacement of an electronic transferable record with a paper instrument (article 18).[105] Such changes of medium may be necessary where, for example, there are different levels of acceptance of electronic bills of lading among parties and across borders.[106] These are matters not covered by the underlying substantive law (for instance the fact that the paper instrument shall be made inoperative and will cease to have any effect or validity in terms of article 17(3)), so the inclusion is to be welcomed and brings legal certainty.

Although the discussion here focused on only a few of the articles of the Model law, it is submitted that the Model Law can – and should – be made part of South African law with very few amendments. It is further submitted that the minister may make the Model Law part of regulations envisaged in terms of section 9(1)(a) of the Sea Transport Documents Act.

SYMBOLIC DELIVERY[107]

The requirements for symbolic delivery are:[108]

> "(a) the parties must have the intention to resort to this form of delivery; (b) the keys must be delivered with the intention that the contents of the warehouse and so forth are thereby transferred; and (c) the keys must supply the transferee with exclusive

---

102 See *Explanatory Note* par 150-152.

103 art 16. *Cf* Du Toit (n 6) 123-124 and *Numill Marketing CC v Sitra Wood Products Pte Ltd* 1994 3 SA 460 (C).

104 See the definition of a "transferable document or instrument" in art 2 of the Model Law.

105 See *Explanatory Note* par 161-179.

106 See *Explanatory Note* par 161 and 176; *cf* Du Toit (n 6) 317-319.

107 The terms *clavium traditio* and *traditio symbolica* are also used.

108 Van der Merwe "Things" 2014 27 *LAWSA* par 221; *Sakereg* (1989) 316; Du Toit (n 6) 108. Delivery is only one of the requirements for the derivative acquisition of ownership. See also Van der Merwe supra (1989) 301-305.

control over the contents of the warehouse and so forth".

It has long been held that transferring (or negotiating) the bill of lading can amount to symbolic delivery of the goods:[109]

> "The key [the handing over of which effects delivery of the goods in a warehouse] is the symbol of the property in the goods placed in the warehouse, in the same way as the bill of lading is the symbol of the property in the goods shipped on board".

Although it may be more correct to refer to a form of delivery "closely analogous"[110] to symbolic delivery, or even "an effective form of constructive delivery *sui generis*",[111] such distinction is not made by the courts. It is not, however, about the symbol as such; the symbol must enable the transferee to exercise control over the goods:

> "No doubt a mere symbol is not sufficient to effect delivery; the goods must be subjected to the power of the person to whom delivery is to be made. … The key is in one sense symbolical, but it is more than that, for it is the means by which the pledgee is enabled to have access to and retain control of the goods".[112]

As stated in *Knight v Lensvelt*, [113]

> "the change of physical control can be effected by placing the purchaser in possession of the *means* of dealing effectively with the property … or in other words, placing the property in the power of the purchaser".

---

109   *London and South African Bank v Donald Currie & Co* (1875) 5 Buch 29 34. For a full analysis of the preceding and subsequent case in South Africa and England, see Du Toit (n 6) 91 *et seq.*

110   Van der Merwe (n 108 (2014)) par 221.

111   Carey Miller "Transfer of ownership" in Zimmermann and Visser (eds) *Southern Cross – Civil Law and Common Law in South Africa* (1996) 727 741 – thus "not so much symbolic delivery as the only appropriate means of dealing with the goods in transit".

112   *Heydenrich v Saber* (1900) 17 SC 73, 76-77; *S v Magxwalisa* 1984 2 SA 314 (N) 321A. Carey Miller ("Transfer of ownership" in Feenstra and Zimmermann (eds) *Das römisch-holländische Recht – Fortschritte des Zivilrechts im 17. und 18. Jahrhundert* (1992) 521 529; (n 111) 740) points out that the Roman and Roman-Dutch authorities are inconclusive on the question.

113   1923 CPD 444 447 (own emphasis).

The question is whether these "means" can also include some form of electronic bill of lading. Most of the Roman[114] and Roman-Dutch[115] texts refer to no more than the "key" or "keys" of, *inter alia*, a warehouse. Voet[116] wrote that

> "[i]t is symbolical or figurative when it takes place by a symbol, that is to say an external token given in place of delivery". The use of the word "token" in Gane's translation of Voet is an interesting quirk because the term is today also used within the context of blockchain – but of course it is not suggested that anything turns on this. According to Huber,[117] "[s]ymbolical delivery is when in place of delivering the property itself you hand over something that has the significance of such property".

It is submitted that a blockchain bill of lading can be the "means", "token" or "something that has the significance of such property" for purposes of effecting symbolic delivery – quite apart from any development regarding symbolic delivery or an analogous form of delivery that courts must surely sanction in the era of the Fourth Industrial Revolution. Depending on its implementation, it is further submitted that the publicity requirement[118] may be fulfilled better by the information in the distributed ledger, than would have been the case when using a paper bill of lading to effect delivery.

CONCLUSION

The idea to embody personal rights in a piece of paper was revolutionary. Some time ago, Malan[119] wrote:

> "The ingenuity of the bill of exchange lies in its tangibility. ... The achievement of the medieval merchants was to incorporate their intangible rights of action against their trading partners in the corporeal paper and to make transfer of these rights dependent

---

114 *I* 2 1 45; *D* 18 1 74; *D* 41 1 9 6; *D* 41 2 1 21.

115 De Groot *Inleidinge* 2 5 12; Van Leeuwen *Simon van Leeuwen's Commentaries on Roman-Dutch Law* (trans Kotzé 1886) 2 7 2; Van der Keessel *Praelectiones Iuris Hodierni ad Hugonis Grotii Introductionem ad Iurisprudentiam Hollandicam* (Afrikaans trans Gonin assisted by Pont) in addition deals with the delivery of documents showing ownership of a movable.

116 *Commentarius ad Pandectas* 41 1 34 (trans Gane 1957); a different translation (Krause), referring to an "outward token" is quoted in *Meintjes v Wilson* 1927 OPD 183 187-188; and, in *Laljee v Omdadutt* (1883) 4 NLR 117 118-119, a translation referring to an "external symbol or sign" is mentioned.

117 *Heedensdaegse Rechtsgeleertheyt* 2 9 14 (trans Gane 1939).

118 See Van der Merwe (n 108 (1989)) 300-301.

119 Malan "Legal implications of electronic storage" 1990 *Stell LR* 153 154.

on the fate of the instrument. They flouted existing and traditional legal norms and subjected them to the requirements of the marketplace. They made law and lawyers have never ceased to wonder at their audacity".

It may be rather early to express an opinion on the matter, but blockchain technology may well have a similar impact on the law as the notion of embodying rights in paper had a long time ago. It is submitted that, in the case of blockchain bills of lading, a sensible interpretation of current legislation, together with the flexibility of the common law, would be able to provide the necessary legal framework for such bills of lading. It is nevertheless suggested that the Model Law will bring further legal certainty and harmonisation with other jurisdictions, for the benefit of global maritime trade.

CONTRIBUTION LIABILITY COMPENSATION FOR SHIP-SOURCED OIL POLLUTION DAMAGE IN SOUTH AFRICA

CHLOE JOHANNES[*]

[*] Lecturer of Mercantile Law, University of Johannesburg.

INTRODUCTION

The transportation of oil by sea poses the risk of marine oil pollution. Approximately half of global crude oil is transported by sea.[1] In 2018, the United Nations Conference on Trade and Development estimated the global crude oil trade at 1.9 billion tonnes.[2] In the same year, tanker shipments of oil, gas and chemicals accounted for 29 percent of the globally traded goods transported by sea.[3] As international maritime trade continues to grow, ships increase in number and size.[4] Larger quantities of bunker fuel are being carried over the sea to fuel those vessels,[5] a factor that increases the risk of marine oil pollution. Although large-scale ship-sourced oil pollution incidents have decreased over the last few decades,[6] the threat of oil pollution persists because a single incident can cause significant damage. Following such an incident, costly clean-up measures may be required, the marine environment and marine organisms may be adversely impacted and individuals may suffer damage to their property, other economic loss or injury to their health. In addition, the whole national economy of the Coastal State may be negatively affected as industries such as tourism and fisheries, which often make significant contributions to economic growth, suffer a (hopefully temporary) decline.[7] The large quantities of oil imported into South Africa, make our economy and marine and coastal environment vulnerable to pollution damage.[8] Moreover, the Cape of Good Hope, at the south-western tip of South Africa, is an important global trade route acting as a point of transit for oil tanker

---

1   United Nations Conference on Trade and Development (UNCTAD) "Liability and compensation for ship source oil pollution: an overview of the international legal framework for oil pollution damage from tankers" (2012) 1 https://unctad.org/en/PublicationsLibrary/dtltlb20114_en.pdf (25-01-2019).

2   UNCTAD "Review of maritime transport" (2019) 9 https://unctad.org/en/PublicationsLibrary/rmt2019_en.pdf (05-09-2020).

3   ibid 4.

4   UNCTAD (n 1) 5.

5   ibid 1.

6   ibid 5.

7   ibid 1.

8   In 2018, the South African oil industry received over 20 million tonnes of contributing oil. See International Oil Pollution Compensation Funds (IOPC) "Annual Report" (2019) 28 https://iopcfunds.org/wp-content/uploads/2020/03/Final-Annual-Report_2019_e-1.pdf (31-07-2020).

shipments en route to the East and West[9] carried by tankers that are too large to transit through the Suez Canal.[10]

Oil incidents that have occurred in South Africa include spills from the *Castillo de Bellver*,[11] the *Apollo*[12] and the *Treasure*.[13] The *Apollo* and the *Treasure* required costly clean-up measures and had significant impacts on the marine environment and marine life. Indeed, the oil contamination caused by the *Apollo* led to an enormous environmental catastrophe killing thousands of seabirds, including endangered African penguins,[14] while the grounding of the *Treasure* caused the worst oiling incident in South Africa yet as more than 19 000 penguins were oiled, of which approximately 2 000 adults and 4 350 chicks died.[15]

As a result of the adverse economic and environmental impacts of oil spills, liability for oil pollution damage must be clearly defined. Victims of oil pollution damage need to know where to turn for compensation of their losses.

---

9   US Energy Information Administration, International Energy Statistics "World Oil Transit Chokepoints" (2017) 18 https://www.eia.gov/international/content/analysis/special_topics/World_Oil_Transit_Chokepoints/wotc.pdf (29-08-2020).

10   Holloway "South Africa's practical approach to dealing with oil pollution prevention and ships in need of assistance" 2005 *China Ocean's LR* 141 141. In 2015, the crude oil transiting around the Cape made up approximately 9 percent of globally traded oil transported by sea. See US Energy Information Administration (n 9) 18.

11   The Spanish registered tanker MV *Castillo de Bellver* caught fire approximately 70 nautical miles WNW of Cape Town and, seven hours later, the vessel broke in two. The following morning, the stern section capsized and sank some 24 nautical miles due west of Saldanha Bay. The *Castillo de Bellver* was carrying 242 262 tonnes of light crude oil of which approximately between 160 000 and 190 000 tonnes were discharged into the ocean. The oil spill occurred near an ecologically sensitive area and in the locality of important commercial fishing grounds. Little environmental damage, however, occurred because favourable wind conditions drove the oil slick away from the shore into the Benguela current thus resulting in its natural dispersal. See Moldan, Jackson, McGibbon and Van Der Westhuizen "Some aspects of the *Castillo de Bellver* oil spill" 1985 *Marine Pollution Bulletin* 97 97.

12   The *Apollo Sea* sank off the coast of Cape Town between Dassen Island and Robben Island. Approximately 2 400 tonnes of heavy fuel oil were spilled and washed ashore at both Dassen and Robben Islands. Some 10 000 African penguins were oiled, resulting in the worst oiling incident in South Africa at the time. 4 718 of the collected oiled birds were successfully cleaned by the Southern African National Foundation for the Conservation of Coastal Birds (SANCCOB) and later returned to the wild. See Wolfaardt, Underhill, Altwegg, Visagie and Williams "Impact of the Treasure oil spill on African penguins Spheniscus demersus at Dassen Island: case study of a rescue operation" 2008 *Afr J Mar Sci* 405 405-406; Crawford, Davis, Harding, Jackson, Leshoro, Meÿer, Randall, Underhill, Upfold, Van Dalsen, Van der Merwe, Whittington, Williams and Wolfaardt "Initial effects of the 'Treasure' oil spill on seabirds off western South Africa" 2000 *SA J Mar Sci* 157 159.

13   In June 2000, the bulk ore carrier *MV Treasure* sank off western South Africa between Dassen and Robben islands (important bird areas). The *MV Treasure* was carrying 1 344 tonnes of heavy fuel oil, 56 tonnes of diesel oil and 64 tonnes of lubricating oil of which all excluding 205 tonnes of heavy fuel were discharged into the waters. More than 19 000 penguins (mostly African Penguins) were oiled as a result of the spill. See Crawford et al (n 12) 157 and 169; Wolfaardt et al (n 12) 406 and 414.

14   Crawford et al (n 12) 159. Following the *Apollo*, 5 000 birds died, many of them during transit to SANCCOB rescue stations or shortly after arrival at the stations.

15   Wolfaardt et al (n 12) 405-406 and 414; Crawford et al (n 12) 157 and 171.

Questions of liability may result in protracted litigation, which can hinder and delay compensation for victims of oil pollution damage. Following the ecological catastrophe caused by *Torrey Canyon*,[16] the global community recognised the need for international co-operation regarding oil pollution and, under the auspices of the International Maritime Organization (IMO),[17] the 1969 International Convention on Civil Liability for Oil Pollution Damage (CLC 1969)[18] was adopted. CLC 1969 places strict liability on tanker owners for oil pollution damage,[19] accompanied by the right to limit such liability to financial caps set out in the Convention.[20] Tanker owners are required to obtain and carry evidence of insurance covering their liability.[21] Part of the compromise that led to the adoption of the CLC 1969 was the establishment of an international fund, to which the oil industry would contribute, by means of the 1971 International Convention on the Establishment of an International Fund for Compensation for Oil Pollution Damage (FUND 1971).[22]

The *Amoco Cadiz* oil spill occurred less than a decade after the adoption of FUND 1971.[23] The spill revealed that the limits of liability under CLC 1969 and FUND 1971 were not enough to adequately cover the costs of an oil spill that large.[24] This led, in 1992, to the amendment of the compensation regime created in terms of the two conventions by means of two protocols which entered into

---

16 In March 1967, the Liberian registered tanker *Torrey Canyon* ran aground on the Seven Stones Reef near Lands End in Cornwall. The tanker was carrying 117 000 tonnes of Kuwait crude oil of which approximately 80 000 tonnes were discharged into the sea. This resulted in the contamination of beaches on the Cornish coast, a threat to the French coast, contaminated oyster beds and fisheries and extensive damage to bird life. See Nanda "The *Torrey Canyon* disaster: Some legal aspects" 1967 *Denver LJ* 400 400–401.

17 Gurumo and Han "The role of international oil pollution liability legislation in the protection of the marine environment" 2012 *IJESD* 183 184.

18 973 *UNTS* 3, (1969) 9 *ILM* 45. Adopted: 29-11-1969; EIF: 19-06-1975.

19 art III.

20 art V.

21 art VII.

22 1110 *UNTS* 57, (1972) 11 *ILM* 284. Adopted: 18-12-1971; EIF: 16-10-1978; NLIF: 24-05-2002. See the sixth paragraph of the preamble to the Convention.

23 In March 1978, the Amoco Cadiz ran aground 130 miles off the coast of Brittany and spilled 230 000 tonnes of crude oil into the surrounding waters. The spill resulted in the contamination of the French coastline, contaminating beaches and fishing ground. This was, at the time, the worst oil tanker casualty. See Bartlett "In re Oil Spill by the Amoco Cadiz – choice of law and a pierced corporate veil defeat the 1969 Civil Liability Convention" 1985 *Mar Law* 1 1; Rosenthal and Raper "*Amoco Cadiz* and limitation of liability for oil spill pollution: Domestic and international solutions" 1985 *Virginia J Nat Res L* 259 259-260.

24 Faure and Hui "Economic analysis of compensation for oil pollution" 2006 *J Mar L & Com* 179 196.

force in 1996.[25] These protocols increased the financial limits for compensation of oil pollution damage[26] and extended the geographical area within which tanker owners incur strict liability for pollution damage.[27] The amended conventions are known as the 1992 International Convention on Civil Liability for Oil Pollution Damage (CLC 1992)[28] and the 1992 International Convention on the Establishment of an International Fund for Compensation for Oil Pollution Damage (FUND 1992).[29] The International Oil Pollution Compensation Fund 1992 ("the Fund")[30] is managed by a Secretariat located in London[31] and provides compensation where cover under CLC 1992 is insufficient.[32] Through becoming a state party to FUND 1992, a state becomes a party to the Fund.[33] FUND 1971 ceased to be of force in 2002 when the number of States parties became less than 25.[34] Twelve years later, the International Oil Pollution Compensation Fund 1971 ceased to exist.[35] A large number of States, including South Africa, have denounced CLC 1969.[36]

The Civil Liability Act was enacted to give effect in South African law to the 1992 Protocol that amended CLC 1969 and to provide for matters related therewith,[37] while the Compensation Act gives effect to the 1992 Protocol that amended FUND 1971 and provides for matters related therewith.[38] The

---

25 The 1992 Protocol to Amend the 1969 International Convention on Civil Liability for Oil Pollution Damage (CLC PROT 1992) (1956 *UNTS* 255; adopted: 27-11-1992; EIF: 30-05-1996) and the 1992 Protocol to Amend the 1971 International Convention on the Establishment of an International Fund for Compensation for Oil Pollution Damage (FUND PROT 1992) (1956 *UNTS* 330; adopted: 27-11-1992; EIF: 30-05-1996).

26 art V of CLC PROT 1992 and art V of Fund PROT 1992.

27 art II of CLC PROT 1992. The Convention applies to pollution damage in a Contracting State's territory, territorial waters and exclusive economic zone.

28 art 11(2) of CLC PROT 1992. The text of the Convention is available in IOPC *Liability and Compensation for Oil Pollution Damage* (2018) 5-19.

29 art 27(2) FUND PROT 1992. The text of the Convention is available in IOPC (n 28) 23-41.

30 art 2(1) of FUND 1992.

31 International Oil Pollution Compensation Funds (IOPC) "Explanatory Note" (2020) 1   https://iopcfunds.org/wp-content/uploads/2020/09/explanatory-note_e.pdf (01-08-2020).

32 art 2(1)(a) FUND 1992.

33 IOPC (n 31) 1.

34 See IMO *Status of IMO Treaties* (2020) 288. See also art 2 of FUND PROT 1992.

35 IOPC (n 31) 1.

36 See IMO (n 34) 260-261.

37 long title. See also s 2(1) of the Act.

38 long title. See also s 2(1) of the Act.

Contributions Act provides for the imposition of the International Oil Pollution Compensation Fund Contributions Levy ("the levy") on specific persons and sets out how the levy is determined and paid to the Fund.[39] The Administration Act provides for administrative issues related to the levy imposed by the Contributions Act and connected matters.[40]

Prior to the enactment of the Civil Liability Act, the Marine Pollution (Control and Civil Liability) Act ("the Marine Pollution Act"),[41] which was modelled partly on CLC 1969, was the only piece of legislation governing the liability of ship owners for ship-sourced oil pollution damage. The Civil Liability Act only removed from the Marine Pollution Act the provisions relating to liability covered by CLC 1992 or FUND 1992 or both.[42] This means that "liability for bunker spills from non-tanker vessels [remains] covered by the [Marine Pollution] Act. Similarly, many administrative and intervention rights ... remain unaltered".[43]

In light of the economic and environmental threat posed by oil spills, it is vital that South Africa has adequate legislation in place to overcome the adverse effects of ship-sourced oil pollution damage. The domestic force given to CLC 1992 and FUND 1992 in South Africa is an important step in the right direction. This chapter examines the two conventions as they apply in South Africa as well as the domestic legislation which currently fills the gaps of their combined regime. Measures to enhance the existing liability and compensation regime for ship-sourced oil pollution damage in South Africa are explored.

---

39   long title.

40   long title.

41   6 of 1981.

42   s 17 of the Civil Liability Act.

43   Hare *Shipping Law & Admiralty Jurisdiction in South Africa* (2009) 566.

EVALUATION OF CLC 1992 AND FUND 1992 AS ENACTED INTO SOUTH AFRICAN LAW

Types of vessels and oil pollution covered by CLC 1992

CLC 1992 defines the term "ship" narrowly as "any seagoing vessel and sea-borne craft of any type whatsoever constructed or adapted for the carriage of oil in bulk as cargo provided that a ship capable of carrying oil and other cargoes shall be regarded as a ship only when it is actually carrying oil in bulk as cargo and during any voyage following such carriage unless it is proved that is has no residues of such carriage in bulk aboard".[44] CLC 1992 thus only applies to tanker vessels which are designed to carry oil in bulk and ore-bulk-oil carriers (OBOs), which are capable of carrying other cargo (dry cargo) and wet cargo such as oil.[45] All other seaborne vessels, such as bulk carriers, container ships, general cargo ships, cruise ships and other vessels carrying passengers, tugs, dredgers, car carriers, fishing vessels, diving support vessels and drilling ships, are not covered by the Convention, even though these vessels often carry bunker oil fuel on board.[46]

The CLC 1992 definition of "oil" is limited to "any persistent hydrocarbon mineral oil such as crude oil, fuel oil, heavy diesel oil and lubricating oil, whether carried on board a ship as cargo or in the bunkers of such a ship".[47] These persistent oils are composed of a considerable amount of heavy hydrocarbon fractions or high boiling material that does not disintegrate rapidly in the environment.[48] These persistent oils present a threat to the environment and marine life, and remain in the environment long enough to necessitate responsive measures which may be costly.[49] Compensation for responsive measures such as reasonable reinstatement

---

44 International Oil Pollution Compensation Funds (IOPC Funds) "Guidance for Member States Consideration of the Definition of 'ship'" (2016) 2 https://www.iopcfunds.org/uploads/tx_iopcpublications/IOPC_definition_of_ship_ENGLISH_web.pdf (23-02-2019).

45 ibid.

46 ibid.

47 art I(5).

48 Anderson "Persistent vs non-persistent oils: What you need to know" *Beacon (Skuld Newsletter)* (2001) 1 https://www.itopf.org/fileadmin/data/Documents/Papers/persistent.pdf (24-02-2019).

49 ibid.

measures, including clean-up operations following persistent oil pollution spills, are covered by CLC 1992 and the Fund.

CLC 1992 does not cover non-persistent oils such as light diesel, gasoline and kerosene, composed of lighter hydrocarbon fractions which disintegrate rapidly through evaporation and seldom require responsive measures or only require limited responsive measures.[50] However, although non-persistent oil dissipates rapidly through evaporation and rarely requires active responses, they nevertheless pose a threat, especially in high volumes, to private property and the environment. Indeed, non-persistent oils can impact paint coatings in marinas and harbours, causing damage to property.[51] In addition, high concentrations in water are severely toxic to marine organisms, such as plants and animals.[52] The death of marine organisms in turn impacts those who rely on marine life for their livelihood, such as commercial fishers, shrimpers and oystermen. It is thus important that liability and compensation be provided adequately not only in damage caused by persistent oil, but also in the case of damage caused by non-persistent oil. As indicated earlier, liability and compensation for oil pollution damage caused by vessels other than oil tankers and/or non-persistent oil are regulated by the Marine Pollution Act, the adequacy of which will be examined in greater detail later.[53]

Geographical application of CLC 1992

CLC 1992 has a more extended geographical application than CLC 1969. The latter only applied to pollution damage within the States parties' land territories, internal waters and territorial seas.[54] By contrast, CLC 1992 applies also in the exclusive economic zone (EEZ) or any equivalent area.[55] The enactment of CLC 1992 thus provides for liability and compensation for damage occurring not only within South Africa's territory, including its internal and territorial waters,

---

50   ibid.

51   ibid.

52   ibid.

53   Act 6 of 1981.

54   art II.

55   art II.

but also its EEZ. This ensures that liability and compensation exist not only for damage to the environment beyond the outer limit of the territorial sea up to the outer limit of the EEZ, but also for damage to the resources within that zone, over which South Africa has sovereign rights.[56]

Strict liability

According to CLC 1992, "the owner of a ship at the time of an incident, or, where the incident consists of a series of occurrences, at the time of the first such occurrence, shall be liable for any pollution damage caused by the ship as a result of the incident".[57] CLC 1992 thus imposes strict liability for pollution damage on tanker owners, but provides for very limited cases in which they do not incur such liability.[58] Strict liability is channelled exclusively to the ship owner, who is entitled to claim recourse from any contributing parties.[59] Claims against the servants or agents of the ship owner, a charterer, a "pilot or any person who, without being a member of the crew, performs services for the ship", a "manager or operator of the ship" or a salvor are expressly excluded unless "the damage resulted from their personal act or omission, committed with the intent to cause such damage, or recklessly and with knowledge that such damage would probably result".[60] The benefit of channelling liability to the tanker owner is that victims of tanker oil pollution need not determine exactly who is liable in delict and can turn directly to the ship owner for compensation.[61] Tracking down the exact party or parties at fault, and as such liable in delict, is often a time-consuming and costly process because a number of parties are usually involved in the navigation and management of a vessel. Another

---

56 See art 56(1)(a) of the 1982 United Nations Convention on the Law of the Sea (1833 *UNTS* 3, (1982) 21 *ILM* 1261; adopted: 10-12-1982; EIF: 16-11-1994; LOSC). See also s 7(2) of the Maritime Zones Act 1994 (15 of 1994).

57 art III(1).

58 In terms of art III(2), a tanker owner does not incur liability for oil pollution damage: (a) caused by an act of war, hostilities, civil war, insurrection or a natural phenomenon of an exceptional, inevitable or irresistible character; (b) caused wholly by an act or omission done with intent to cause damage by a third party; or (c) caused wholly by the negligence or other wrongful act of any Government or other authority responsible for the maintenance of lights or other navigational aids in the exercise of its function. In addition, art III(3) provides that, if the pollution damage was caused wholly or partly from an act or omission with intent to cause damage by the person who suffered the damage, or from the negligence of that person, the owner may be exonerated wholly or in part of liability to such person.

59 IOPC (n 31) 3.

60 art III(4).

61 Faure and Hui (n 24) 179 188.

benefit of channelling liability to the ship owner is that victims of oil pollution damage need not prove the extent of each contributing parties' liability, something which is difficult to do and often delays compensation. In addition, channelling liability to the owner prevents a duplication of the same claim, which could give rise to lengthy proceedings.[62] While it has been submitted that, in the interest of promoting deterrence, third parties who have contributed to the loss should be exposed to liability,[63] it should be noted that the CLC 1992's objective is only to ensure adequate and prompt compensation for victims of oil pollution damage,[64] which strict liability channelled exclusively to the ship owner underpins.

Financial limits on strict liability and compulsory insurance under CLC 1992

Tanker owners are entitled to limit their liability to the financial limits set out in CLC 1992[65] unless "it is proved that the pollution damage resulted from [their] personal act or omission, committed with the intent to cause such damage, or recklessly and with knowledge that such damage would probably result".[66] The owner of a tanker carrying more than 2 000 tonnes of oil as cargo must take out insurance or another financial security "to cover his liability for pollution damage under" the Convention[67] and a certificate attesting that insurance or other financial security is in force must be carried on board the vessel.[68] This means that the strict liability of the owner, although limited, is accompanied by an assurance of payment in the form of compulsory insurance. The assurance of payment is strengthened by provisions enabling the victim of oil pollution damage to take direct action against the insurer to obtain compensation.[69] The compulsory insurance provisions ensure that finances, although capped, are available to compensate victims of oil pollution damage. By contrast, uncapped liability that is not accompanied by such a financial

---

62   Faure and Hui "International regimes for compensation of oil pollution: Are they effective" 2003 *RECIEL* 242 250.

63   Faure and Hui (n 24) 188.

64   See the preamble to CLC PROT 1992.

65   art V(1).

66   art V(2).

67   art VII(1).

68   art VII(4).

69   art VII(8).

guarantee might result in under compensation or no compensation at all when the ship owner is unable to pay. The combination of strict, but limited liability, with the assurance of payment provides the first tier of compensation for victims of oil pollution damage occurring in South Africa's land territory as well as its internal waters, territorial waters and EEZ.

Compensation under Fund 1992

The second tier is offered by the Fund set up in accordance with FUND 1992.[70] The Fund compensates victims of tanker oil pollution damage where the ship owner is exempt from liability, unable to meet its financial obligations or the damage exceeds the financial caps on the ship owner's liability.[71] The aggregate amount of compensation available under the Fund for a single incident is 203 million Special Drawing Rights ("SDR"),[72] which includes the sum paid by the tanker owner (or its insurer) in accordance with CLC 1992.[73] The Fund is financed by entities who receive more than 150 000 tonnes of crude oil or heavy fuel oil (referred to as "contributing oil") a year at a port or terminal within a state party.[74] The Fund relies on reports provided by States parties to determine which oil-receiving entities within the States are liable to pay the levy.[75] The ten highest contributing States parties to the Fund (based on contributing oil received and reported to the Fund in 2018) are: India (14.59%), Japan (12.10%), the Republic of Korea (9.32%), Italy (7.28%), the Netherlands (7.19%), Singapore (6.25%), Spain (5.09%), France (3.83%), Thailand (3.40%) and the United Kingdom (3.28%).[76] According to reports on contributing oil received and reported to the Fund

---

70   IOPC (n 31) 1.

71   art 4(4)(a).

72   The SDR is a unit of account utilised by the International Monetary Fund (IMF). The value of the SDR is based on a basket of five national currencies namely the British pound sterling, the United States dollar, the Euro, the Japanese yen and the Chinese renminbi. The SDR is not a monetary system or claim against the IMF. It is a prospective claim on the freely utilisable currencies of IMF members. SDR can be changed for any of the basket currencies. See International Monetary Fund "Fact Sheet Explaining SDRs (Special Drawing Rights)" (2018) https://www.imf.org/en/About/Factsheets/Sheets/2016/08/01/14/51/Special-Drawing-Right-SDR (22-02-2019).

73   art 4(4)(a).

74   art 10(1) read with art 1(3).

75   IOPC (n 8) 28–29.

76   ibid 29.

in 2018, South Africa received 20 426 819 tonnes of contributing oil, which amounted to 1.33% of the total amount. [77]

A problem faced by the Fund is that some States parties do not submit the necessary reports,[78] with the result that the Fund is unable to levy contributions in respect of those States.[79] In 2018, 15 States failed to meet their reporting obligation, while four States have outstanding reports for 5 years or more and 2 States have not submitted a single report since becoming States parties to the FUND 1992.[80] The latter does not contain any provisions enabling the Fund to take action, such as withholding payment from the Fund, when a state fails to meet its reporting obligation.[81] The Fund has nevertheless adopted the policy of assessing for admissibility, but withholding payments for claims from States that have 2 or more reports outstanding.[82]

Since South Africa became a party to FUND 1992, it benefits from the second tier of compensation offered to victims of tanker oil pollution damage. However, oil pollution incidents such as those related to the *Erika*[83] and the *Prestige*[84] have revealed that the aggregate amount available for compensation under CLC

---

77   ibid.

78   Jacobsson "The international liability and compensation regime for oil pollution damage from ships – International solutions for a global problem" 2007 *Tul Mar LJ* 1 7. States parties are obliged to submit reports in term of art 15(2) of FUND 1992 on the oil receiving entities and quantities received.

79   States parties in which there are no entities receiving an excess of 150 000 tonnes of contributing oil for the year are still obliged to report a nil to the Fund's secretariat. In 2018, 43 States reported receiving no contributing oil within their territories. See IOPC (n 8) 28-29.

80   As at 31 December 2019, oil reports for the calendar year 2018 had not been received for the territories of 15 States parties. There are four States parties with outstanding reports for five or more years. Two States parties have not submitted any reports to the 1992 Fund since becoming Member States. IOPC (n 8) 29.

81   Jacobsson (n 78) 7.

82   IOPC "Annual Report" (2008) 38 https://www.iopcfunds.org/wp-content/uploads/2018/12/2008_ENGLISH_ ANNUAL_REPORT.pdf (24-07-2020). This policy was adopted by the Fund Assembly at its session in October 2008.

83   The Maltese-registered tanker broke in two off the coast of Brittany in France on 12 December 1999. The *Erika* was carrying a cargo of 31 000 tonnes of heavy fuel oil, of which approximately 19 800 tonnes were spilled. Around 400 kilometres of the coastline were affected by oil. Clean-up operations followed which quite swiftly removed most of the oil from the coastline. See IOPC "Incidents involving the IOPC Funds" (2013) 6 https://iopcfunds.org/ wp-content/uploads/2018/12/incidents2013_e.pdf (25-02-2019).

84   In 2002, the Bahamas-registered tanker carrying 76 972 tonnes of heavy fuel oil started leaking oil off the coast of Galicia in Spain. While being towed away from the coast, the vessel broke in two and sank. Over the weeks that followed, oil continued to leak from the wreck at a declining rate. Approximately 63 200 tonnes of heavy fuel oil were spilled and approximately 13 700 tonnes of cargo remained in the wreck. The west coast of Galicia was severely contaminated by the oil, which eventually moved to affect the north coast of Spain and France. See IOPC (n 83) 12.

1992 and FUND 1992 is sometimes inadequate to cover such large oil spills.[85] In acknowledgement of that fact, a third tier of compensation was established in the form of an opt-in Supplementary Fund. The latter was introduced by the IMO through the Protocol of 2003 to FUND 1992 (FUND PROT 2003).[86] The Supplementary Fund provides cover where the limits of the Fund are reached.[87] FUND PROT 2003 provides a significant increase in the amounts available for compensation under CLC 1992 and FUND 1992 because the total aggregate amount available for compensation of a single tanker oil spill by the Supplementary Fund is 750 million SDR, which includes the amounts payable under CLC 1992 and FUND 1992. [88]

The annual contributions to the Supplementary Fund are levied in a similar manner as the contributions to the Fund because entities receiving more than 150 000 tonnes of contributing oil per year within the States parties must also contribute to the Supplementary Fund.[89] States parties are also obliged to submit reports providing information on the oil-receiving entities and the quantities of oil received to the Director of the Supplementary Fund.[90] The submission of information on oil receipts submitted in accordance with article 15 of FUND 1992 to the Director of the Fund is deemed to have been submitted also under FUND PROT 2003.[91] The Supplementary Fund's contribution system differs, however, from that of the Fund in that contributions are based on a minimum presumed receipt of 1 million tonnes of contributing oil per year within a member state, even where no contributing oil is received or less than 1 million tonnes of contributing oil is received.[92] This does not apply to South Africa in practice because, since FUND PROT 2003 came into effect, South Africa has reported

---

85   UNCTAD (n 1) 11.

86   Adopted: 16-05-2003; EIF: 03-03-2005. The text of the Protocol is available at https://www.iopcfunds.org/fileadmin/IOPC_Upload/Downloads/English/WEB_IOPC_-_Text_of_Conventions_ENGLISH.pdf (20-01-2019). The Supplementary Fund was established in terms of art 2(1) of the Protocol.

87   art 4(1) of FUND PROT 2003.

88   art 4(2)(a).

89   art 10(1).

90   art 13(1).

91   ibid.

92   art 14(1)-(2).

receiving well in excess of 10 million tonnes of contributing oil per year.[93] South Africa, in any event, has not yet acceded to the Supplementary Fund. This also means that it cannot benefit from the third tier of compensation offered by the Supplementary Fund.[94]

As indicated above, the Supplementary Fund provides greater cover than that available under CLC 1992 and FUND 1992 and, as a result, it is less likely that the pollution damage caused by a single incident would exceed the Fund's limits of liability.[95] Accession to FUND PROT 2003 would thus go a long way towards ensuring that the South African victims of a large oil spill are not without compensation or under-compensated.

Pollution damage covered by CLC 1992 and FUND 1992

Environmental damage covered by CLC 1992 and FUND 1992

The CLC 1992 definition of "pollution damage" is broad enough to cover "the costs of preventive measures and further loss or damage caused by preventive measures"[96] as well as compensation for the "impairment to the environment other than loss of profit from such impairment", but it limits that compensation to the "costs of reasonable measures of reinstatement actually undertaken or to be undertaken" to restore the environment to its pre-spill condition.[97] "Impairment to the environment" is not defined in CLC 1992, but it is understood to mean "an adverse alternation to the environment leading to the deterioration or weakening of its functioning".[98] The term "reasonable measures" is not defined in CLC 1992, but it is understood to include reasonable measures to enhance the recovery process of the environment that do not cause further degradation and are proportionate,

---

93   See the International Oil Pollution Fund's annual reports from 2015 to 2018 https://iopcfunds.org/publications/iopc-funds-publications/ (24-07-2020). In 2018, the South African oil industry received over 20 million tonnes of contributing oil. See IOPC (n 8) 28-29.

94   Hare (n 43) 557.

95   Billah "The role of insurance in providing adequate compensation and in reducing pollution incidents; the case of the international oil pollution liability regime" 2011 *PELR* 42 47.

96   art 1(6)(b).

97   art 1(6)(a).

98   IOPC "Guidelines for presenting claims for environmental damage" (2018) 5 https://iopcfunds.org/wp-content/uploads/2018/12/IOPC_Environmental_Guidelines_ENGLISH_2018_WEB_01.pdf (27-07-2020).

feasible and connected to the spill.[99] Compensation for post-spill studies with a sufficiently close link of causation to the spill are also covered.[100]

Extensive studies and past pollution incidents reveal that the marine environment is resilient enough to recover without any intervention because oil spills rarely impact the marine environment permanently.[101] For that reason, CLC 1992 does not make provision for the compensation of environmental damage in and of itself, that is pure environmental damage based on abstract quantification, calculated in accordance with theoretical models is not provided.[102] The Fund has thus rejected abstract quantifications, for instance, in the *Volgoneft* incident[103] when a "Methodika" claim, the amount of which was calculated by multiplying the quantity of oil spilled by a number of roubles per tonne, had been submitted by Russia.[104] The Fund's rejection of the claim was affirmed by the Arbitration Court of Saint Petersburg and Leningrad Region in September 2010 on the basis that compensation for "impairment to the environment" under article 1(6) of CLC 1992 is restricted to the costs of reasonable reinstatement measures.[105]

Although France, like Russia, is a member of CLC 1992, the French Criminal Court of First Instance in Paris awarded compensation for pure environmental damage resulting from the *Erika* incident.[106] The award included moral damages (including loss of enjoyment), damage to reputation and the brand image of several regions and municipalities as well as moral damages resulting from damage to natural heritage.[107] The Criminal Court in Paris recognised the right of an environmental association, with special powers for the protection, management and conservation

---

99 IOPC "Claims Manual" (2019) 39–40 https://iopcfunds.org/wp-content/uploads/2018/12/2019-Claims-Manual_e-1.pdf (27-07-2020).

100 IOPC (n 98) 15.

101 ibid 39.

102 IOPC (n 99) 14.

103 On 11 November 2007, the Russian-registered tanker *Volgoneft* broke in two in the Strait of Kerch linking the Sea of Azov and the Black Sea between the Russian Federation and Ukraine. While at anchor, the tanker got caught in a severe storm and heavy seas. The tanker was carrying 4 077 tonnes of heavy fuel oil almost half of which spilled into the sea. Approximately 250 kilometres of the coastlines of the Russian Federation and Ukraine were affected by the oil. More than 30 000 birds reportedly died. See IOPC (n 83) 25–26.

104 ibid.

105 ibid.

106 ibid 8.

107 ibid.

of an area, to claim compensation for moral and environmental damage to the area it is tasked with safeguarding.[108] At the Fund's Executive Committee's 40th session, in March 2008, numerous delegates expressed concern that the Criminal Court had awarded compensation for pure environmental damage although CLC 1992 restricts compensation for the environment to reasonable reinstatement measures.[109] Several delegations stated that the decision could have significant impacts for the CLC 1992 and Fund regime.[110] At that point in time, however, the Fund was unable to ascertain the impact of the decision since it was pending appeal.[111] In March 2010, the decision of the Criminal Court in Paris was affirmed on appeal by the French Court of Appeal in Paris.[112] In delivering its judgement the French Court of Appeal appeared to have little regard for the Fund's interpretation of Article 1(6) of CLC 1992, but instead controversially held that the provision does not rule out compensation for pure environmental damage.[113] When requested not to channel strict liability on the basis that the latter decision was founded on national law and not the CLC 1992 and Fund regime the court rejected such possibility, emphasising that Article 1(6) does not preclude compensation for pure environmental damage.[114] The award of pure environmental and moral damages was further affirmed by the French Court of Cassation (the highest court in the French Judiciary) in March 2010.[115] The French courts acknowledged and quantified compensation for pure environmental damage even though such compensation is not permitted under CLC 1992 and the Fund as affirmed in the IOPC Fund's Claims Manual.

The Fund Committee has noted that the judgment of the French Court of Cassation is not binding on the Fund because the Fund was not party to

---

108 ibid.

109 IOPC (n 82) 81.

110 ibid.

111 ibid.

112 IOPC (n 83) 8-9.

113 Kopela "Civil and criminal liability as mechanisms for the prevention of oil marine pollution" 2011 *RECIEL* 313 320.

114 ibid.

115 IOPC (n 83) 10.

the criminal proceedings.[116] Nonetheless the French courts' interpretation and application of CLC 1992 is contentious.[117] They highlight that the CLC 1992 is reliant on its interpretation and application within national jurisdictions.[118] The uniform interpretation and application of CLC 1992 is an important factor of the regime's success.[119] While awarding compensation for pure environmental damage is in line with developments in environmental law and the polluter-pays principle and may also have a deterring effect on future spills and substandard shipping in the oil industry,[120] varying interpretations of CLC 1992 might derail the international regime created by CLC 1992 and FUND 1992.[121] Indeed, admitting claims for pure environmental damage which are not covered by CLC 1992 may widen the ambit of liability of the Fund further than intended, something which may impact its viability.[122] Furthermore, the aim of CLC 1992 and the Fund regime is only to provide adequate and prompt compensation for oil pollution damage rather than to address deterrence and sub-standard shipping.[123] The French courts' decisions pose questions as to whether the objectives of CLC 1992 should be re-evaluated as far as substandard shipping is concerned.[124] In addition, the decisions also illustrate the views expressed by France in support of extending compensation under CLC 1992 for pure environmental damage.[125] While States parties have expressed concerns about substandard shipping and some delegations supported

---

116 IOPC "Annual Report" (2013) 31 https://iopcfunds.org/wp-content/uploads/2018/12/annualreport2013_e.pdf (01-09-2020).

117 Kopela (n 113) 323.

118 ibid.

119 ibid. See also IOPC (n 82) 48. Assemblies of the Funds have expressed the view that a uniform definition of "pollution damage" is essential for the CLC 1992 and the Fund regime.

120 Kopela (n 113) 323.

121 ibid.

122 See Jacobsson (n 78) 24, who notes that it is important for the future viability of the CLC 1992 and Fund regime that States parties adhere to the Fund's policies.

123 Kopela (n 113) 323.

124 ibid.

125 ibid. See also the 2000 submission by the French delegation (Review of the International Compensation Regime Third Intersessional Working Group (Doc. 92FUND/WGR.3/2/1 28 June 2000) par 2.2) where France expressed the view that there is a trend in the national legislation of some States to award more than "mere reinstatement measures" based on the influence of public perceptions and increased environmental awareness; and the 2001 submission by the French delegation (Review of the International Compensation Regime Third Intersessional Working Group (Doc. 92FUND/WGR.3/5/6 08 March 2001) par 4) where the delegation pointed out that international environmental law is slowly extending the boundaries of damage covered in respect of "related interests", including "amenity values".

using the civil liability regime as a measure of deterrence, others have opposed such an extension in light of the regime's objectives.[126] The European Commission has also suggested that the civil liability regime be amended to contribute to the deterrence of sub-standard shipping in the oil industry.[127] In future, the courts of States parties may thus, in the interest of increased global environmental awareness, the protection of environmental rights, the deterrence of substandard shipping and the prevention of oil spills, be more inclined to hold the polluter liable for pure environmental damage. This may result in other States parties of the Fund taking the same stance as France to award pure environmental damage even though the Fund has noted that it is not bound by the *Erika* decision.

In Spain, in relation to the *Prestige* oil spill, the Spanish Criminal Court in Corcubión awarded around €1 241 million for pure economic loss.[128] On appeal, on 20 December 2018, the Spanish Supreme Court held, however, that the Fund does not incur liability to compensate victims for pure environmental and moral damage because article 1(6) of CLC 1992 excludes such damages and only covers reasonable reinstatement measures.[129]

In South Africa, the polluter-pays principle is entrenched in domestic environmental legislation. Section 2(4)(p) of the National Environmental Management Act (NEMA)[130] obliges the polluter to pay the costs of remedying the effects of pollution as well as preventing, minimising or controlling further pollution.[131] Section 28 of NEMA places a duty on the polluter to take "reasonable measures",[132] which include measures to:

> "(a)   investigate, assess and evaluate the impact on the environment;

---

126 Kopela (n 113) 323. See also Report on the Ninth Meeting of the Third Intersessional Working Group (Doc 92FUND/A10/7 10 May 2005) par 7.1, 7.5 and 7.7.

127 Kopela (n 113) 323. See also Directive 2004/35/CE of the European Parliament and of the Council of 21 April 2004 on environmental liability with regard to the prevention and remedying of environmental damage *Official Journal* L 143/56 of 30 April 2004 0056–0075.

128 IOPC (n 83) 16.

129 Cassation appeal/606/2018 23-25 https://iopcfunds.org/incidents/incident-map#1916-13-November-2002 (30-08-2020). See further IOPC "Recent developments in the Prestige incident – December 2018 Judgment" (2019) https://iopcfunds.org/news/recent-developments-in-the-prestige-incident-december-2018-judgment/ (30-08-2020).

130 107 of 1998.

131 s 2(4)(p).

132 s 28(1).

(b)   inform and educate employees about the environmental risks of their work and the manner in which their tasks must be performed in order to avoid causing significant pollution or degradation of the environment;

(c)   cease, modify or control any act, activity or process causing the pollution or degradation;

(d)   contain or prevent the movement of pollutants or the causant of degradation;

(e)   eliminate any source of the pollution or degradation; or

(f)   remedy the effects of the pollution or degradation".[133]

Section 30A of NEMA applies to "emergency situations"[134] such as oil spills and requires the person who caused the emergency situation to take measures to mitigate, prevent, control and rehabilitate the impact thereof on the environment.[135] These legislative measures do not appear to extend to compensation for pure environmental damage, but they hold the polluter financially liable for reasonable measures to prevent, minimise, rectify and control the effects of oil pollution damage. This is aligned to CLC 1992, as interpreted in the Fund's Claims Manual, which limits compensation for the impairment of the environment to "reasonable reinstatement measures".

Section 24 of the Constitution of the Republic of South Africa, 1996, grants everyone a right "to an environment that is not harmful to their health or well-being" and to have their environment protected by the State through reasonable legislative and other measures that prevent pollution and ecological degradation, promote conservation and secure ecologically sustainable development". This right is supported by the locus standi clause in the Constitution, "granting anyone acting in the public interest" the right to challenge any violation of the environmental right before a court.[136] The concept of "health" relates to human health, which

---

133 s 28(3).

134 s 30A (7) defines an "emergency situation" as "a situation that arises suddenly and poses an imminent and serious threat to the environment, human life, property, including a disaster". This definition is broad enough to include an oil spill.

135 s 30A(3).

136 See s 38(d) of the Constitution. See also Witbooi "Restrictive environmental measures: (When) do they justify compensation for the property owner"2001 *SAJELP* 215 231.

includes both mental and physical health.[137] While "well-being" could be broadly interpreted so as to include spiritual or psychological characteristics including an individual's need to be able to connect with nature,[138] to do so would bring environmental issues, such as conservation and the maintenance of biodiversity, within the ambit of the environmental right enshrined in the Constitution.[139] Such a broad interpretation could also be the basis upon which compensation for pure environmental damage is awarded in South Africa. The South African courts have, however, been hesitant to broadly interpret "well-being" to include aesthetic or spiritual dimensions and have limited it to physical discomfort.[140] The South African courts have thus not granted compensation for pure environmental damage and have limited compensation for the impairment of the environment to measures to prevent, rectify, minimise and control pollution. However, the possibility of the South African courts awarding compensation for pure environmental damage cannot be permanently excluded because increased global environmental awareness, the need to deter substandard shipping and the prevention of oil spills may lead to the courts more broadly interpreting the concept of "well-being" so as to accommodate compensation for pure environmental damage.

Pure economic loss

The CLC 1992 definition of "oil pollution damage" is broad enough to encompass loss of profits, including such losses sustained as a result of the "impairment of the environment".[141] The Convention however does not specify which such losses are covered. There is a broad range of profit losses which can be sustained following an oil spill. A person or entity may suffer loss of profits as a result of damage to his, her or its private property. For example, a fisher whose nets have been contaminated by the spill may suffer a loss of profit for the time period

137 Warnich "Environmental Right in Terms of the Constitution" (2018) https://www.polity.org.za/article/environmental-right-in-terms-of-the-constitution-2018-02-14 (25-07-2020).

138 ibid. See also Witbooi (n 136) 233.

139 Warnich (n 137).

140 ibid. See also *Hichange Investments v Cape Produce Co (Pty) Ltd t/a Pelts Products* 2004 2 SA 393 (E).

141 art 1(6) of CLC 1992.

that the fishing nets are being cleaned, repaired or replaced.[142] This type of loss of profits, which is linked to property damage, is known as a "consequential loss".[143] Other parties or entities may suffer a loss of profits without sustaining any loss or damage to private property; such losses may arise solely from the "impairment of the environment" upon which they rely for their livelihood or business.[144] These losses are known as pure economic losses and such losses can be quite widespread following a damaging spill.[145] Indeed, oil spills often severely impact the marine environment, marine organisms and the coastline, upon which many parties rely directly for their livelihood and business such as commercial fishers, fish farms, restaurants, hotels and campsites on the coastline.[146] A fisher might, for example, sustain pure economic losses following an oil spill due to reduced fishing stocks (due to mortalities or contamination), interruption of fishing activities, a loss of market or reduced sale prices.[147] As far as it is concerned, the tourism industry might face a loss of income due to a reduction in tourists as a result of the spill and may incur additional costs of promotion.[148] Secondary or indirect pure economic losses can also be sustained by other industries that rely on the directly affected industries.[149] For example, the industries providing fuel, ice and nets as well as fish wholesalers and retailers who depend on the fishing industry may suffer a decline in business and profits where fishing and fishing business decrease.[150] Likewise, the industries providing goods and services to the tourism industry might incur losses if the tourist industry takes a dip because the number of tourists visiting the contaminated area decline.[151]

---

142 IOPC (n 99) 14.

143 ibid.

144 ibid.

145 ibid. See also Palmer "The great spill in the Gulf…and a sea of pure economic loss: Reflections on the boundaries of civil liability" 2011 *Penn State Law Review* 105 110.

146 IOPC (n 99) 32 and 36.

147 For a full discussion of losses in the fishing industry, see IOPC "Guidelines for presenting claims in the fisheries, mariculture and fish processing sector" (2019) https://iopcfunds.org/wp-content/uploads/2017/04/2019-Fisheries_e.pdf (27-07-2020).

148 For a full discussion of losses in the tourism industry, see IOPC "Guidelines for presenting claims in the tourism sector" (2018) https://iopcfunds.org/wp-content/uploads/2018/08/IOPC-Tourism-Guidelines_ENGLISH-2018-WEB.pdf (27-07-2020).

149 IOPC (n 99) 32 and 37.

150 ibid 32.

151 ibid 14 and 37.

The decision as to which of the above-discussed claims for pure economic loss are admissible for compensation is left largely to the courts of the States parties. While the admissibility of claims for consequential economic loss is not controversial and is affirmed by the Fund in its Claims Manual, claims for pure economic loss are more problematic.[152] In order to assist the domestic courts in determining where the cut-off line should be drawn in respect of claims for loss of profits, the Fund provides guidelines in its Claims Manual. The latter sets out that claims for pure economic loss by the tourism sector and those relating to fisheries and mariculture activities will only be admissible for compensation where there is "a sufficiently close link of causation" between the contamination and the loss claimed.[153] In determining whether such a "sufficiently close link of causation exists", the Fund looks at: (1) the geographic proximity of the claimant's business activity to the contaminated area; (2) the degree to which the claimant's business is financially reliant on the impacted resource (such as the polluted area of the sea); (3) the extent to which the claimant had other sources of supply or alternative markets; and (4) the extent to which the claimant's business forms an integral part of the economic activity within the contaminated area.[154] When applying those criteria, the Fund has accepted claims for pure economic loss from those directly reliant on the impaired environment such as those involved in mariculture, fishing and shellfish gathering, fish processors/vendors, fishers as well as beachfront restaurants, campsites and hotels that suffered a loss of income due to a decline in tourism activities.[155] At the same time, the Fund has rejected claims of a more secondary and indirect nature for lacking a sufficient link of causation. Examples are the claims of a food merchant selling frozen food to restaurants, a salt-producer who suffered loss due to a self-imposed quota rather than the spill, a fish wholesaler whose business was located outside the contaminated region and a subrogated claim from a hotel insurer for the cancellation of a millennium party due to a storm and not the spill.[156]

---

152 ibid 14: "Under certain circumstances, claims for pure economic loss are payable".

153 ibid 15.

154 ibid 32–33 and 36–37.

155 IOPC (n 82) 84–87.

156 ibid.

The Fund's criteria are not binding on the courts of States parties,[157] but they should be taken into account when interpreting the provisions of CLC 1992, according to article 31(3)(b) of the 1969 Vienna Convention on the Law of Treaties.[158] The Fund's criteria are quite general and flexible to make accommodation for new and existing claims as they are applied to assess each case on its own merits.[159] The criteria are also "pragmatic" and accommodate the financial climate, geographic location and political influences which may influence the admissibility of claims for pure economic loss.[160] Therefore, even where a court considers the Fund's criteria or makes reference to them, it retains a large degree of flexibility in determining which claims for pure economic loss are admissible.[161] In addition, this inherent flexibility in the criteria leaves room for the legal background of a state party and its approach to claims for economic loss to influence its courts' interpretation of the criteria. As a result, the courts in one state party might interpret the Fund's criteria narrowly, while the courts in another state might interpret the criteria more broadly to admit a greater range of claims for pure economic loss. The inherent flexibility built into the Fund's criteria makes this possible and may in itself threaten uniformity.

In the United Kingdom, the courts are very restrictive in their approach to claims for pure economic loss, which were traditionally precluded in the absence of property damage by the "economic loss rule", but have made an exception to accept claims for loss of profit by fishermen directly reliant on the contaminated area even in the absence of property damage.[162] The restrictive approach of the courts in the United Kingdom was evident following the grounding of the

---

157 ibid 49. See also Jacobsson (n 78) 27.

158 1155 *UNTS* 331, (1969) 8 *ILM* 679. Adopted: 23-05-1969; EIF: 27-01-1980: "There shall be taken into account, together with the context: … (b) any subsequent practice in the application of the treaty which establishes the agreement of the parties regarding its interpretation".

159 IOPC (n 82) at 87.

160 Soyer "Ship-sourced oil pollution and pure economic loss: The quest for overarching principles" 2009 *Torts LJ* 1 6.

161 ibid.

162 Huang *Recoverability of Pure Economic Loss Arising from Ship-Source Oil Pollution* (2011) 254.

BRAER [163] in Scotland and the *Sea Empress*[164] in Wales where the courts in these jurisdictions had to grapple with the admissibility of claims for pure economic loss. The courts applied the criteria of proximity (both physical and causal) between the contamination and the loss.[165] On that basis, a claim for loss of profits by a smolt producer (Landcatch Ltd), located 500 km from the contaminated region, was denied because the loss was caused by customers' unwillingness to purchase smolt after the spill, rather than by the contamination itself.[166] Likewise, a claim for loss of income (due to a decline in passengers) by the main ferry operator from the Shetland Islands to the mainland was denied on the basis that the loss was not a direct consequence of the spill, but rather an indirect result, caused by negative publicity affecting the image of the Shetland area as a holiday destination.[167] After the *Sea Empress* ran aground, a fish processing company located out of the contaminated area, Tilbury, claimed loss of profits following a fishing ban in the contaminated area. Tilbury alleged that it lost £643 557 in profits that it would have made from processing whelks obtained from fishers fishing in the contaminated area and selling them to the Korean market. Tilbury's claim was denied due to a lack of proximity, rendering the claim too remote, "secondary" and "indirect".[168] On appeal, the court emphasised that the term "damage" was restricted to physical contamination and its consequences and that Tilbury's loss

---

163 In January 1993, having experienced an engine failure, the oil tanker BRAER ran aground, amidst severe weather conditions in the Shetland Islands area. The tanker was carrying about 85 000 tonnes of oil, almost all of which spilled into the surrounding waters. The oiling of the coastline was relatively minimal in comparison to the scale of the spill and clean-up operations were limited, but many birds and mammals died and a wide range of fish and shellfish over a fairly large area became contaminated with oil. The latter resulted in the implementation of a fishing ban in the contaminated region and millions of farmed salmon (more than 25% of the total production for the Shetlands that year) could not be sold and had to be destroyed. See Goodlad "Effects of the Braer oil spill on the Shetland seafood industry" 1996
The Science of the Total Environment 127 127–128 and 130.

164 In February 1996, the oil tanker Sea Empress ran aground in the entrance to Milford Haven in the South-West of Wales and around 72 000 tonnes of light crude oil and 480 tonnes of heavy fuel oil were released into the surrounding waters contaminating approximately 200 km of the Pembrokeshire coastline, much of which is part of a national park, is well known for its natural beauty and is used for a variety of purposes including tourism, fisheries and mariculture. See Nikitik, Andrew and Robinson "Patterns in benthic populations in the Milford Haven waterway following the Sea Empress oil spill with special reference to amphipods" 2003 *Marine Pollution Bulletin* 1125 1125.

165 Soyer (n 160) 14.

166 *Landcatch Ltd v International Oil Pollution Compensation Fund* [1999] 2 *Lloyd's Rep* 316, affirming the decision of Lord Gill in *Landcatch Limited v Braer Corporation and Another* [1998] 2 *Lloyd's Rep* 552.

167 *Skerries Salmon Ltd v The Braer Corporation* [1999] SLT 1196.

168 ibid.

resulted instead from its inability to process whelks at a location far away from the contaminated regions.[169] All the aforementioned decisions are consistent with the Fund's criteria in rejecting claims of a secondary and indirect nature, being without a sufficiently close link to the contamination. That approach appears to be premised on the general inadmissibility of claims for pure economic loss, with the exception of claims by those directly reliant on the affected resource.[170]

In China, claims for pure economic loss have not garnered much attention from the courts.[171] The *Tasman Sea* oil spill was the first public case where commercial fishers directly dependent on the affected environment were granted compensation for economic loss due to the disruption in fishing and harvesting activities caused by the spill. [172] In that case, directness rather than the Fund's criteria was used to determine the scope of admissibility of the claims for pure economic loss. It remains to seen whether the Chinese courts will admit claims for pure economic loss that have a close causal link to the contamination, but are not directly caused by it.

In French law, there is no rule precluding claims for pure economic loss.[173] A claim for negligently inflicted pure economic loss is not likely to face many technical burdens and the French courts are quite open to finding in favour of the plaintiffs in tort.[174] To limit the claims admissible for pure economic loss, the French courts have required a link of causation and applied the requirements of foreseeability and directness.[175] Following the *Erika* oil spill, some French courts relied on the Fund's criteria to admit claims for pure economic loss while others did not, emphasising that the Fund's criteria are not binding on the courts.[176] In most instances, the French courts reached the same decisions as the Fund

---

169 *R J Tilbury & Sons (Devon) Ltd (t/a East Devon Shellfish) v Alegrete Shipping Co Inc* [2003] 2 All ER (Comm) 1, [2003] 1 *Lloyd's Rep* 327, [2003] 1 CLC 325.

170 Jacobsson (n 78) 27.

171 Huang (n 162) 262.

172 ibid.

173 Huang (n 162) 255.

174 ibid 256.

175 ibid.

176 Jacobsson (n 78) 28.

would have reached and, where they differed, they were overturned on appeal and brought in line with the decisions of the Fund.[177]

In South Africa, the courts are cautious to grant claims for pure economic loss where doing so would lead to indeterminate liability.[178] Under Roman-Dutch law, claims for pure economic loss without related loss or damage to property were precluded.[179] Although the courts have been cautious to extend delictual liability to claims for pure economic loss, such claims may be successful where the elements of a delict are met.[180] This means that wrongfulness needs to be established, something which ordinarily requires establishing whether a legal duty exists.[181] In South Africa, no general duty exists in respect of negligently inflicted pure economic loss. As a result, each court will have to decide, on a case-by-case basis, whether a duty exists.[182] That decision is likely to be made taking into account the *boni mores*,[183] the environmental right entrenched in the Constitution as well as environmental legislation and societal environmental awareness. There has not been any case in South Africa dealing with claims for pure economic loss caused by an oil spill yet[184] and it remains to be seen to which extent such claims will be accepted by the courts.

It appears that, in most instances, the courts in the States parties have admitted claims for pure economic loss that align with the Fund's criteria, although reference has not always been made to the criteria. In a number of States parties, case law in respect of claims for pure economic loss still appears to be developing and it is unclear whether such development will lead to claims for pure economic loss being narrowly admitted, to prevent indeterminate liability and a multitude of claims, or more broadly admitted in light of social and political considerations. In the absence of a uniform approach, the outcome of a claim for pure economic

---

177 ibid.

178 Kotze "Interpretation of claims for pure economic loss under art 1(6)(c) of the Hazardous and Noxious Substances Convention" 2002 *SAYIL* 171 178-179.

179 ibid 177.

180 ibid.

181 ibid.

182 ibid 177-178.

183 ibid 178.

184 ibid 180.

loss following an oil spill remains largely uncertain and dependent on where the incident takes place and where the claim is subsequently instituted. A very broad interpretation of the Fund's criteria leading to a broad admissibility of claims for pure economic loss should be cautioned against in order to avoid unwarranted costs (for losses that are too remote) being incurred with the risk of endangering the Fund's viability.[185] At the same time, one should avoid an overly restrictive approach, which might preclude genuine claims for pure economic losses linked to the contamination.

In instances of very large-scale spills, it is particularly hard for the domestic courts to decide exactly where to draw the line between admissible and inadmissible claims for pure economic loss because of the broad range of potential victims and the far-reaching effects of the oil spill. An example is the *Deepwater Horizon* incident in April 2010. In this case, the platform exploded while in use at the Macondo Prospect (a seabed location) approximately 40 miles from the southeast coast of Louisiana, releasing some 4.9 million barrels of oil and becoming the largest marine oil spill in United States,[186] contaminating the marine environment and shore along the Gulf Coast and causing multibillion losses in the fisheries sector and tourist industry.[187] Many beaches and marshes in a number of Gulf regions were impacted by the blowout, beachfront hotels and their employees were impacted by a decline in hotel reservations, real-estate agents selling and renting properties on the Gulf Coast were affected by a decline in property values in the region, drillers were precluded from drilling by a federal moratorium on deep-water drilling, and commercial fishers as well as those reliant on fish and other seafood from the Gulf waters, such as seafood restaurants, fish markets, wholesalers and grocery stores, suffered a decline in business.[188] Unsurprisingly, the majority of

---

185 Davis "Pure economic loss claims under the Oil Pollution Act: Combining policy and congressional intent" 2011 *Colum JL & Soc Probs* 1 44, who states that unwarranted costs can flow from a more liberal interpretation of provisions relating to pure economic loss (in the case of the United States Oil Pollution Act, 1990); Jacobsson (n 78) 24, who notes that it is important for the future viability of CLC 1992 and the Fund regime that States parties adhere to the Fund's policies.

186 Selby "In re: Oil Spill by the Oil Rig Deepwater Horizon on the Gulf of Mexico, on April 20, 2010, Order, Aug 26, 2011" 2012 *Harv Env LR* 533 533; Perry "The Deepwater Horizon oil spill and the limit of civil liability" 2011 *Wash LR* 1 1.

187 Perry (n 186) 2.

188 Davies "Deepwater Horizon: Removal costs, civil damages, crimes, civil penalties and State remedies in oil spill cases" 2011 *Tul LR* 1 24.

the claims resulting from the incident were for pure economic loss.[189] In fact, the potential liability following a spill of this magnitude is endless because everyone who suffers some sort of setback as a result of the spill influences the business of another.[190]

The United States of America are not a party to CLC 1992 and FUND 1992. The applicable federal legislation is the Oil Pollution Act (OPA) of 1990,[191] enacted in response to the *Exxon Valdez* spill.[192] Until then, claims for pure economic loss were precluded under general maritime law by the *Robins Dry Dock* rule, which only permitted claims for economic loss linked to loss or damage to property.[193] By contrast, the OPA expressly permits a claimant to recover economic loss, even in the absence of any damage to the claimant's property. Under section 2702(b)(2)(E) of the OPA, "loss of profits or impairment of earning capacity due to the injury, destruction, loss of real property, personal property, or natural resources" can be recovered by "any claimant".[194] The exact causal nexus required by the phrase "due to" is however not set out in the OPA.[195] There are very few judicial decisions clarifying the scope of that provision and the causal link required by the words "due to" has been the subject of varying interpretations, which have vacillated from requiring the oil pollution damage to be sole cause or proximate cause of the loss, on the one hand, to a contributing cause of the loss, on the other.[196] In an unreported decision of the United States District Court for the Eastern District of Louisiana, a proximate cause test was applied to establish which

---

189 BDO Consulting "Independent Evaluation of the Gulf Coast Claims Facility Report of Findings & Observations to the U.S. Department of Justice" (2012) 60 https://www.justice.gov/iso/opa/resources/66520126611210351178.pdf (10-08-2020).

190 Palmer (n 145) 110.

191 Pub L No 101-380, Aug 18, 1990, 104 Stat.

192 In March 1989, the oil tanker Exxon Valdez ran aground in Prince William Sound, Alaska, and spilled an estimated 42 million litres of crude oil. The oil subsequently spread over more than 26 000 km2 of water in other parts of the Gulf of Alaska contaminating over 1 000 km of the coastline. The spill resulted in high mortalities of seabirds and other marine mammals, hundreds of thousands of seabirds, several thousand sea otters and a significant proportion of killer whales. Other wildlife species were also impacted. See Eslera, Ballacheya, Matkinb, Cushingc, Kalerd, Bodkina, Monsona, Esslingera and Kloeckera "Timelines and mechanisms of wildlife population recovery following the Exxon Valdez oil spill" 2018 *Deep-Sea Research Part II: Topical Studies in Oceanography* 36 36

193 *Robins Dry Dock & Repair Co v Flint* 275 US 303 (1927).

194 33 US Code § 2702.

195 Davis (n 185) 21.

196 Davies "Liability issues raised by the Deepwater Horizon blowout" 2011 *A&NZ Mar LJ* 35 38.

claims for pure economic loss were admissible according to section 2702(b)(2)
(E).[197] In terms of that test, claims for economic loss by those who rely directly on
the affected natural resource, such as fishers, are admissible while claims by those
indirectly reliant on the resource, such as seafood restaurants, are not.[198]

After the *Deepwater Horizon* spill, British Petroleum (BP) set up a Gulf Coast
Claims Facility (GCCF) that aimed to fully compensate victims who suffered
oil pollution damage as a result of the spill.[199] The GCCF was backed by a $20
billion trust fund accompanied by an open-ended commitment in the event that
the amount proved insufficient.[200] The GCCF sought to resolve private claims
(from individuals and businesses) against BP resulting from the spill outside the
court system in an expeditious manner.[201] The GCCF made emergency payments,
for which claimants were not required to sign a release and final settlements.[202]
By contrast, claimants who accepted final payment from the GCCF had to sign
an undertaking not to pursue action against BP in court.[203] In admitting claims
for pure economic loss flowing from the spill, the GCCF applied a proximate
cause test, requiring claimants to show that the spill was the proximate cause
of their loss.[204] In practice, the GCCF liberally applied the proximate cause test
and granted cover not only to those directly reliant on the Gulf's resources and
within its immediate vicinity but also to those who were physically unaffected by
the oil spill but suffered a decline in business due to a decrease in tourists.[205] In
fact, in its Final Payment Methodology the GCCF indicated that neither physical
proximity to the spill nor a particular type of work or industry is a precondition

---

197 ibid.

198 ibid.

199 Issacharoff and Rave "The BP oil spill settlement and the paradox of public litigation" 2014 *Loyola LR* 398 398.

200 ibid.

201 ibid 400.

202 ibid 421.

203 ibid 420–421; BDO Consulting (n 189) 29.

204 BDO Consulting (n 189) 38. See also Gulf Coast Claims Facility (GCCF) "Protocol for Emergency Advance
Payments" (2010) 5 https://www.restorethegulf.gov/sites/default/files/imported_pdfs/library/assets/gccf-
emergency-advance-payments.pdf. (07-08-2020), which indicated that the GCCF would apply a "proximate cause
test" and claimants would have to demonstrate geographic proximity, describe the nature of the industry and explain
their reliance on the natural resources in order to successfully claim for pure economic loss resulting from the
Deepwater Horizon incident.

205 Davis (n 185) 31.

for compensation, although the latter played a role in the type of proof needed to substantiate a claim.[206] By the end of 2011, the GCCF had processed more than 1 million claims and paid out over $6.2 billion to individuals and businesses.[207] Approximately 99.8% of the claims and 99.6% of the amounts paid by the GCCF related to claims for pure economic loss.[208] Although the majority of the payments for compensation (74%) were made to claimants in the immediate vicinity, a sizeable portion of the amount paid for compensation went to businesses in regions which were physically unaffected by the spill.[209]

Many individuals and entities impacted by the spill questioned the decisions made by the administrator of the GCCF, who was remunerated by BP itself, and opted to pursue their claims in court rather than accept payment from the GCCF.[210] The Department of Justice expressed concerns regarding the inconsistent outcomes in respect of claimants who were similarly situated.[211] An independent review uncovered instances in which the GCCF made errors in the claims evaluation process but found that, for the most part, the GCCF had applied its protocols and methodologies consistently.[212] In respect of similarly situated claimants being met with different outcomes by the GCCF, the independent evaluation revealed that it may have been impacted by a number of factors, including a change in the methodologies of the GCCF while it operated.[213] The independent evaluation of the GCCF claims process revealed that approximately 7 300 claimants were negatively impacted by errors (such as underpayment and claims being denied), requiring the GCCF to make additional payments and/or first payments of more than $64 million.[214]

---

206 GCCF "Final Rules Governing Payment Options, Eligibility, and Substantiation Criteria and Final Payment Methodology" (2011) 2-3 https://eng2viet.files.wordpress.com/2011/02/gccf-final-rules.pdf (30-07-2020).

207 BDO Consulting (n 189) 71.

208 ibid 60.

209 ibid.

210 ibid.

211 ibid 71.

212 ibid 58.

213 ibid 72.

214 ibid.

In 2010, the Judicial Panel on Multidistrict Litigation (JPML) centralised all federal actions in the United States District Court for the Eastern District of Louisiana.[215] This led to the consolidation of thousands of individual claims, including private claims for economic loss and property damage, with this multidistrict litigation.[216] In February 2011, BP began settlement negotiations with the plaintiffs in the class action lawsuit *In Re: Spill by the Oil Rig "Deepwater Horizon" in the Gulf of Mexico on April 20, 2010*, which was pending in the United States District Court for the Eastern District of Louisiana.[217] On 2 March 2012, the parties reached an in-principle agreement for two class action settlements, a Medical Claims Settlement and an Economic and Property Damages Settlement, which are of relevance for this discussion.[218] As part of the litigation *In Re: Spill by the Oil Rig "Deepwater Horizon"*, the District Court Judge Carl Barbier issued a transition order, on 8 March 2012, for the transition from the GCCF claims process to a court-supervised Settlement Programme with its own framework for processing claims as established by the Economic and Property Damage Settlement.[219] According to that order, the GCCF would no longer admit, process or pay any claims other than the claims for which final payment had already been accepted by the claimant and which were not pending appeal, all other claims having to be submitted under the Settlement Programme.[220] The transition order also terminated the GCCF appeal process for all claims unless still pending.[221] In December 2012, a District Court order was issued granting the final approval of the Economic and Property Damages Settlement, confirming a class-wide release and barring class members from instituting legal action against BP.[222]

215 *In Re Oil Spill by the Oil Rig "Deepwater Horizon" in the Gulf of Mexico, on April 20, 2010 MDL No 2179* Order and Reasons (Document: 8138) 1.

216 ibid.

217 ibid 2. See also BDO Consulting (n 189) 56.

218 *In Re Oil Spill* (n 219) 2; BDO Consulting (n 189) 56-57.

219 *In Re Oil Spill* (n 219) 3; BDO Consulting (n 189) 56-57.

220 BDO Consulting (n 189) 56-57.

221 ibid 57.

222 *In Re Oil Spill by the Oil Rig "Deepwater Horizon" in the Gulf of Mexico, on April 20, 2010 MDL No 2179* Order and Judgement (Document: 8139) 1, 3, 4.

The Economic and Property Damages Settlement aims to settle all claims by private individuals and entities who suffered economic loss and property damage as a result of the *Deepwater Horizon* incident.[223] In terms of the Settlement, the class consists of individuals and businesses defined by geographic zones (ranging from most impacted to least impacted) and the nature of their loss or damage.[224] The geographic bounds are Gulf Coast areas (Louisiana, Mississippi, Alabama, certain coastal counties in east Texas and west Florida) including specified adjacent Gulf waters. Individuals must have "lived, worked, owned property" in the specified zones, while businesses must have conducted business within the specified zones, within a specified time period.[225] The Settlement recognises six categories of damage: (1) economic loss (covering claims by businesses and individuals who suffered a loss of income or profits as a result of the *Deepwater Horizon* incident); (2) property damage (which includes the loss of use/enjoyment of real property and covers property damage of coastal property and wetlands property, including property sales loss); (3) vessel of opportunity ("VoO") charter payment; (4) vessel physical damage; (5) subsistence damage (which covers claims for loss of subsistence from those who fished or hunted in the region to harvest, catch, barter, consume or trade Gulf resources, including seafood and game, in a traditional or customary manner, to sustain their basic or family dietary, financial security, shelter, tool or clothing needs, and who relied upon subsistence resources that declined in the region due to the *Deepwater Horizon* incident); and (6) seafood compensation covered by its own fund of $2.3 billion (including claims by eligible commercial fishers, seafood boat captains, seafood crew, oyster leaseholders and seafood vessel owners who have their home port or landed seafood on the Gulf Coast, including damages suffered by oyster leaseholders).[226] The Settlement presumes causation for certain zones and/or industries more likely to have been impacted by the spill on the basis that these industries would prove causation in litigation. In those cases,

---

223 *In Re Oil Spill* (n 219) 6. See also *In Re Oil Spill by the Oil Rig "Deepwater Horizon" in the Gulf of Mexico, on April 20, 2010 MDL No 2179* Preliminary Approval Order (Document: 6418) 4.

224 *In Re Oil Spill by the Oil Rig "Deepwater Horizon" in the Gulf of Mexico, on April 20, 2010 MDL No 2179* Order and Judgement (Document: 8139) Appendix A: Class Definition A-1. See also *In Re Oil Spill* (n 223) 5.

225 ibid.

226 *In Re Oil Spill* (n 215) 10–16.

the claimants are only required to prove that they suffered a financial loss and need not prove a causal link between their loss and the *Deepwater Horizon* incident.[227]

Since the court's approval of the Settlement, BP has challenged the claims administrator's interpretation thereof resulting in protracted litigation over many years. According to BP, the claims administrator's misinterpretation of the terms of the Settlement has resulted in the payment of "artificial claims" where the claimant's loss is not linked to the *Deepwater Horizon* incident, the losses have been inflated and/or there are no losses at all.[228] BP asserted that this misinterpretation led to obscure results and was not aligned with the goal of the Settlement, which is to compensate actual loss of profits rather than artificial claims by unaffected claimants.[229] In this respect two issues raised by BP merit mention. Firstly, BP was displeased with the method according to which losses were calculated, because the financial statements of the claimants were not in all instances being properly "matched" (their expenses were not being matched to their revenue).[230] Secondly BP was dissatisfied that presumed causation resulted in claimants not having to show any causal link between their loss and the incident.[231] After extended litigation the issue of matching was addressed, the claims administrator was directed to match the revenue and expenses of claimants and to draft a policy in this regard.[232] In respect of causation BP's request to change the terms of the Settlement was rejected, the rejection was affirmed on appeal and BP was held to be bound by the settlement which the parties negotiated.[233] Only recently, in respect of causation, the Fifth Circuit held that where credible evidence of an intervening

---

227 ibid 12.

228 *Lake Eugenie Land & Dev Inc v BP Exploration & Prod Inc (In re Deepwater Horizon)* No 13-30315 (5th Cir Nov 5 2013), consolidated with *In Re: Deepwater Horizon* No 13-30329 (5th Cir 2013) (Document: 00512394834) 7, 9 and 25.

229 ibid 9.

230 ibid 6 and 13-19. See also *Lake Eugenie Land & Dev Inc v BP Exploration & Prod Inc (In re Deepwater Horizon)* No 17-30727 (5th Cir June 26 2019) 4.

231 *Lake Eugenie* (n 228) 4-6.

232 *Lake Eugenie* (n 228) 4. See "Policy 495", which sets out two categories of methods for the matching of financial statements. One group of methodologies, namely the industry-specific methodologies ("ISMs"), which enables the administrator to "reallocate" or "smooth" the claimants' otherwise large profits on an industry-wide basis, was rejected by the Fifth Circuit. By contrast, the other method, namely the annual variable margin methodology ("AVMM"), which allows expenses and corresponding revenue to be recorded in the same month, regardless of when the expenses were incurred, was accepted. See at 3-6 and 8-9.

233 *Lake Eugenie* (n 228) 4.

(superseding) cause can be shown the claimant's attestation can be examined.[234] On this basis an award of $77 million was reversed because BP was able to show that the claimant's loss resulted from an increase in the price of fertilizer rather than the *Deepwater Horizon* incident.[235] This decision may provide BP with partial relief against "artificial claims" caused by presumed causation, in that at least where credible evidence of an intervening cause can be shown the claimant's attestation of a loss may be further investigated.

The difficulties faced by GCCF in admitting claims for pure economic loss indicate how complex determining the exact "causal nexus" required between the spill and the loss becomes when large numbers of claims are submitted. It also highlights how important clear causation rules or policies establishing the required link between the contamination and the loss are. The inconsistencies in the GCCF's admission of claims of claimants who are similarly situated further highlights the importance of interpreting and applying the same rules and policies consistently and throughout. The protracted litigation following the court's approval of the Economic and Property Damage Settlement emphasises the importance of interpreting and applying policies in a manner that precludes the payment of artificial and/or inflated claims. Large-scale spills raise social and political considerations and garner far greater publicity, which may influence the number of claims submitted and may lead to claimants submitting claims solely on the basis of public perception rather than actual impact by the spill. The latter is a cause for concern and further increases the importance of approaching claims for economic loss resulting from an oil spill (especially a large spill) with consistency. Inconsistencies in admitting claims for pure economic loss can result in protracted litigation.[236] For those reasons, in instances of large-scale spills with a multitude of claims for pure economic loss, the courts of the tates parties to CLC 1992 and FUND 1992 must be careful to ensure consistency in their decisions and consistency with the Fund's criteria. Likewise, the courts in States parties should ensure that "artificial" and/or inflated claims for pure economic loss are

234 *BP Exploration & Production, Incorporated; BP America Production Company; BO PLC v Claimant ID 100191715* No 19-30264 (5th Cir 2020) (Document: 00515329840) 4–6.

235 ibid 1 and 5.

236 Palmer (n 145) 141.

not admitted. The Fund's criteria (where applied) should be interpreted so as to exclude such claims. Large-scale, or a multitude of artificial and/or inflated claims for pure economic loss could potentially affect the Fund's viability where the Fund's involvement becomes necessary. The approach followed in the case of the GCCF should arguably not be followed because it was backed by a $20 billion trust fund and an open-ended commitment, which were unique and made it possible for the GCCF administrator to apply liberally the proximate cause test.[237]

THE MARINE POLLUTION ACT'S COVERAGE OF NON-PERSISTENT-OIL AND NON-TANKER-OIL POLLUTION DAMAGE

As previously explained, the CLC 1992 and FUND 1992 regimes only cover persistent-oil pollution from tanker vessels.[238] The regime does not cover bunker-oil pollution discharged from a non-tanker vessel and non-persistent-oil pollution. In South Africa, bunker-oil pollution damage caused by non-tanker vessels and pollution damage caused by non-persistent oil is presently covered by the Marine Pollution Act, which defines the terms "ship" and "oil" more broadly than the Civil Liability Act. The Marine Pollution Act defines the term "ship" so as to include "any kind of vessel or other sea-borne object from which oil can be discharged".[239] The words "any kind of vessel" and "sea-borne object" are broad enough to encompass a wide range of non-tanker vessels such as, for example, bulk carriers, container ships, general cargo ships, cruise ships and other vessels carrying passengers, tugs, dredgers, car carriers, fishing vessels, diving support vessels and drill ships previously mentioned.

In addition, the Marine Pollution Act applies to non-persistent-oil pollution because it defines the word "oil" expansively as "any kind of mineral oil [including] spirit produced from oil and a mixture of such oil and water or any other substance".[240] The words "any kind of mineral oil" are broad enough to

---

237 Davis (n 185) 38.

238 art 1(5) of CLC 1992.

239 s 1.

240 ibid.

encompass both persistent and non–persistent mineral oil. In addition, the Marine Pollution Act applies to harmful substances, which are defined to include oil and any other substance subject to control by the 1973 International Convention for the Prevention of pollution from Ships[241] as modified by its 1978 Protocol ("MARPOL 1973/78")[242] as well as "mixtures of such substances and water or any other substance".[243] MARPOL 1973/78 defines "oil" as "petroleum in any form including crude oil, fuel oil, sludge, oil refuse and refined products" other than petrochemicals.[244] The Marine Pollution Act therefore applies to many forms of oil, including non-persistent oil. In other words, where CLC 1992 through its incorporation by means of the Civil Liability Act does not apply to the form of oil pollution or type of vessel involved, the Marine Pollution Act will apply.

The Marine Pollution Act is a combination of CLC 1969 and MARPOL 1973.[245] Modelled partly on CLC 1969, the Marine Pollution Act imposes strict liability on ship owners for oil pollution damage,[246] with limited exceptions.[247] Strict liability is channelled exclusively to the ship owner and victims are barred from claiming against the servants and/or agents of the ship owner under the Marine Pollution Act or otherwise.[248] Furthermore, because ship owners incur strict liability, they can limit the extent of their liability to 133 SDR per tonne or 14 million SDR, whichever amount is smaller.[249] The compulsory insurance provisions in the Marine Pollution Act have been repealed by the Civil Liability Act, but the latter Act only applies to tankers.[250] There is thus no assurance of

---

241 1340 *UNTS* 184, (1973) 12 *ILM* 1319. Adopted: 02-11-1973; EIF: 10-02-1983.

242 1340 *UNTS* 61, (1978) 17 *ILM* 546. Adopted: 17-02-1978; EIF: 02-10-1983.

243 s 1(1).

244 reg 1(1) of Annex I. See also Appendix I to Annex I.

245 Hare (n 43) 560.

246 s 9(1)(a)-(c).

247 In terms of s 9(3), ship owners are exempt from liability where the "loss, damage or costs": "(a) resulted from an act of war, hostilities, civil war, insurrection or an exceptional, inevitable and irresistible natural phenomenon; or (b) was wholly caused by an act or omission on the part of any person, not being the owner or a servant or agent of the owner, with intent to do damage; or (c) was wholly caused by the negligence or other wrongful act of any government, or other authority responsible for the maintenance of lights or other navigational aids in the exercise of that function".

248 s 10(2).

249 s 9(5).

250 s 17 read with the schedule to the Civil Liability Act.

payment accompanying the strict, but limited, liability imposed on ship owners for oil pollution damage by the Marine Pollution Act. While ship owners may elect to take out insurance, it appears that vessel owners (with the exception of tanker owners) have no obligation to do so.

There is no fund accompanying the Marine Pollution Act. As a result, where the ship owner is exempt from liability, unable to meet its financial obligations or the damage exceeds the limits on the ship owner's liability, victims of oil pollution damage may be under-compensated or not compensated at all. The victims could claim from contributing parties who are not regarded as "servants or agents" of the ship owner, such as the oil cargo interests. However, in the absence of strict liability, proof of the contributing parties' liability and the extent thereof is required, something which may hinder or delay compensation.

Under the Marine Pollution Act, ship owners can only be prevented from limiting their liability if it is shown that the damage was "due to the fault of the owner or with the knowledge or concurrence of the owner".[251] This means that it is easier to prevent ship owners from capping their liability under the Marine Pollution Act than under the Civil Liability Act. Indeed, proving that the owner knew the "damage would probably ensue" is a more onerous burden to bear than simply showing fault or privity on the part of the ship owner. It is therefore more likely that a ship owner will be prevented from limiting his, her or its liability under the Marine Pollution Act.

A major shortcoming of the Marine Pollution Act is that it only applies strict liability to pollution damage within South Africa, which is defined to include its territorial waters.[252] The Act does not apply strict liability to incidents occurring within South Africa's EEZ, meaning that, in instances of non-tanker or non-persistent-oil pollution in that zone, strict liability does not apply. Victims of such pollution damage therefore have to prove the fault of the responsible party or parties, something which, as previously mentioned, may turn out to be a difficult, lengthy and costly endeavour hindering compensation.

---

251 s 10(4). The ship owner may not limit its liability where the damage resulted from a wilful act or omission of the owner.

252 s 9(1)(a) read with s 1.

While, pending the introduction of new legislative measures and its repeal, the Marine Pollution Act with all its shortcomings continues to regulate bunker-oil pollution damage as well as non-persistent-oil pollution damage in South Africa, the 2001 International Convention on Civil Liability for Bunker Oil Pollution Damage (BUNKERS 2001)[253] can address the shortcomings of the Act in respect of bunker-oil pollution damage and the 1996 International Convention on Liability and Compensation for Damage in Connection with the Carriage of Hazardous and Noxious Substances by Sea[254] (HNS 1996) as amended by its 2010 Protocol[255] (2010 HNS Convention)[256] can provide a solution in respect of non-persistent-oil pollution damage. These conventions are examined below.

THE APPLICATION OF BUNKERS 2001 TO BUNKER-OIL POLLUTION DAMAGE

BUNKERS 2001 was adopted to provide effective compensation to victims of bunker-oil pollution damage. Claims relating to bunker-oil pollution represents nearly half of the total amount of oil pollution claims globally,[257] making the Convention an essential aspect of the international compensation regime for ship-sourced oil pollution. BUNKERS 2001 is modelled on CLC 1992 in that it lays down strict liability for ship owners, entitles ship owners to limit their liability under an applicable national or international regime and requires compulsory insurance in respect of bunker-oil pollution.[258] To date, South Africa has not acceded to BUNKERS 2001. The latter defines "bunker oil" as "any hydrocarbon mineral oil, including lubricating oil, used or intended to be used for the operation or propulsion of the ship, and any residues of such oil".[259] BUNKERS 2001 defines a "ship" as "any seagoing vessel and seaborne craft, of any type whatsoever"

---

253 (2001) 40 *ILM* 1493. Adopted: 23-03-2001; EIF: 21-11-2008.

254 (1996) 35 *ILM* 1415. Adopted: 03-05-1996; EIF: not yet.

255 adopted: 30-04-2010; EIF: not yet. The text of the Protocol is available at https://www.hnsconvention.org/wp-content/uploads/2019/04/2010-HNS-Protocol_e.pdf (02-09-2020).

256 The consolidated text is available at http://www.imo.org/en/OurWork/Legal/HNS/Documents/HNS%20Consolidated%20text.pdf (02-09-2020).

257 Wu "Liability and compensation for bunker pollution" 2002 *J Mar L & Com* 553 555.

258 art 3, 6 and 7.

259 art 1(5).

excluding vessels or seaborne crafts not fuelled by bunker oil and tankers.[260] BUNKERS 2001 is therefore applicable to bunker-oil pollution from a broad range of ships currently regulated by the Marine Pollution Act in South Africa.

BUNKERS 2001 has a wider geographical application than the Marine Pollution Act in that it extends to a state's EEZ or equivalent area.[261] This means that South Africa's accession to BUNKERS 2001 would introduce strict liability for bunker-oil pollution damage occurring in South Africa's EEZ and the incorporation of its provisions into domestic law would make it possible for the victims of bunker-oil pollution in the EEZ to benefit from the strict liability regime and, therefore, no longer have to prove liability or the extent of the responsible parties' liability.

In addition, BUNKERS 2001 defines the term "ship owner" more broadly than the Marine Pollution Act to include "the registered owner, bareboat charterer, manager and operator of the ship".[262] The Convention therefore extends the strict liability to all the persons who are involved in the navigation and management of the vessel. There are thus a wider range of parties whom victims of bunker oil pollution are able to hold jointly and severally liable for victim reparation in terms of the Bunker Convention.[263] This broad definition is highly beneficial because there is no accompanying fund to which a claimant can look for compensation where the ship owner in the narrow sense of the term is unable to meet his, her or its financial obligations or where the damage exceeds the limits of liability set out in the Convention. In other words, thanks to this broad definition, a claimant has at least a number of parties to whom it can turn for compensation in the case of any shortfall or where the registered ship owner is unable to meet his, her or its financial obligations.[264] It should, however, be noted that only the registered ship owner of the vessel is required to take out insurance.[265] This means that,

---

260 art 1(1).

261 art 2(a)(i)–(ii).

262 art 1(3).

263 Zhu "Can the Bunkers Convention Ensure Adequate Compensation for Pollution Victims" 2009 *J Mar L & Com* 1 3.

264 ibid.

265 art 7(1).

while there is no assurance of payment when pursuing a claim against any of the other parties who are liable, the claimant has at least a number of parties whom it can hold jointly and severally liable for compensation and, where one party is insolvent, it can turn to the other.[266] This is in contrast to the Marine Pollution Act, under which the victims of bunker-oil pollution can only turn to the registered ship owner and, where the latter is insolvent or otherwise unable to pay, they have no other recourse.

Furthermore, BUNKERS 2001 does not expressly set out a limitation on a ship owner's liability. Indeed, the Convention merely provides that it does not detract from a ship owner's right to limit its liability under a national or international regime,[267] such as the 1976 Convention on the Limitation of Liability for Maritime Claims[268] as amended by its 1996 Protocol (LLMC 1996).[269] The limits of liability are thus determined by an applicable national regime or LLMC 1996. The latter limits the ship owner's liability to claims for "loss of life or personal injury" and "other claims", a limitation that does not exclude claims for damage caused by bunker spills.[270] The limitation, which was amended in 2012,[271] is set as follows: for "other claims" relating to ships not exceeding a gross tonnage of 2 000, liability is limited to 1.51 million SDR, for each tonne from 2 001 to 30 000 tonnes 604 SDR, for each tonne from 30 001 to 70 000 tonnes 453 SDR and for each tonne exceeding 70 000 tonnes 302 SDR. This means that, for a vessel of 30 000 tonnes, the amount recoverable is 1.51 million SDR + (604 SDR x 28 000 tonnes) = 18 422 000 SDR, while for a vessel of 70 000 tonnes the amount recoverable is 18 422 000 SDR + (453 SDR per tonne x 40 000 tonnes) = 36 542 000 SDR and for a vessel exceeding 70 000 tonnes an amount in excess of 36 542 000 SDR is claimable. This indicates that the amounts claimable under LLMC 1996 may be significantly higher than the total aggregate of 14 million SDR claimable under the Marine Pollution Act.

266 Zhu (n 263) 3.

267 art 6.

268 1456 *UNTS* 221, (1977) 16 *ILM* 606. Adopted: 19-11-1976; EIF: 01-12-1986.

269 (1996) 35 *ILM* 1433. Adopted: 02-05-1996; EIF: 13-05-2004.

270 art 3.

271 Resolution LEG 5(99) 2012 on amendments to the 1996 Protocol.

The LLMC 1996 limitations, however, only apply when the state involved has incorporated the Convention into its domestic law. In instances where it has not done so, LLMC 1996 is not applicable and the only limits available are those set in national legislation, if any. The extent of the ship owners' liability under BUNKERS 2001 is therefore left to be determined in each case on the basis of the applicable national or international regime. The fact that BUNKERS 2001 does not set limits on the ship owners' liability is seen as a shortfall of the Convention because ship owners and their insurers are not sure of the exact amounts to which the ship owners' liability may be limited, although the insurance need not exceed the limit on the ship owners' liability in LLMC 1996.[272] In the absence of specified limits on liability, claimants under BUNKERS 2001 suffering similar loss or damage may be faced with significantly different limits on liability, depending on where the spill occurs and claims are instituted.[273] Another downside is that there is no limitation fund under LLMC 1996 exclusively for bunker-oil pollution claims and those claims would have to compete with other limitable claims under the applicable regime.[274] However, history reveals that there have been very few instances in which the claims of victims of bunker oil pollution damage had to compete with other claims under the LLMC 1996.[275]

South Africa, however, has not acceded to LLMC 1996[276] and, as a result, the limits on liability set out therein do not apply. Should South Africa accede to Bunkers 2001 and incorporate it into domestic law, the existing limits on liability set out in national law will continue to apply rather than those provided in the LLMC 1996 until South Africa accedes to the LLMC 1996 and incorporates it into domestic law. The 14 million SDR limit in the Marine Pollution Act may thus continue to apply to bunker oil pollution damage, except if the provision containing this limitation is repealed by the legislation enacting BUNKERS 2001 into national law. Alternatively, a ship owner may limit its liability for loss or damage to property resulting from a single occasion, in the absence of any fault

272 art 7(1). See Wu (n 257) 562.

273 Wu (n 257) 562.

274 Wu (n 257) 564.

275 ibid.

276 See IMO (n 34) 393-394.

or privity, according to the general limitation in the Merchant Shipping Act.[277] According to this general limitation a ship owner's liability for all claims for loss or damage to property only resulting from a single incident is limited to 66,67 SDR for each tonne of the vessel.[278] For a vessel of 2000 tonnes this limitation offers as little as 133 340 SDR cover (66,67 SDR x 2000 = 133 340 SDR). This is far less cover for bunker oil pollution damage than the cover offered by the limits on a ship owner's liability in respect of a vessel of the same size in the LLMC 1996. The general limitation on a ship owner's liability set out in the Merchant Shipping Act is thus unlikely to provide suitable coverage for bunker oil pollution damage in South Africa. It would be useful for legislation enacting Bunkers 2001 into South African law to expressly increase the present limit of 14 million SDR for bunker oil pollution damage. Alternatively, South Africa could accede to and incorporate both BUNKERS 2001 and LLMC 1996 into domestic law. Nonetheless increased limits on liability to cater for large-scale bunker-oil pollution damage will prove extremely useful as the quantities of bunker oil transported by sea increase as international maritime trade grows.[279]

An added positive feature of BUNKERS 2001 is that it compels the registered owners of all ships in excess of 1 000 tonnes to take out compulsory insurance[280] and carry evidence thereof on board.[281] The insurance taken must cover the limits on liability set out under the applicable national or international limitation regime, but should, in all instances, not be greater than an amount calculated in accordance with the limits set out in LLMC 1996.[282] In this regard, BUNKERS 2001 enables victims of oil pollution damage to take direct action against the insurer, an avenue which promotes compensation.[283] In contrast, it has already been pointed out that the compulsory insurance provisions in the Marine Pollution Act have been repealed and ship owners other than tanker owners are not obliged to take out compulsory

---

277 s 261 Merchant Shipping Act 57 of 1951.

278 ibid.

279 UNCTAD (n 1) 1.

280 art 7(1).

281 art 7(2).

282 art 7(1).

283 ibid.

insurance, and there is no accompanying right to take direct action against the insurer. The compulsory insurance provisions imposed by BUNKERS 2001, accompanied by the ability to take direct action against the insurer, are far more beneficial than those of the Marine Pollution Act, which does not impose such obligation.

Under the Marine Pollution Act, it is considerably easier for a claimant to prevent a ship owner from capping its liability than under BUNKERS 2001. As previously mentioned, under the Marine Pollution Act a claimant need only prove "actual fault or privity" on the part of the ship owner to prevent the owner from limiting its liability.[284] By contrast, ship owners can only be prevented from limiting their liability on the basis of BUNKERS 2001 if "the pollution was a result of a personal act or omission, committed with the intent to cause such damage, or recklessly and with knowledge that such damage would probably result".[285] As previously mentioned, having to prove that the ship owner knew that the "damage would probably result" is much more cumbersome than only proving fault or privity on the part of the ship owner.[286] Although the fact that it is easier to prevent a ship owner from limiting its liability under the Marine Pollution Act can be seen as a positive feature thereof, it should be pointed out that unlimited liability of the ship owner would in any event not be accompanied by an assurance of payment and may thus prove to be of no value where the ship owner is insolvent.

Acceding to BUNKERS 2001 and incorporating it into our domestic law would address some of the shortfalls of the Marine Pollution Act. Indeed, strict liability for bunker-oil pollution would be extended to South Africa's EEZ and beneficial compulsory insurance provisions for all ships exceeding 1 000 tonnes would be incorporated into domestic law. In addition, increased limits on liability such as those found in the LLMC 1996 can be introduced into South African law by expressly including such limits in the legislation enacting BUNKERS 2001 or by acceding to LLMC 1996 and incorporating it into national law. The limits on

---

284 s 10(6).

285 Art 6 of BUNKERS 2001 refers to LLMC 1996. See art 4 of LLMC 1976 as amended by LLMC PROT 1996. See art 9 of the LLMC PROT 1996.

286 s 10(4) of the Marine Pollution Act.

a ship owner's liability in LLMC 1996 may prove more beneficial than the low limits on liability in the Marine Pollution Act.

THE APPLICATION OF 2010 HNS CONVENTION TO NON-PERSISTENT-OIL POLLUTION DAMAGE.

Although it is not a contracting State to HNS 1996,[287] South Africa became in 2019 the fifth State to ratify or accede to HNS PROT 2010.[288] This is not an issue because, in terms of the latter's article 18(1), once the Protocol comes into effect, HNS 1996 and HNS PROT 2010 will, as between the parties to the Protocol, "be read and interpreted together as one single instrument".

2010 HNS Convention defines a ship as "any seagoing vessel and seaborne craft" of any type whatsoever,[289] a definition that is broad enough to cover a wide range of vessels and does not refer only to tankers. The Convention covers hazardous and noxious substances which includes oils, other liquid substances defined as noxious or dangerous, liquefied gases, liquid substances with a flashpoint not exceeding 60°C, dangerous and hazardous and harmful substances (carried in packaged form or in containers) and solid bulk material possessing chemical hazards.[290] The Convention does not cover persistent-oil pollution damage, which is regulated by CLC 1992,[291] but it covers non-pollution damage caused by persistent oil, such as damage caused by a fire or explosion.[292] Because 2010 HNS Convention will cover a broad range of oils (namely those defined in regulation 1 of Annex I of MARPOL), including non-persistent oils,[293] once it is incorporated into South African domestic law and the overlapping provisions in the Marine

---

287 IMO (n 34) 497.

288 ibid 501.

289 art 1(1) of 2010 HNS Convention.

290 IMO "The HNS Convention Why it is needed" (2016) 3 http://www.imo.org/en/MediaCentre/HotTopics/ Documents/HNS%20ConventionWebE.pdf (29-07-2020). See also the definition of hazardous and noxious substances in art 1(5), which covers a broad range of substances.

291 art 4(3)(a).

292 IOPC "An overview of the International Convention on the Liability and Compensation for Damage in Connection with the Carriage of Hazardous and Noxious Substances by Sea, 2010 (The 2010 HNS Convention)" (2018) 1 https://www.hnsconvention.org/wp-content/uploads/2018/08/HNS-Convention-Overview_e.pdf (29-07-2020).

293 art 1(5)(a)(i) read with appendix I of Annex I to MARPOL 1973/1978.

Pollution Act are repealed, it will provide cover for claims relating to pollution caused by all the non-persistent oils which are not covered by CLC 1992 and BUNKERS 2001. The incorporation of 2010 HNS Convention would also result in strict liability for persistent-oil pollution damage being extended to South Africa's EEZ.[294] The Marine Pollution Act, which is currently applicable until it is repealed, only imposes strict liability for non-persistent-oil pollution damage caused in South Africa's territory and territorial waters and does not extend to the EEZ.

2010 HNS Convention is modelled on CLC 1992, together with FUND 1992.[295] The Convention channels strict liability (with limited exceptions) to vessel owners in cases where damage is caused by an incident involving a hazardous and noxious substance (HNS), provided that there is a causal link between the damage and the HNS carried on board.[296] The owner of a ship that carries HNS is entitled to limit his, her or its liability[297] and is obliged to take out insurance to cover the limits on that liability.[298] In turn, victims of oil pollution damage caused by an HNS may pursue their claims directly against the insurer.[299] These provisions would be a largely beneficial introduction because compulsory-insurance provisions no longer apply in South Africa in respect of non-tanker vessels. The strict liability and compulsory-insurance provisions in 2010 HNS Convention offer the first tier of compensation for victims of damage caused by an HNS, while a second tier of compensation will be offered by the International Hazardous and Noxious Substances Fund (HNS Fund).[300] The HNS Fund will be financed by entities receiving HNS substances within the States parties, like the contributions to the Fund, and those contributions will be calculated according to the quantities of HNS received within each state party in a calendar year.[301] The HNS Fund will pay out where the vessel owner is exempt from liability, incapable of meeting

294 art 3(a)–(b).
295 IOPC (n 292) 2.
296 art 7(1).
297 art 9(1).
298 art 12(1).
299 art 12(8).
300 established by art 13(1).
301 art 19–23.

its financial obligations or because the damage exceeds the limits of liability,[302] with the maximum amount of compensation payable for a single incident under the HNS Fund being set at 250 million SDR, including the sum paid by the vessel owner (or its insurer).[303] This aggregate amount far exceeds the 14 million SDR recoverable for a single incident under the Marine Pollution Act. This is one reason in support of incorporating 2010 HNS Convention into South African domestic law. Another reason is that non-persistent-oil pollution damage will be covered by a Fund, thereby offering an assurance of payment that is currently not offered under the Marine Pollution Act.

In addition, 2010 HNS Convention will apply more broadly than CLC 1992, together with FUND 1992, because it will not only cover pollution damage caused by an HNS, but also the loss of life, personal injury and damage to property, loss or damage caused by contamination of the environment, the loss of income resulting from such contamination and the costs of preventative measures.[304]

To sum up, 2010 HNS Convention will address the shortfalls of the Marine Pollution Act in respect of non-persistent-oil pollution damage. The geographical scope of application of the Convention to a more extended geographical area, the higher limitations on the ship owner's liability and the provisions enabling direct action against the insurer will improve the coverage of non-persistent-oil pollution damage in South Africa. Most importantly, strict liability will be introduced for non-persistent-oil pollution damage in South Africa's EEZ and the victims of such pollution damage will no longer need to prove the vessel owner's liability.

CONCLUSION

The South African liability and compensation regime for ship-sourced oil pollution damage has been significantly improved by the domestic force given to CLC 1992 and FUND 1992. CLC 1992 and the Fund regime applicable to tanker-oil pollution has a number of positive aspects such as its application to an extended geographical area, strict liability for tanker-oil pollution, compulsory

302 art 14(1).
303 art 14(5)(a).
304 art 1(6).

insurance and the right of direct action against the insurer. In addition, the caps on a tanker owner's liability for pollution damage caused in South Africa have been increased by CLC 1992 and the Fund regime. The compensation regime is supported by the financial backing offered by the Fund. The compensation regime could, however, be further improved through South Africa's accession to FUND PROT 2003. Until South Africa does so, the costs of a large oil spill exceeding the limits of the CLC 1992 and the Fund regime will not be covered sufficiently. This means that, in such instances, numerous victims may go uncompensated or undercompensated. Furthermore, the Marine Pollution Act that currently fills the gap in respect of non-persistent and non-tanker bunker-oil pollution damage has a number of shortfalls such as its limited territorial application and its low limits of liability. Thus, until South Africa accedes to BUNKERS 2001, incorporates it into domestic law and repeals any overlapping provisions in the Marine Pollution Act, the latter, with its shortfalls, will continue to regulate bunker-oil pollution damage in South Africa. At the same time, non-persistent-oil pollution damage will also continue to be regulated by the Marine Pollution Act until the 2010 HNS Convention comes into force, is incorporated into domestic law and the overlapping provisions in the Marine Pollution Act are repealed. In other words, while the South African liability and compensation regime for oil pollution damage has numerous positive features, it can still be improved through the accession to BUNKERS 2001 and the incorporation of the 2010 HNS Convention into domestic law once it comes into force. This will ensure that victims of bunker-oil pollution and other oil pollution from non-tanker vessels are able to benefit from the application of strict liability in an extended geographical area, from the compulsory-insurance obligations placed on the ship owner and the accompanying right to take action against the insurer as well as guaranteed increased limits on the ship owners' liability under HNS 2010 and the possible increased limits through acceding to and enacting both BUNKERS 2001 and LLMC 1996 into domestic law. Likewise, accession to FUND PROT 2003 will offer victims of tanker-oil pollution damage the highest level of cover for the compensation of their losses.

UTMOST GOOD FAITH IS DEAD, LONG LIVE UTMOST GOOD FAITH? A HISTORICAL OVERVIEW OF GOOD FAITH IN (MARINE) INSURANCE IN ENGLAND AND SOUTH AFRICA

DALEEN MILLARD[*]

SAMANTHA HUNEBERG[**]

[*] Professor in Private Law, University of Johannesburg.
[**] Lecturer in Mercantile Law, University of Johannesburg

INTRODUCTION

Marine insurance is by all accounts the oldest form of insurance, dating back to the *lex mercatoria,* which was absorbed into the laws of different countries and resulted, *inter alia*, in insurance law being almost identical in most countries in Western Europe, including Holland.

Debate in South Africa on the true origins of insurance law was therefore much ado about nothing as, save for the principles that govern some aspects of the actual insurance contract, insurance is insurance! Nevertheless, the then Appellate Division found it necessary to state that the source of *South African insurance law* is Roman-Dutch law and *Mutual & Federal Insurance Co Ltd v Oudtshoorn Municipality*[1] remains one of the much-quoted precedents on insurance contracts.

Although insurance contracts have always been truly international, the ruling in *Oudtshoorn* teaches that although English law is not a source of *South African insurance law*, it has persuasive authority in some matters. In addition, insurance law in modern-day South Africa should be developed with the local markets in mind. Marine insurance, although anchored in the South African legislative framework, takes cognisance of standards in other jurisdictions as vessels inevitably negotiate waters outside the jurisdiction of South African courts. It is also submitted that all marine vessels, regardless of their country of origin, face the same perils once at sea. It is therefore informative to compare the South African perception of good faith in insurance to the English one.

Two recent cases on marine insurance provide examples of the kinds of perils that may be insured against. In the English case of *Sealion Shipping Limited and Toisa Horizon Inc v Valiant Insurance Company: The MV "Toisa Pisces"*,[2] the insured vessel was an oil production and storage unit which was chartered to a third party. The owners procured so-called "loss of hire" insurance and, because of a series of break-downs, the vessel was placed off-hire for a number of periods, due *inter alia* to failure of a port motor, a subsequent hydraulics failure which necessitated dry-docking and failure of a starboard motor. When the owners instituted a claim, the

---

1   [1985] 1 All SA 324 (A).
2   [2012] EWHC 50 (Comm); [2012] EWCA Civ 1625.

insurers refused to pay based on material non-disclosure and want of due diligence. Both the courts of first instance and the court of appeal found the insurers liable. In the trial court, Blair J stated that the design fault in the engines that was allegedly not disclosed was not material because it would not have caused the insurers to reject the risk. In addition, there was also not a want of due diligence as no negligence pertaining to the vessel could be attributed to the owner.[3] The court relied on the Canadian decision in *Secunda Marine Services v Liberty Mutual*.[4] On appeal, the court relied on the policy wording, came to the same conclusion and, as a result, the issue of non-disclosure was said to be immaterial. This case illustrates that various risks pertaining to marine operations may be insured, including so-called "loss of hire". Whatever the risk, (utmost) good faith plays an important role.

The recent decision in South Africa in *Viking Inshore Fishing (Pty) Ltd v Mutual and Federal Insurance Co Ltd*[5] considered the role of promissory warranties in marine insurance and brings a different aspect of good faith to the fore. On 8 May 2005, the fishing vessel *Lindsay* collided with the *Ouro do Brasil* off the coast near Cape St Francis. The court ruled that mere breach of a promissory warranty is not itself a ground for repudiation. Rather, if such breach is inconsequential to the loss, it should not be a ground for repudiation. It should be mentioned that the relevance of warranties in the context of good faith is as important as misrepresentation, as warranties in insurance provide the insured with a more favourable alternative than misrepresentation, meaning that insurers may ask policyholders to make a presentation pertaining to certain facts (or warrant something pertaining to the risk, to be more precise). Breach of warranty then constitutes breach of contract and, as was evident in the *Viking Inshore* case, repudiation based on breach of warranty may be just as problematic as repudiation based on misrepresentation.[6] In both cases, the right to avoid the contract is restricted by statute.[7]

It is therefore evident that marine insurance is vital to marine enterprises and that all aspects of marine insurance have an international and a domestic-law

3   par 69–76.

4   (2006) NSCA 82.

5   [2016] 2 All SA 730 (SCA), 2016 6 SA 335 (SCA).

6   See par 5.3 below.

7   s 53(1)(a) of the Short-term Insurance Act (53 of 1998).

component, which makes a comparative study of any aspect of marine insurance both interesting and vital. With all this in mind, this contribution aims to sketch the development of the doctrine of utmost good faith from the Marine Insurance Act, 1906 (MIA), to the Insurance Act, 2015, in the United Kingdom and asks whether this doctrine has in fact stood the test of time. In addition, the contribution asks whether the South African approach to good faith in marine insurance in fact yields better results. To this end, this overview will evaluate the most prominent cases in marine insurance over the years and will specifically focus on misrepresentation in marine insurance contracts in England and South Africa. The reader will also find that, because marine insurance in South Africa is (but) a form of short-term or non-life insurance, the principles that apply to marine insurance also apply to all other short-term or non-life insurance contracts, with a few exceptions.[8] Finally, the contribution evaluates the role of the Financial Advisory and Intermediaries Services Act (FAIS Act),[9] the Policyholder Protection Rules (PPRs)[10] and the new Insurance Act[11] as legislative instruments that influence good faith in insurance contracts, including marine insurance contracts.

ENGLISH LAW

The common law position on utmost good faith

The concept of good faith stemmed from *Carter v Boehm*,[12] where Lord Mansfield stated: "Good faith forbids either party by concealing what he privately knows, to draw the other into a bargain, from his ignorance of that fact, and his believing the contrary".[13]

It was in this case that Lord Mansfield introduced certain duties of disclosure for both the insurer and the insured.[14] The duty to disclose material information,

---

8   One such exception is that average is a *naturale* of a marine insurance contract but not of a short-term or non-insurance contract. For the latter, the contract must specifically include an average clause. See Reinecke, Van Niekerk and Nienaber *South African Insurance Law* (2013) 327.

9   37 of 2002.

10   2018.

11   18 of 2017.

12   (1766) 3 Burr 1905 (97 ER 1162).

13   ibid 1164.

14   Lowry "Whither the duty of good faith in UK insurance contracts" 2009 (16) *Connecticut Insurance Law Journal* 97.

therefore, underpins the duty of good faith.[15] The consequence of this is that the general contractual duty expected by both contracting parties to avoid any misrepresentation is extended and reinforced by the additional obligation to disclose all material facts that would induce an insurer to underwrite the specific risk.[16] In order to understand the principle that emanates from the case, it is insightful to know the facts. Carter was the Governor of Fort Marlborough, a fort that was situated in Indonesia. The fort was built by the British East India Company. Carter took out an insurance policy with Boehm to insure against the fort being taken by a foreign enemy. A witness, Captain Tryon, testified that Carter knew that the fort was built to resist attacks from local enemies, but would be unable to repel European enemies. Apparently, Carter knew that the French were likely to attack the fort and, when they did so successfully, Boehm refused to honour the agreement. It is against these facts that Lord Mansfield explained, in the *Carter* case,[17] that the policy considerations underlying the duty of disclosure are the prevention of fraud and the furtherance of good faith. The duty, therefore, fulfils mostly a preventative role and is used as a deterrent to acting in bad faith.[18] Lord Mansfield based the duty upon the concept of "concealment" but, over time, this developed beyond "deliberate concealment" to encompass all types of non-disclosures, even if innocent, of a material fact,[19] thus drawing distinctions between "deliberate concealments" and misrepresentations (bad faith), on the one hand, and innocent, mistaken non-disclosure (good faith), on the other.[20]

What is interesting to note is that Lord Mansfield avoided the terminology "utmost good faith" in the *Carter* case; yet this is exactly to what section 17 of the Marine Insurance Act (MIA)[21] refers.[22]

---

15   ibid.

16   Lowry (n 14) 98.

17   *Carter* case (n 12) 1164.

18   Lowry (n 14) 104. See also *Re Yager & Guardian Assurance Co* [1912] 108 LT 38 (KB), where Channel J stated that the rationale underlying the duty of disclosure is not the need to prevent harm to the insurer, but the need for a true and fair agreement whereby risk is transferred (44-45).

19   Lowry (n 14) 104.

20   ibid 104-105.

21   1906.

22   Lowry (n 14) 107.

The obvious question which comes to mind is when exactly did the disclosure duty morph into "utmost" good faith. The MIA codified the common-law principles that had been developed in the eighteenth and nineteenth centuries, largely from marine cases, such as *Carter v Boehm*,[23] *Noble v Kennoway*,[24] *Mayne v Walter*[25] and *Friere v Woodhouse*.[26] These cases illustrate that it is in fact the underwriter who is generally the passive recipient of information supplied by the insured when presenting the risk.[27] Therefore, it is for the insured to supply all the necessary information to the insurer.[28] The duty of good faith plays a vital role in that it transforms non-disclosures into misrepresentation because an insured who fails to disclose a material fact is essentially misrepresenting the true state of affairs.[29] What is of importance is that inducement is vital to these two terms: for misrepresentation, the consequence is therefore the same as with untainted non-disclosure, namely avoidance of the contract *ab initio*.[30] What is fascinating is that the *Carter*, *Noble*, *Mayne* and *Friere* cases never directly referred to the principle of "utmost good faith", but rather canvassed various forms of concealments and non-disclosures.[31] Interestingly, Sir Mackenzie Chalmers was responsible for the codification of a body of case law into the Digest upon which the 1906 Act is based.[32] He simply interpreted the case law at the time and this is where utmost good faith was introduced.[33] The view that insurance required nothing less than utmost good faith became firmly entrenched in English insurance law in this way.[34] The duty of utmost good faith was subsequently entrenched in section 17 of the MIA.

23 n 12.
24 (1780) 2 Doug KB 511 (2 ER 326 326-327).
25 (1782) 3 Doug KB 79 (99 ER 548 548-549).
26 (1817) Holt NP 572 (171 ER 345).
27 Lowry (n 14) 108.
28 Lowry (n 14) 105.
29 ibid.
30 s 17 of the MIA.
31 Lowry (n 14) 107. Those non-disclosures were either deliberate or innocent.
32 ibid.
33 ibid.
34 ibid.

The Marine Insurance Act, 1906

The duty of utmost good faith

The MIA, as an Act of Parliament regulated not only marine insurance but also other types of insurance[35] as a codification of English common law.[36] As was stated in paragraph 2.1 above, this Act saw the codification of the duty of utmost good faith,[37] which is the cornerstone of insurance law.[38] To this end, section 17 of the MIA provides:

> "A contract of marine insurance is a contract based upon the utmost good faith, and, if the utmost good faith be not observed by either party, the contract may be avoided by the other party".[39]

This duty is observed in all insurance contracts and applies before the contract is entered into (that is, at the pre-contractual stage) as well as during the performance of the contract (post-contractual stage, hence a continuing

---

35 The most important sections of this Act include: s 17 (imposes a duty on the insured of *uberrima fides*; ie that questions must be answered honestly and the risk not misrepresented); s 18 ("The assured must disclose to the insurer, before the contract is concluded, every material circumstance which is known to the assured, and the assured is deemed to know every circumstance which, in the ordinary course of business, ought to be known by him. If the assured fails to make such disclosure, the insurer may avoid the contract".); s 33(3) (If [a warranty] be not [exactly] complied with, then, subject to any express provision in the policy, the insurer is discharged from liability as from the date of the breach of warranty, but without prejudice to any liability incurred by him before that date); s 34(2) (where a warranty has been broken, it is no defence to the insured that the breach has been remedied, and the warranty complied with, prior to the loss); s 34(3) (a breach of warranty may be waived by the insurer); s 50 (a policy may be assigned); ss 60–63 (deal with the issues of a constructive total loss – by contrast an actual total loss describes the physical destruction of a vessel or cargo); and s 79 (deals with subrogation; ie the rights of the insurer to stand in the shoes of an indemnified insured and recover salvage for his own benefit). Schedule 1 of the Act contains a list of definitions and schedule 2 contains the model policy wording.

36 Law Commission and the Scottish Law Commission *Insurance Contract Law: Business Disclosure; Warranties; Insurers' Remedies for Fraudulent Claims and Late Payment* (presented to the Parliament of the United Kingdom by the Lord Chancellor and Secretary of State for Justice by Command of Her Majesty, July 2014) (Law Com No 353; Scot Law Com No 238) par 1.16.

37 ibid par 1.27; Longmore "Good faith and breach of warranty" 2004 *Lloyd's Maritime and Commercial Law Quarterly* 158 and Ivamy *Chalmer's Marine Insurance Act 1906* (1983) 24.

38 Lowry (n 14) 100.

39 Longmore (n 37) 158. See also Birds, Lynch and Milnes *MacGillivary on Insurance Law* (2014) 453; *Bell v Lever Bros Ltd* [1932] AC 161 227 and *Mutual and Federal Insurance Co Ltd v Oudtshoorn Municipality* 1985 1 SA 419 (A) for the South African position. See also s 17 of the MIA 1906 and Birds, Lynch and Milnes (supra) 453. The remedy for a breach of utmost good faith, therefore, is that of avoidance of the contract *ab initio* under s 17. This is a severe remedy that has retrospective effect and no right to damages. See also s 14 of the Insurance Act, 2015, which changes the consequence of non-compliance with the duty of utmost good faith.

duty).[40] Regarding good faith as a continuing duty, Hirst J in *Black King Shipping v Massie (The Litsion Pride)*[41] remarked that a post-contractual duty of good faith clearly existed between both the insurer and the policyholder.[42] There is a marked difference between English law, where a continuing duty of good faith exists, and South African law, where the duty of good faith only exists during the pre-contractual stage. In English law, the continuous duty of good faith entails that the policyholder should not make any untrue statements or misrepresentations during the pre-contractual stage and that the parties should generally act with good faith towards one another during the contract.[43] More specifically, prior to the contract being concluded, utmost good faith mainly comprises the policyholder's duty to disclose and not misrepresent all material facts to the insurer.[44] The post-contractual position means that the policyholder must act honestly when making any claim under the policy.[45]

If one party breached the duty of utmost good faith, the only remedy under the MIA was for the other party to avoid the contract in its entirety, in other words, treat the policy as if it never existed.[46] This remedy was much criticised.[47]

---

40   *London Assurance Co v Mansel* (1897) 11 Ch D 363 367 and Birds, Lynch and Milnes (n 39) 453. However, the application of the post-contractual duty of good faith requires consideration of why the insurer is avoiding the contract, ie whether the insurer's decision to avoid the policy had been made in breach of good faith or whether the insurer's conduct involving claims handling amounts to a breach – in other words, whether the claim is a fraudulent one.

41   [1985] 1 *Lloyd's Rep* 437.

42   The *Litsion Pride* case, however, was subsequently overruled by *Versloot Dredging BV v HDI Gerling Industrie Versicherung AG* [2016] UKSC 45; [2016] WLR (D) 403 (appeal from [2014] EWCA Civ 1349).

43   Birds, Lynch and Milnes (n 39) 453–454.

44   s 17 of the MIA.

45   ibid.

46   ibid.

47   Lowry (n 14) 150.

The duty of disclosure

Section 18 of the MIA deals with pre-contractual disclosures.[48] The central element of section 18 is that it places an onerous duty on the insured (the policyholder) to disclose to the insurer "every material circumstance" which the policyholder "knows or ought to know" before concluding a contract.[49] Under section 18(2), a material circumstance is defined as "every circumstance which would influence the judgment of a prudent insurer in fixing the premium, or determining whether he will take the risk".[50]

This section effectively required the policyholder to look into the mind of a hypothetical sensible insurer and to work out what exactly would influence it, with little additional guidance by the insurers.[51] Through an analysis of section 18, it is suggested that the insurer plays a relatively passive role, without asking questions or indicating what it wishes to know.[52] As a result, this led to policyholders burdening the insurers with large amounts of unnecessary information in an attempt to ensure that nothing was omitted.[53]

Section 20(1) of the MIA provides for the issue of misrepresentations and stipulates that

---

48 S 18 provides as follows: "The assured must disclose to the insurer, before the contract is concluded, every material circumstance which is known to the assured, and the assured is deemed to know every circumstance which, in the ordinary course of business, ought to be known by him. If the assured fails to make such disclosure, the insurer may avoid the contract". See also Ivamy (n 37) 26.

49 *Manifest Shipping Co Ltd v Uni-Polaris Insurance Co Ltd (The Star Sea)* [2001] UKHL 1, [2003] 1 AC 469 (per Lord Hobhouse) par 54. See also Law Commission (n 36) par 3.7 and 3.8.

50 In *Pan Atlantic Insurance Co Ltd v Pine Top Insurance Co Ltd* [1995] 1 AC 501, the House of Lords confirmed that a material circumstance is one that would have an effect on the mind of the prudent insurer in assessing the risk. It is not necessary that it would have a decisive effect on the insurer's acceptance of the risk or on the amount of premium charged.

51 *Pan Atlantic Insurance Co Ltd v Pine Top Insurance Co Ltd* [1995] 1 AC 501 508. See also *Lishman v Northern Maritime* (1875) LR 10 CP 179. Section 18(3) deals with the exceptions to the duty to disclose: "Unless the insurer makes an enquiry, – an insured need not disclose: (a) any circumstance which diminishes the risk; (b) any circumstance which is known or presumed to be known to the insurer. The insurer is presumed to know matters of common notoriety or knowledge, and matters which an insurer in the ordinary course of his business, as such, ought to know; (c) any circumstance as to which information is waived by the insurer; and (d) any circumstance which it is superfluous to disclose by reason of any express or implied warranty".

52 ibid. See also Issues Paper 1: Misrepresentation and Non-Disclosure (September 2006) http://lawcommission. justice.gov.uk/docs/ICL1_Misrepresentation_and_Non-disclosure.pdf and http://www.scotlawcom.gov.uk/index. php/download_file/view/214/107/ (02-02-2018).

53 ibid. Note that s 19 made the matter even more complicated by placing a stand-alone duty of disclosure on the policyholder's broker or any other agent, although the insurer's remedy for breach is against the policyholder.

> "[e]very material representation made by the assured or his agent to the insurer during the negotiations for the contract, and before the contract is concluded, must be true. If it be untrue the insurer may avoid the contract".[54]

The definition of a material representation in section 20(2) repeats the test for "material circumstances" in section 18(2).[55] Section 20(3) of the MIA provides that "a representation may be either a representation as to a matter of fact, or as to a matter of expectation or belief".

The MIA provided only one remedy for the insurer in the case of misrepresentations and non-disclosures, namely avoidance of the contract.[56] In other words, the contract is treated as if it has never been made and all claims made under it are refused.[57] Avoidance of the contract normally required restitution, meaning that the parties must be restored to the positions they were in prior to the contract being made, except where one was guilty of fraud.[58]

Criticism

By way of summary, it may be stated that the duty of disclosure in terms of the MIA was excessively wide.[59] The policyholder was under a burden to disclose "every material circumstance" which might be relevant to an insurer, while the insurer was able to play a relatively passive role. This was an unfair practice, placing the already vulnerable policyholder in a detrimental position.[60] These problems were further exacerbated by the fact that the only remedy for non-disclosure was avoidance of the contract.

---

54 *Economides v Commercial Union Assurance Co Plc* [1998] QB 587 593.

55 In that it must influence the judgment of a prudent insurer in fixing the premium or deciding whether to take on the risk.

56 s 17 of the MIA.

57 ibid.

58 Regarding marine insurance, s 84(3)(a) of the MIA provides as follows: "Where the policy is void, or is avoided by the insurer as from the commencement of the risk, the premium is returnable, provided that there has been no fraud or illegality on the part of the assured".

59 Tyldesley "Consumer insurance law – reform at last?" 2010 *Amicus Curiae* 1 3.

60 Tyldesley "Insurance law – unfair, unclear, archaic and inaccessible?" 2006 *Amicus Curiae* 1.

Judges were not silent in expressing their unease over the rigours of the disclosure duty in terms of sections 17 and 18 of the MIA.[61] In *Anglo-African Merchants Ltd v Bayley*,[62] Megaw J queried whether the insured should be bound to disclose that which he does not appreciate to be material.[63] In *Lambert v Co-operative Insurance Society Ltd*,[64] all three judges in the Court of Appeal took the opportunity to criticise the prudent insurer test.[65] At the time, the judges even called for parliamentary intervention to address the inequalities caused by the severity of the duty.[66] With respect to the insurer's right of avoidance in terms of the duty, the judiciary also condemned the results which flowed from exercising the remedy.[67] In *Kausar v Eagle Star Insurance Co Ltd*,[68] Staughton LJ stated:

> "Avoidance for non-disclosure is a drastic remedy. It enables the insurer to disclaim liability after, and not before, he has discovered that the risk turns out to be a bad one; it leaves the insured without the protection which he thought he had contracted and paid for...I do consider there should be some restraint in the operation of the doctrine. Avoidance for honest non-disclosure should be confined to plain cases".[69]

The "all-or-nothing" avoidance rule of section 17 was viewed as largely "disproportionate".[70] This was due to the fact that no matter the type of breach and whether it occurred at the pre-or post-contractual stage, avoidance was the sole remedy.[71] However, this distinction is of less importance today following the amendment to section 17 of the MIA brought about by section 14 of the Insurance Act, 2015.[72]

---

61   Lowry (n 14) 115–116.

62   [1970] 1 QB 311.

63   ibid 319.

64   [1975] 2 *Lloyd's Rep* 485 (AC).

65   ibid 491–493.

66   ibid.

67   Lowry (n 14) 117.

68   [1997] CLC 129.

69   ibid 132-33.

70   Birds, Lynch and Milnes (n 39) 453-454 and Lowry (n 14) 117-118.

71   ibid.

72   Thanasegaran *Good Faith in Insurance and Takaful Contracts in Malaysia* (2016) 17. S 14 of the 2015 Insurance Act provides that insurance contracts are still contracts of utmost good faith, however, "any rule of law permitting a party to a contract of insurance to avoid the contract on the ground that the utmost good faith has not been observed by the other party, is abolished".

The need for legislative reform

In 1978, the Law Commission was given the opportunity to review non-disclosure.[73] The recommendations put forward by the Commission included a noticeably revised duty of disclosure that, had it been implemented, would have resulted in moving the focus away from the "prudent insurer" as the decisive test of materiality.[74]

The Commission proposed a reformed duty of disclosure for both consumers and businesses.[75] This modified duty would require an insured to disclose those facts that a reasonable person in the position of the applicant would disclose.[76] Notwithstanding the fact that many were optimistic that such legislative reform would take place, this slowly faded out over time.[77]

It was only after the 2006 Law Commission enquiry that change eventually occurred.[78] This resulted in the culmination of a few new statutes, namely the Consumer Insurance (Disclosures and Representations) Act, 2012 (applicable to consumer contracts), the Consumer Rights Act, 2015, and the Insurance Act, 2015.

The sections on disclosures and utmost good faith, as highlighted above, have since undergone reform in terms of the Insurance Act, 2015.[79] The statutory reforms to the duty of utmost good faith as introduced in this Act will be discussed below. The duty of fair presentation as introduced in this Act has also had an effect on the duty of utmost good faith, as will be seen in paragraph 3 below.

---

73   Lowry (n 14) 118. See also Law Commission (n 36) par 4.2.

74   Lowry (n 14) 119. See also Law Commission (n 36) par 6.2.3.

75   ibid.

76   ibid. See also Law Commission (n 36) par 4.47.

77   Lowry (n 14) 119.

78   n 52 above.

79   Jaffe "Reform of the insurance law of England and Wales – separate laws for the different needs of businesses and consumers" 2013 *Tulane Law Review* 1075 1078.

THE INSURANCE ACT 2015

Introduction

The newly enacted Insurance Act, 2015, seeks to strike a fairer balance between policyholders and insurers.[80] The Act creates new duties for both the insurer and policyholders[81] and regulates the duty of disclosure, both before a contract comes into being and when such contract is amended.[82] The Act also addresses warranties (including the basis-of-contract clauses), terms not relevant to the actual loss, fraudulent claims by an insured party and good faith. It also amends some provisions of the Third Parties (Rights Against Insurers) Act, 2010.

The Act does not anticipate to be a full codification of insurance laws and, alongside it, other laws on insurance law will continue to apply, such as the Marine Insurance Act, 1906, and the Third Parties (Rights Against Insurers) Act, 2010.[83] The Act applies in England, Wales, Scotland and Northern Ireland.[84] The new law, rather than being a strict code, sets out principles to be followed, with the aim of being adequately flexible to cater for from the smallest business to major corporations.[85]

The new duty of fair presentation and the new effect of a breach of the duty of good faith apply only in relation to contracts of insurance entered into on or after 12 August 2016 and to variations agreed to on or after 12 August 2016 in respect of contracts agreed at any time.[86]

---

80   Merkin and Gurses "The Insurance Act 2015: Rebalancing the interests of the insurer and the assured" 2015 *Modern Law Review* 1004 1008.

81   ibid.

82   See Hertzell and Burgoyne "The Law Commissions and insurance contract law reform: An update" 2013 *Journal of International Maritime Law (JIML)* 105 110.

83   This Act is aimed at protecting a claimant who has a claim against an insolvent, but insured defendant by transferring the insured's rights under the insurance policy to the third party and enabling the latter to proceed against the insurer. See also Soyer "Insurance Act 2015 coming into force: Overhauling commercial insurance law in the UK" 2016 *JIML* 253 256.

84   See Hertzell and Burgoyne (n 82) 123.

85   ibid; Soyer (n 83) 253 254. It is important to note that the Act will not apply retrospectively. See Merkin and Gurses (n 80) 1004–1027.

86   ibid. The new law on warranties, terms not relevant to the actual loss and fraudulent claims will apply only in relation to contracts of insurance entered into on or after 12 August 2016, and to variations of such contracts. See Merkin and Gurses (n 80) 1027.

In this Act,[87] the concept of "consumer insurance contract" has the same meaning as in the Consumer Insurance (Disclosure and Representations) Act, 2012. The term "non-consumer insurance contract" means a contract of insurance that is not a consumer insurance contract.

The duty of fair presentation

Starting with the legislation, section 2 of the Act sets out the application and interpretation of the new duty of fair presentation. It stipulates that this duty applies to non-consumer contracts and the variation thereof.[88]

Section 3 defines what is meant by the duty of fair presentation. Before a contract of insurance is entered into, the insured must make a fair presentation of the risk to the insurer.[89] Subsection 2 states that the duty imposed by subsection 1 is referred to in the Act as "the duty of fair presentation". A fair presentation of the risk is described in subsection 3 as one which makes the disclosure required by subsection 4.[90] In addition, the representation or the disclosure must be made in a manner which would be reasonably clear and accessible to a prudent and in such a manner that "every material representation as to a matter of fact is substantially correct, and every material representation as to a matter of expectation or belief is made in good faith".[91]

Section 4 sets out what constitutes knowledge of the policyholder and stipulates that a policyholder is an individual who knows only what is actually known to him or her or what is known to one or more individuals who are

---

87   apart from Part 6.

88   Subs 2 provides that "this Part applies in relation to variations of non-consumer insurance contracts as it applies to contracts, but (a) references to the risk are to be read as references to changes in the risk relevant to the proposed variation, and (b) references to the contract of insurance are to the variation". A non-consumer insurance contract "means a contract of insurance that is not a consumer insurance contract". See the Insurance Act, 2015.

89   s 1 of the Act.

90   S 4 reads as follows: "The disclosure required is as follows, except as provided in subsection (5)— (a) disclosure of every material circumstance which the insured knows or ought to know, or (b) failing that, disclosure which gives the insurer sufficient information to put a prudent insurer on notice that it needs to make further enquiries for the purpose of revealing those material circumstances".

91   s 3(3)(b)–(c) of the Act. S 3(5) goes on to provide for the following: "In the absence of enquiry, subsection (4) does not require the insured to disclose a circumstance if (a) it diminishes the risk, (b) the insurer knows it, (c) the insurer ought to know it, (d) the insurer is presumed to know it or (e) it is something as to which the insurer waives information".

responsible for the policyholder's insurance.[92] Subsection 3 goes on to provide that a policyholder "who is not an individual knows only what is known to one or more of the individuals who are (a) part of the insured's senior management, or (b) responsible for the insured's insurance".[93]

What is significant about this statute is that disclosure of knowledge under the MIA used to be a duty that was placed on the prospective policyholder. The important shift that took place to a shared responsibility between policyholders and insurers is evident from section 5, which describes what is meant by the knowledge of the insurer:

> "(1) For the purposes of section 3(5)(b), an insurer knows something only if it is known to one or more of the individuals who participate on behalf of the insurer in the decision whether to take the risk, and if so on what terms (whether the individual does so as the insurer's employee or agent, as an employee of the insurer's agent or in any other capacity).
>
> (2) For the purposes of section 3(5)(c), an insurer ought to know something only if—
>
>> (a) an employee or agent of the insurer knows it, and ought reasonably to have passed on the relevant information to an individual mentioned in subsection (1), or
>>
>> (b) the relevant information is held by the insurer and is readily available to an individual mentioned in subsection (1).
>
> (3) For the purposes of section 3(5)(d), an insurer is presumed to know—
>
>> (a) things which are common knowledge, and
>>
>> (b) things which an insurer offering insurance of the class in question to insureds

---

92 s 4(2) of the Act.

93 Subsequent relevant subsections of s 4 provide as follows: "(4) An insured is not by virtue of subsection (2)(b) or (3)(b) taken to know confidential information known to an individual if—(a) the individual is, or is an employee of, the insured's agent; and (b) the information was acquired by the insured's agent (or by an employee of that agent) through a business relationship with a person who is not connected with the contract of insurance. (5) For the purposes of subsection (4) the persons connected with a contract of insurance are— (a) the insured and any other persons for whom cover is provided by the contract, and (b) if the contract re-insures risks covered by another contract, the persons who are (by virtue of this subsection) connected with that other contract. (6) Whether an individual or not, a policyholder ought to know what should reasonably have been revealed by a reasonable search of information available to the policyholder (such search may be conducted by making enquiries or by any other means). (7) In subsection (6) 'information' includes information held within the insured's organ or by any other person (such as the insured's agent or a person for whom cover is provided by the contract of insurance)". See subsection 8 for definitions.

in the field of activity in question would reasonably be expected to know in the ordinary course of business".

Remedies for breach of the duty of fair presentation have been set out in section 8 and are far more proportionate than the previous regime of avoidance.[94]

To summarise these provisions, the potential policyholder is now under an obligation to disclose everything that is known to him or her, or which should be known to him or her, which will affect the insurer's decision of whether to accept the risk or not. In addition to this, the potential policyholder must also draw the attention of the insurer to all information which is relevant to the insurance coverage.[95] The policyholder, however, is not obliged to disclose matters already known to the insurer and insurers are required to mention from the start those matters which, in their opinion, are needed for the purposes of accepting the insurance.[96]

Evaluation of the duty of fair presentation

Through the inclusion of the duty of fair presentation, the Act aims to encourage co-operation between the policyholder and the insurer at a pre-contractual stage.[97] The aim of co-operation is reached by introducing a new

---

94 S 8 reads as follows: "(1) The insurer has a remedy against the insured for a breach of the duty of fair presentation only if the insurer shows that, but for the breach, the insurer — (a) would not have entered into the contract of insurance at all, or (b) would have done so only on different terms. (2) The remedies are set out in Schedule 1. (3) A breach for which the insurer has a remedy against the insured is referred to in this Act as a 'qualifying breach'. (4) A qualifying breach is either— (a) deliberate or reckless, or (b) neither deliberate nor reckless. (5) A qualifying breach is deliberate or reckless if the insured— (a) knew that it was in breach of the duty of fair presentation, or (b) did not care whether or not it was in breach of that duty. (6) It is for the insurer to show that a qualifying breach was deliberate or reckless".

95 S 3(4)(a)–(b) of the Act provides as follows: "Insured parties will be considered to have known, or ought to have known: matters that could be expected to be revealed by a reasonable search of information available to the insured party – for example, information held within an organisation or by a broker; anything known by a person responsible for their insurance – for example, a broker; insured organisations will also be deemed to have the knowledge of anyone who is a part of the organisation's senior management, or who is responsible for their insurance".

96 S 3(5) and (6) of the Act reads: "Insurers will be considered to have known, or ought to have known: matters known to individuals who participate on behalf of the insurer in deciding whether to take the risk and on what terms – for example, underwriting teams; knowledge held by the insurer and readily available to the person deciding whether to take the risk; and matters known by an employee or agent of the insurer and which should reasonably have been passed on to the person deciding whether to take the risk". Brokers will no longer be subjected to the old disclosure duties to which they were subjected previously. See also Thomas "The Insurance Act 2015 – a new duty of 'fair presentation'" 2016 Company Secretary's Review 4 49.

97 Birds, Lynch and Milnes (n 39) 575.

obligation on a policyholder to make a fair presentation of the risk to the insurer.[98] This presentation should disclose all the information in a reasonably clear and understandable manner.[99] In addition, the policyholder must ensure that every material representation as to a matter of fact is substantively correct and that every material representation as to a matter of belief or expectation is made in good faith.[100]

Before the Insurance Act, 2015, came into operation, potential policyholders were required to disclose every circumstance that they knew, or ought to have known, would influence an insurer in fixing a premium or deciding whether to underwrite a risk.[101] This generally required policyholders to predict, without much guidance from the insurer, by what factors a hypothetical insurer would be influenced.[102] This burden on the policyholder was somewhat cumbersome. The new Act[103] has created a fairer "duty of fair presentation" aimed at encouraging active, rather than passive, engagement by insurers as well as clarifying and specifying known or presumed to be known matters.[104]

The new obligation of fair presentation has a number of practical implications for both the policyholder and the insurer. Pre-disclosure analysis by the policyholder and sifting of all relevant information will be needed to ensure that disclosure is made in a reasonably clear and understandable manner.[105] If the policyholder does make a misrepresentation, the insurer is entitled to the

---

98 Under the Act, a policyholder is required to disclose every material circumstance which the policyholder knows or ought to know, and to conduct a reasonable search of its records to discharge the duty of fair presentation. See Birds, Lynch and Milnes (n 39) 575.

99 "Data dumping" is therefore no longer permissible.

100 s 3(4). See also Thomas (n 96) 49.

101 Birds, Lynch and Milnes (n 39) 575. Take note that the Consumer Insurance (Disclosures and Representations) Act, 2012, also changed the dispensation under the MIA.

102 The same obligation extended to brokers acting on behalf of policyholders. See Birds, Lynch and Milnes (n 39) 575. See also Law Commissions Report (n 36) par 6.2.

103 in Part 2.

104 The policyholder, before entering into a contract of insurance, will be required to disclose either: every matter which they know, or ought to know, that would influence the judgement of an insurer in deciding whether to insure the risk and on what terms; or sufficient information to put an insurer on notice that it needs to make further enquiries about potentially material circumstances. See Birds, Lynch and Milnes (n 39) 575.

105 Under the Act, disclosure must be made in a reasonably clear and accessible manner, material representations of fact must be "substantially correct" and material representations of expectation or belief must be made in "good faith". Individuals will be deemed to know matters which they suspected and which they would have known about had they not deliberately refrained from confirming or enquiring about them.

proportionate remedies as highlighted in section 8, depending on the type of breach committed by the policyholder.

As indicated, insurers will no longer be able to rely on a passive approach to disclosure.[106] More active engagement is encouraged and, if not in place already, insurers should consider establishing systems and processes to identify when further enquiries need to be made before underwriting risks.[107] Insurers must review what information is readily available to those who decide whether to accept risks and the terms on which to do so.[108]

Section 8 of the Insurance Act (mentioned above) sets out the remedies for the insurer in case of breach of the duty of fair presentation by the policyholder. This section stipulates that if the policyholder is in breach of the duty of fair presentation, either deliberately or recklessly, the insurer can avoid the policy and keep all premiums paid.[109] In the situation where the policyholder's breach is not deliberate or reckless, the insurer can avoid the policy and return all premiums paid, provided that the insurer can prove that it would not have entered into the policy at all. If the insurer would have entered into the policy on different terms, the policy will be treated as if it included those terms. Lastly, if the insurer would have entered into the contract but would have charged the policyholder a higher

---

106 Birds, Lynch and Milnes (n 39) 575 and Law Commission (n 33) par 6.2. In South Africa, this has also been a problem. The court in *Mahadeo v Dial Direct Insurance Ltd* [2008] JOL 21383 (W) stated that insurers must ask the correct questions in order to determine the risk because they have a notion of the kind of information they require. The duty of fair presentation in English law clearly takes cognisance of this thorny issue. In South Africa, the General Code of Conduct (GCC) adopted in terms of the FAIS Act has detailed rules on the pre-contractual duties of insurers when selling products. See s 7 of the FAIS GCC. These stipulations are supplemented by rule 11.3.4 of the 2018 Policyholder Protection Rules (PPRs): "Information provided must enable a policyholder to understand the features of the policy and help the policyholder understand whether it meets the policyholder's requirements. In determining the level of information to be disclosed the insurer must consider (a) the factually established or reasonably assumed knowledge and experience of the policyholder or average targeted policyholder at whom the communication is targeted; (b) the policy terms and conditions, including its main benefits, exclusions, limitations, conditions and its duration; (c) the policy's overall complexity, including whether it is entered into together with other goods and services; and (d) whether the same information has been provided to the policyholder previously and if so, when". It is evident that there is a growing trend in both England and South Africa to compel insurers to take a more active role in determining the risk and in assisting prospective policyholders in disclosing the correct information.

107 Law Commission (n 36) par 6.2. See also Thomas (n 96) 49.

108 Insurers should consider keeping internal records of the names and roles of individuals responsible for these decisions and establish appropriate processes and lines of communication to ensure that relevant information is shared with other insurers.

109 s 8 of the Insurance Act, 2015.

premium, the insurer may reduce proportionately the amount to be paid on a claim to reflect that premium adjustment.[110]

Previously, an insurer was able to refuse all claims under an insurance contract if the pre-contractual disclosure duty was breached, even if the breach was committed by the broker.[111] The 2015 Act has now introduced a range of *proportionate* remedies, which are applied according to the type of breach committed.[112] It is important to note that these proportionate remedies are much fairer. To bring an action for relief for non-disclosure, insurers will need to be able to prove how they would have acted differently if the breach had not occurred.[113]

Good faith

As was stated in paragraph 2.1, in terms of section 17 of the MIA of insurance were based on utmost good faith and, if the policyholder breached this duty, the insurer could avoid the contract in its entirety.[114] In terms of section 14 of the 2015 Act, no party may now avoid the contract based on the ground that the duty of utmost good faith has not been complied with.[115] Section 14 deals with good faith and reads as follows:

> "(1) Any rule of law permitting a party to a contract of insurance to avoid the contract on the ground that the utmost good faith has not been observed by the other party is abolished.
>
> (2) Any rule of law to the effect that a contract of insurance is a contract based on the utmost good faith is modified to the extent required by the provisions of this Act and the Consumer Insurance (Disclosure and Representations) Act 2012.

---

110 ibid.

111 Birds, Lynch and Milnes (n 39) 588-589 and Law Commission (n 36) par 11.37.

112 ibid.

113 Birds, Lynch and Milnes (n 39) 589. See also Law Commission (n 36) par 11.44-11.46. Disclosure of underwriting guides and other relevant documents may now be required, along with records of underwriting decisions made and factors considered in particular cases. The link between pre-contractual presentations and fraud is that all failures to disclose are intentional or even remotely fraudulent. However, if parties are confronted with a situation where pre-contractual misstatements may perhaps be fraudulent, the law is now just and clear.

114 See the South African position on good faith which stemmed from the decision in *Mutual and Federal Co Ltd v Oudtshoorn Municipality* 1985 1 SA 419 (A).

115 s 14(1).

(3)   Accordingly—

(a) in section 17 of the Marine Insurance Act 1906 (marine insurance contracts are contracts of the utmost good faith), the words from ", and" to the end are omitted, and

(b) the application of that section (as so amended) is subject to the provisions of this Act and the Consumer Insurance (Disclosure and Representations) Act 2012.

(4)   In section 2 of the Consumer Insurance (Disclosure and Representations) Act 2012 (disclosure and representations before contract or variation), subsection (5) is omitted".

It is thus clear that section 14 does *not* repeal section 17 of the MIA in its entirety. Rather, section 14 repeals only the part of section 17 which states that the insurer may avoid the contract in its entirety if the duty of utmost good faith has not been complied with. This means that contracts of insurance are still based on utmost good faith and this concept still plays a significant role in a contract of insurance. The duty of fair presentation coincides with the duty of utmost good faith as both duties essentially require that policyholders not make any misrepresentations to the insurer.

Evaluation of good faith

Before the enactment of the 2015 Act, either party could avoid the insurance contract if the other failed to act in accordance with "utmost good faith".[116] Part 5 of the Act has now removed avoidance of contract as a remedy for breach of this duty and abolished any parts of legislation prescribing this as a remedy.[117] Insurance contracts will still be based on utmost good faith and clauses and obligations will be interpreted in a way that favours compliance with this duty.[118] In a sense, the Act aligns the English position with the South African position. It brings about a fairer dispensation in that avoidance is no longer permissible and more equitable remedies are to be sought.

---

116 See the South African position as laid out in the *Oudtshoorn Municipality* case (n 1).

117 s 14 of the Insurance Act. See also Birds, Lynch and Milnes (n 39) 591.

118 s 14 of the Insurance Act. See also *Axa General Insurance Ltd v Clara Gottlieb and Joseph Meyer Gottlieb* [2005] EWCA Civ 112 (CA).

HAS THE DUTY OF UTMOST GOOD FAITH STOOD THE TEST OF TIME?

What is evident from the above discussion on utmost good faith is that English law still seems very much "married" to this concept. The fact that the 2015 Act still refers to this concept shows a reluctance to move away from what has been conceptualised ages ago and may very well be out of pace with modern insurance business practices. When Carter insured Fort Marlborough, Boehm had no way of knowing whether the fort would hold against enemy attack and Boehm had no choice but to rely on Carter's word. It is no wonder then that good faith in this context found its way into legislation and that the remedy under the original 1906 Act was avoidance of the contract. Insurers needed to be protected due to the general asymmetry of information that existed between the insurer and the insured. During the 1800s, communications were slow and unreliable. It was virtually impossible for the insurer to inspect the subject-matter being insured or the scene of the risk. Modern-day insurance contracts are concluded on a different basis and underwriters have other methods at their disposal (such as detailed statistical data) with which to calculate risk. This is why it is not surprising that the remedy of avoidance was repealed by the 2015 Act.[119] The old remedy was always held to be controversial and led to unfair results.[120] Now, a fairer dispensation is observed. No longer is avoidance of the contract the sole remedy for breach of the duty of disclosure. Therefore, although contracts of insurance are still recognised as contracts of utmost good faith, it seems that the concept of utmost good faith is being transformed into something more fair and equitable for both the insurer and the insured.

The introduction of the duty of fair presentation has also led to the repeal of sections 18 and 20 of the MIA and the fact that the 2015 Act has introduced a fairer dispensation involving a duty of "fair presentation" shows that the duty of utmost good faith no longer serves its original purpose. One may therefore conclude that the duty of utmost good faith no longer serves the original purpose as envisaged by Lord Mansfield when he introduced the duty of disclosure in

119 s 15 of the Insurance Act, 2015.

120 Lowry (n 14) 150.

the eighteenth and nineteenth centuries.[121] The previous dispensation relating to disclosure was undoubtedly necessary during that period when the context was mainly marine. The insured was generally in a much better position with regard to knowledge of the risk and utmost good faith, in this context, served a purpose. It stands to reason that, as the asymmetry of information relative to a particular transaction being negotiated is less significant, utmost good faith similarly became less significant. That is why the duty to disclose, together with the remedies for non-disclosure, needed to be reformed. This deficiency is capable of being treated by requiring the insurer to ask specific questions, which is in fact now the case with the duty of fair presentation.[122] Consequently, it is no longer the sole duty of the policyholder to burden the insurer with unnecessary information. Insurers now play a more active role in establishing the risk to be insured and the duty of utmost good faith does not seem to serve its original purpose as set out in the nineteenth century.

In conclusion, what remains of utmost good faith is only the shell and, thankfully, its content is more equitable and leads to a fairer dispensation.

GOOD FAITH IN MARINE INSURANCE LAW IN SOUTH AFRICA

Legislative and conceptual framework

South African marine insurance can be traced back to the *lex mercatoria* and, therefore, has the same roots as English insurance law.[123] As marine insurance inevitably has an international character, comparisons between jurisdictions often show that standard insurance practices, such as subrogation and salvage, apply across the board. As was alluded to in paragraph one above, English law is not a source of South African law as such, but it does have persuasive authority.[124]

---

121 *Carter* case (n 12).

122 See the discussion above on the duty of fair presentation.

123 Reinecke et al (n 8) 19.

124 *Oudtshoorn Municipality* case (n 1).

As in England, insurance in South Africa is often classified in order to refer to the kind of cover offered by a specific kind of insurance.[125] It is therefore common to refer to motor insurance, life insurance, aviation insurance and marine insurance, to name but a few.[126] In this case, the insurance is classified according to the so-called "line" of cover provided by the particular insurance contract. Reinecke, Van Niekerk and Nienaber are of the opinion that, in most instances, differentiations are retained "for the sake of habit" and not because different principles are applied to these different types of contracts.[127] This is, of course, correct. It must be stated, however, that, in South Africa, licensing requirements often inform decisions to categorise insurance business. To that end, two statutes have for some time distinguished between life insurance and non-life insurance. The Long-term Insurance Act (LTIA)[128] and the Short-term Insurance Act (STIA)[129] have contained rules pertaining to life and non-life insurance respectively and these two statutes contain very similar stipulations. Marine insurance as a line of business was regulated by the STIA.

On 1 July 2018, the Insurance Act (IA)[130] came into operation. This statute is of significance for the remainder of the discussion because it repealed key sections of the LTIA and STIA. In addition, the IA abolishes the concepts "long-term insurance" and "short-term insurance" and, henceforth, uses life and non-life insurance, thereby developing the South African conceptual framework in line with international standards. The IA classifies marine insurance as category 5, sub-category a) being "personal lines" and b) "commercial lines".[131] The Act stipulates that these two classes of marine insurance cover "damage or loss resulting from the possession, use or ownership of vessels used on or in a river, canal, dam, lake or sea". Category 10(a) further provides for liability (marine) insurance, denoting liability to another person caused by marine risks. This distinction between property and

---

125 Reinecke et al (n 8) 10.

126 ibid.

127 ibid.

128 52 of 1998.

129 53 of 1998.

130 18 of 2017.

131 See table 2 of the IA, which contains classes and sub-classes of insurance.

liability insurance is also made for a number of other types of niche insurance, such as aviation and rail insurance. The purpose of this contribution, however, is to evaluate the concept of good faith and to compare this aspect of marine insurance as it is currently applied in the two jurisdictions in question.

Good faith in South African insurance contracts

One of the two main differences between English insurance law and *South African insurance law* is that the concept of utmost good faith is still used in England regardless of the fact that the meaning of utmost good faith has changed from the MIA to the current statutory framework. In South Africa, it has been emphatically stated that there is no such thing as *utmost* good faith, but rather that insurance contracts, like any other contracts in South Africa, are contracts in good faith.[132] The second difference is that the duty of good faith in South Africa has always been a pre-contractual duty.[133] In England, however, the same duty does not only exist at the pre-contractual stage, but continues for the duration of the contract. This means that it is generally expected that the duty of utmost good faith be observed throughout the continued existence of the contract. This is clearly different from the South African purely pre-contractual duty.

It is important to keep in mind that the duty of good faith in relation to the duty of disclosure resting on a prospective policyholder pertains to the fact that an insurer must be in a position to quantify the possibility of loss "to a degree of probability", based on facts disclosed by the prospective policyholder.[134] The insurer, therefore, requires information about all the facts that will affect the risk. It is only then that the insurer can calculate the risk, decide whether or not to insure the risk and, ultimately, impose restrictions on the insured amount and other conditions and exclusions in the contract.

It is therefore predominantly in the pre-contractual phase that good faith plays a very important role. This exposition of South African law on good faith will,

---

132 *Oudtshoorn Municipality* case (n 1). See Reinecke and Becker "Die openbaringsplig by versekering: *Uberrima fides* oorboord: *Mutual and Federal Insurance Co Ltd v Oudtshoorn Municipality*" 1985 *TSAR* 86 88.

133 Reinecke et al (n 8) 140.

134 ibid 142.

however, argue that the role of good faith in insurance law has changed somewhat over the past two decades, mainly because of three events, namely the introduction of the FAIS Act, the promulgation of the PPRs and the most recent promulgation of the Insurance Act.[135] As a result, it is submitted that marine insurance as a form of non-life insurance is currently subject to exactly the same rules pertaining to good faith and misrepresentation as any other form of non-life insurance.

However, before the FAIS Act is discussed, it is necessary to provide a brief overview of good faith and misrepresentation in South Africa.

Good faith and misrepresentation

Generally speaking, misrepresentation has the effect of influencing consensus.[136] South African law regards culpable misrepresentation as a wrongful act or a delict.[137] Misrepresentation may be by way of an omission (non-disclosure) or positive conduct and, furthermore, non-disclosure of certain facts entails a failure to speak where there is a duty to speak, while a misrepresentation by positive conduct takes place if a prospective policyholder creates by his conduct a wrong impression relating to a fact.[138] When further classifying misrepresentations, a distinction is made between innocent, negligent and intentional misrepresentations.[139] Innocent misrepresentations occur when a reasonable person in the position of the insured would not have realised that the statement was untrue or that it would harm the insurer.[140] Intentional misrepresentation is where the person making the disclosure is aware of the fact that the statement is incorrect.[141] Negligent misrepresentation occurs where the insured does not realise that his statement is untrue or that it would harm the insurer, while a reasonable person would have realised this and

---

135 18 of 2017.

136 Prozesky-Kuschke "Specific aspects of insurance contracts and indemnity and non-indemnity insurance" in Nagel (ed) *Commercial Law* (2015) 367.

137 Reinecke "Remedies for misrepresentation inducing a long-term insurance contract: The Didcott principle" 2009 *SA Merc LJ* 387-395.

138 ibid.

139 Millard *Modern Insurance Law in South Africa* (2013) 72.

140 Reinecke (n 137) 388.

141 ibid.

would also have foreseen it.[142] In the context of insurance, it is the prospective policyholder who bears the duty of disclosing to the insurer certain information prior to the conclusion or the renewal of his insurance contract.[143] During the pre-contractual stage, parties are still to negotiate the contract and this means that the duty to disclose cannot be a contractual one, which is why breach of this duty (misrepresentation) is a delict.[144] More specifically, where the insured discloses the wrong information or fails to disclose essential, material information and where the insurer acts to his detriment by accepting a risk that has not been fully comprehended, these acts of the (then) prospective policyholder becomes actionable. Not all misrepresentations, however, are material to the risk. Generally speaking, a misrepresentation is material if: (a) it would have induced a reasonable person to contract in reliance on it; (b) it was reasonably likely to convince someone to contract; or (c) it has the probable effect of influencing the mind of the insurer.[145] The common law position was, in fact, codified by section 59 of the LTIA and section 53 of the STIA, which contained the exact same wording. The essence of these sections was found in sub-sections 59(1)*(b)* and 53(1)*(b)*, which stated that the misrepresentation or non-disclosure in question,

> "shall be regarded as material if a reasonable, prudent person would consider that the particular information constituting the representation or which was not disclosed, as the case may be, should have been correctly disclosed to the insurer so that the insurer could form its own view as to the effect of such information on the assessment of the relevant risk".

The effect of these sections was that an insurer could only exercise its contractual remedies if the misrepresentation or non-disclosure *materially* influenced the assessment of the risk under the policy at the time of its conclusion. This is the position even where the policyholder warranted that he had provided the correct

---

142 ibid.

143 Van Niekerk "The insured's duties of disclosure: delictual and contractual; before the conclusion and during the currency of the insurance contract: *Bruwer v Nova Risk Partners Ltd*" 2011 *SA Merc LJ* 135 135.

144 Millard (n 139) 73; Reinecke et al (n 8) 136.

145 Nortje "A new look at materiality" 2012 *TSAR* 468.

information, the only difference being that, because the warranty was breached, the misrepresentation or non-disclosure amounts to breach of contract.[146]

The essence of the issue remains the matter of good faith. As misrepresentation goes to the very heart of the agreement to take over the risk, the importance of this doctrine cannot be over-emphasised. Note that section 59 of the LTIA and section 53 of the STIA only pertained to the voidability of contracts in the instance of misrepresentations that could materially influence the assessment of the risk under the policy at the time of its conclusion.[147] As was stated before, the IA repealed section 59 of the LTIA and section 53 of the STIA. This means that the common law position as it was before the enactment of these two sections is restored, namely that the insurer may repudiate a claim and cancel a contract if the misrepresentation was wrongful or, in other words, material to the risk. If a warranty was included in the contract in terms of which the insured warranted that all information was correct, the contract can be avoided based on breach of warranty, which is breach of contract.[148] It is argued, however, that elements of the overall legislation currently conspire to create a legal dispensation where it is no longer possible simply to view misrepresentations and non-disclosures in such a narrow way. In essence, the FAIS Act and the PPRs contain rules that, when read together, indicate that insurance companies, as well as their agents and intermediaries, should play a more active role in establishing the true facts before offering insurance cover.

---

146 Reinecke et al (n 8) 159; Van Niekerk "Goodbye to the duty of disclosure in insurance law: reasons to rethink, restrict, reform or repeal the duty (part 2)" 2005 *SA Merc LJ* 323 337.

147 Reinecke et al (n 8) 165-166.

148 Reinecke et al (n 8) 167. Breach of warranty *per se*, however, cannot simply warrant cancellation of the contract by the insurance company. Section 53(1)(a) of STIA provides that, if a representation that is the subject of a warranty turns out to be untrue, an insurer may only cancel the contract if the representation is "such as to be likely to have materially affected the assessment of the risk under the policy concerned at the time of its issue or at the time of any variation thereof". This measure brought some relief to policyholders in the wake of widely criticised cases such as *Jordan v New Zealand Insurance Co Ltd* 1968 2 SA 238 (E) and *John v North British and Mercantile Insurance Co* (1902) 19 SC 414, (1902) 12 CTR 771. Reinecke et al (n 8) 311 states that section 53(1)(a) does not provide sufficient protection to policyholders. It is submitted that the measures introduced by the IA for life insurance provide better protection and should also be introduced for non-life insurance. See the discussion in par 5.6 below.

Financial Advisory and Intermediary Services Act

The FAIS Act was introduced to regulate the activities of all intermediaries and advisors who sell financial products. Because the statutory definition of "financial product" includes insurance, the entire Act applies to the insurance business.[149] During the all-important phase where pre-contractual disclosures pertaining to the risk are made by prospective insurers, the FAIS Act and, more specifically, the General Code of Conduct (GCC) in terms of the Act contain stipulations that place a duty on insurance intermediaries and advisors to assist the prospective insured in disclosing information that is relevant to the risk. The GCC is a code under the FAIS Act and, because the FAIS Act is aimed mainly at market regulation, the GCC and other codes of conduct set minimum standards to which financial services providers' conduct must conform when dealing with clients. The obligation to assist the prospective insured to disclose information that is material to the risk is but one of the many obligations provided for by the GCC. This shift in focus brought about a radical move away from the one-sided view that the insured has a duty of disclosure to a more balanced approach that places a duty of enquiry upon the insurer to assist the prospective insured in considering which factors are material to the risk and to disclose these accordingly.

This shift from a one-sided duty upon the prospective insured to disclose regardless of his knowledge of insurance products, to one where the role of the insurer was also considered, was first verbalised by the court in the much-quoted case of *Mahadeo v Dial Direct Insurance Ltd.*[150] *In casu*, the insurer made use of a call-centre script to obtain information from the prospective insured. When a claim was later repudiated based on misrepresentation, the court sided with the policyholder, stating that the scope of the call-centre script provides an indication of the information that is indeed deemed material and that it would be wrong of the insurer to expect the policyholder to provide information outside this script and later to rely on the materiality of such non-disclosure to repudiate a claim. What is manifestly true is that the GCC supports the notion

---

149 See the definition of "financial product" in s 1 of the Financial Sector Regulation Act 9 of 2017. See also Millard and Hattingh *The FAIS Act Explained* (2016) 33-34.

150 [2008] 2 All SA 352 (W); 2008 4 SA 80 (W) 86B-87D.

that insurance advisors and intermediaries have a duty to provide a service: that must be factually correct;[151] that must avoid uncertainty or confusion and not be misleading;[152] that must be provided in plain language,[153] and, where in writing, in a clear and readable print size, spacing and format;[154] that must be be adequate and appropriate in the circumstances;[155] that must be provided timeously so as to afford the client reasonably sufficient time to make an informed decision;[156] that must be rendered in accordance with the contractual relationship and reasonable requests or instructions of the client;[157] that must be executed as soon as reasonably possible and with the interest of the client in mind; and that must be accorded priority over any interest of the provider.[158]

Another part of the GCC that applies to the provision of insurance is clause 15, which regulates the conduct of direct marketers and contains several requirements relating to the information that must be provided to a prospective insured.[159]

---

151 s 3(1)(a)(i) of the FAIS GCC.

152 s 3(1)(a)(ii).

153 ibid.

154 s 3(1)(a)(vi) of the FAIS GCC.

155 s 3(1)(a)(iii).

156 s 3(1)(a)(iv).

157 s 3(1)(a)(v).

158 s 3(1)(d).

159 See s 15(1) and (2) which read as follows: "(1) A direct marketer must, when rendering a financial service to or on behalf of a client, at the earliest reasonable opportunity furnish the client with the following particulars: a) the business or trade name of the direct marketer; b) confirmation whether the direct marketer is a licensed financial service provider and details of the financial services which the direct marketer is authorised to provide in terms of the relevant license and any conditions or restrictions applicable thereto; c) telephone contact details of direct marketer (unless the contact was initiated by the client); d) telephone contact details of the compliance department of the direct marketer; e) whether the direct marketer holds professional and indemnity insurance; Provided that where the direct marketer is a representative, the information contemplated in sub-paragraphs (a) to (c) above must be provided in respect of the provider to which the representative is contracted. (2) When providing a client with advice in respect of a product, a direct marketer must at the earliest reasonable opportunity: a) make enquiries to establish whether the financial product or products concerned will be appropriate, regard being had to the client's risk profile and financial needs, and circumstances; b) furnish the client with the following particulars where appropriate: i) business or trade name of the product supplier; ii) legal status and relationship with product supplier; iii) the following details in respect of the product: (aa) Name, class or type of financial product concerned; (bb) Nature and extent of benefits to be provided; (cc) Manner in which such benefits are derived or calculated, with specific reference to the underlying assets of any investment component and the manner in which the value of such investment component is determined; (dd) Monetary obligations assumed by the client as well as manner of payment; (ee) Whether cooling off rights are offered and, if so, procedures for the exercise of such rights; (ff) Any material investment or other risks associated with the product; c) when advising or being advised by a client that the financial product concerned is to replace an existing financial product held by the client, inform the client of actual and potential financial implications, costs and consequence set out in clause 8(l)(d) of this Code before any transaction is concluded".

It is evident that the primary purpose of the GCC is to force financial services providers to make full and frank disclosures to clients and it is suggested that it is no longer possible for insurance companies to sell products in a "take it or leave it" fashion, only to subsequently rely on misrepresentation to repudiate claims. This, in fact, signals a whole new dispensation in insurance where consumer vulnerability is addressed by statutory measures that are aimed at re-balancing the interests of the insurer and the policyholder. There can be no doubt that the FAIS Act was very important in levelling the playing field between the insurer and the insured. The main question that remains is what the apparent shift in responsibilities from the insured to the insurer means and, to that end, the following two paragraphs provide an exposition of the PPRs and the IA.

The 2018 Policyholder Protection Rules

The PPRs in terms of both Acts (the LTIA and STIA) were first published in 2004[160] in order to provide for issues such as rules for direct marketers,[161] void provisions[162] and general rules[163] regulating the agreement between the insurer and the policyholder. These rules were promulgated in order to provide for the notion of fairness in relation to certain issues surrounding the relationship between insurer and policyholder. Since the rules were promulgated in 2004, there have beefn some significant reforms. The most noteworthy reform was in 2010 with regard to time-bar clauses, following the decision of the Constitutional Court in *Barkhuizen v Napier*.[164] The outcome of the case led to an amendment of the PPRs, at that time in terms of both the LTIA and the STIA, aimed at ensuring more manageable time frames for the institution of claims against insurers.[165] The PPRs have over the years become a well-known tool to safeguard the rights of

---

160 GN 1128 in GG 26853 of 30-09-2004 (PPRs for short-term insurance); GN 1129 in GG 26854 of 30-09-2004 (PPRs for long-term insurance).

161 rule 4.

162 rule 5.

163 rule 6.

164 2007 7 BCLR 691 (CC). The case saw the incorporation of rule 7.4 of the PPRs, that entered into force on 1 January 2010 and states that any time limitation provision may not include the 90-day period within which the insured may make representations to the insurer and must provide for a period of not less than six months after the expiry of the 90-day period for the institution of legal action.

165 See rule 7.4 of the 2010 PPRs.

policyholders and to provide protection where common law and the principles of contract, including good faith, have not yielded equitable results. The value of the PPRs has therefore been significant. In addition, while the GCC applies to *all* financial products, the PPRs apply only to insurance. Furthermore, even though the rules on the pre-contractual duties of insurers as financial services providers have been heralded as infusing fairness into the pre-contractual phase, as illustrated in paragraph 5.4 above, the PPRs as product-specific market regulation were also due for an update in light of the Twin Peaks reforms of the financial services industry that was initiated by the Financial Services Regulation Act (FSRA Act).[166]

The new PPRs came into effect on 1 January 2018.[167] The principle of treating customers fairly ("TCF") is embedded in them and their main theme is to ensure that insurers treat customers fairly throughout the product life cycle. It is submitted that, although this is an important aspect of consumer protection and should under no circumstances be trivialised as a tool that achieves a better balance between insurers and consumers, at the same time it labours from the premises that *all* consumers are vulnerable and in need of protection. However, while well-established, commercial mariners are perhaps not vulnerable. At the same time, it is evident from the Insurance Act that marine insurance is not only available to commercial ventures, but also to individuals who use watercraft for personal purposes. It is even possible for subsistence fishers to obtain micro-insurance policies insuring small risks and limited to a lower amount. Regardless of the nature and extent of the enterprise, the 2018 PPRs adopted in terms of STIA provide for extensive disclosures before, during and after the conclusion of an insurance contract. This may be an indication that good faith is no longer a pre-contractual duty only, but now extends to the contractual relationship and beyond.

As far as pre-contractual disclosures are concerned, it is evident that, even though insurance companies already have duties to assist prospective insureds in disclosing facts material to the risk during the pre-contractual stage according to the FAIS Act, the 2018 PPRs expect even more of insurance companies during

---

166 9 of 2017. See also in this regard Millard and Maholo "Market conduct regulation in perspective: Triumphs and tribulations post Twin Peaks" in Hugo and Möllers (eds) *Legal Certainty and Fundamental Rights: A Cross-Disciplinary Approach to Constitutional Principles in German and South African Law* (2020 – forthcoming).

167 GN 1433 in *GG* 41329 of 15-12-2017.

this stage. The duties set out in rule 11 are stipulated in no uncertain terms. Rule 11.3.1 stipulates that any communication by an insurer to a policyholder in relation to a policy must be in plain language,[168] must not be misleading,[169] must be provided using an appropriate medium, taking into account the complexity of the information being provided,[170] and, where applicable, must be in clear and readable print size, spacing and format.[171] Additionally, the rule states that the basis of calculation "in respect of any amount, sum, premium, value, charge, fee, remuneration or monetary obligation mentioned or referred to therein, [must] be stated in actual monetary terms" and must be clearly and appropriately described.[172] Insurers have the additional duty to ensure that a prospective policyholder receives all the information in good time in order to enable the policyholder to make an informed decision on whether or not to enter into a contract.[173] Rule 11.3.4 further requires insurers to ensure that the information provided enables the policyholder to understand whether the proposed product meets the policyholder's requirements. This, no doubt, poses a challenge. When determining the level of information to be disclosed, the insurer *must* consider: "the factually established or reasonably assumed knowledge and experience of the policyholder or average targeted policyholder at whom the communication is targeted";[174] the policy terms and conditions, including the main benefits, exclusions, limitations, conditions and its duration;[175] the policy's overall complexity;[176] whether the same information has been provided to the policyholder previously and, if so, when.[177] Where an insurer relies on a representative (intermediary or advisor) to provide

---

168 rule 11.3.1*(a)*.

169 rule 11.3.1*(b)*.

170 rule 11.3.1*(c)*.

171 rule 11.3.1*(d)*. The requirement to ensure that an insurer makes the questions in the proposal form clear and unambiguous has for some time been part of South African law and, in that respect, the 2018 PPRs do not add anything new to the existing legal framework. See eg *British America Assurance Co v Cash Wholesale* 1932 AD 70 74 and *Mahadeo v Dial Direct Insurance* 2008 4 SA 80 (W). The latter case did not deal with a printed application form, but with a contract that came into existence telephonically. The same principle, however, applies because questions posed orally must similarly be clear and unambiguous.

172 rule 11.3.1*(e)*.

173 rule 11. 3.2.

174 rule 11. 3.4*(a)*.

175 rule 11. 3.4*(b)*.

176 rule 11. 3.4*(c)*.

177   rule 11. 3.4*(d)*.

any information, the insurer remains responsible to ensure that the information required by rule 11 is communicated to the insured.[178]

In addition to these considerations, rule 11.4.2 is very specific about what needs to be disclosed. It provides as follows:

"An insurer must provide a policyholder with the following information–

(a) the name of the insurer and its contact details;

(b) the type of policy and a reasonable and appropriate general explanation of the relevant policy;

(c) the nature and extent of policy benefits, including, where applicable, when the insurance cover begins and ends, and a description of the risk insured by the policy;

(d) concise details of all of the following, where applicable–

(i) any charges or fees to be levied against the policy or the premium;

(ii) any commission or remuneration payable to any intermediary or binder holder in relation to the policy, and the recipient thereof; and

(iii) any excesses that may become payable by the policyholder, the circumstances under which it will be payable and the consequences of not paying;

(e) in respect of premiums–

(i) the premium that is payable under the policy;

(ii) the frequency at which the premium is payable;

(iii) details of any premium increases, including the frequency and basis thereof;

(iv) whether an increase will be linked to any commensurate increase in policy benefits and any options relating to premium increases that the policyholder may select;

(v) the implications of a failure to pay a premium at the frequency referred to in subparagraph (ii); and

(vi) in the case of policies where the premium (with or without contractual escalations) is not guaranteed for the full term of the policy, the period for which the premium is guaranteed, including the frequency at which or the circumstances

---

178 rule 11.3.6.

in which a review will take place;

(f) what cooling-off rights are offered and procedures for the exercise thereof;

(g) concise details of any significant exclusions or limitations, which information must be provided prominently as contemplated in rule 10.15;

(h) where a policy is entered into in connection with other goods or services (a bundled product), the premium payable in respect of the policy separately from any other prices for such other goods and services and whether entering into the policy or any policy benefit is a prerequisite for entering into or being eligible for any other goods or services;

(i) if the policy to be entered into is a consumer credit insurance policy the insurer must, where this information is known or should reasonably be known to the insurer, disclose to the policyholder whether the policy is a mandatory or optional credit life insurance policy and the difference between the two;

(j) the existence of any circumstance that could give rise to an actual or potential conflict of interest in dealing with the policyholder;

(k) any obligation to disclose material facts, including information to ensure that a policyholder knows what must be disclosed as well as the consequences of non-compliance with the obligations;

(l) where applicable, the right to request recordings of any telephonic disclosures; and

(m) the right to complain, including details on how and where to complain and the contact details of the insurer and contact details of the relevant ombud".[179]

This rule is quoted *verbatim* to illustrate how extensive the duties of disclosure are. Overall, it is crucial to note that the disclosure of material facts is but one of the many duties placed on insurers. Rule 11.4.2*(k)*, which deals with material disclosures, is therefore but one of the many rules that have changed the way in which misrepresentation should henceforth be viewed. It is therefore argued that the requirements for misrepresentation and good faith have now been codified and, although insurers are still able to repudiate claims and cancel contracts where a material misrepresentation was made, it is submitted that any failure to comply with this particular rule will lead to an insurer not being able to cancel an insurance contract. It seems that the duty of a prospective policyholder to disclose

---

179 own emphasis.

has become a duty of an insurer to inform a prospective policyholder that he has a duty to disclose certain information! It will be accurate to conclude that the duty to disclose and the pre-contractual duty of good faith still exist, but that insurers have an active role to play in ensuring that the risk is properly assessed and an appropriate premium is charged.

Insurance Act, 2017

As stated above, the IA came into operation on 1 July 2018. Although the IA is primarily aimed at establishing a prudential framework for insurance, with the majority of market-conduct regulation still seated in the LTIA and STIA (the 2018 PPRs) and in the FAIS Act, the IA did bring about changes to the law pertaining to misrepresentation and insurance warranties.[180] When the IA came into operation, the notice of commencement excluded the repeal of section 53 of the STIA.[181] What is also crucial is that the amendments to the Short-term PPRs that were promulgated on 28 September 2018 did not include a new rule on misrepresentation.[182] This means that section 53 of the STIA remains in place amidst the new, stringent rules on disclosures that are found in rules 1 and 11 of the short-term insurance PPRs[183] and in the GCC in terms of the FAIS Act. The undeniable truth is that insurance companies have pre-contractual duties towards policyholders and that failure to guide prospective insurers to disclose what insurers deem as material is in fact against the PPRs and the GCC. Although the current

---

180 This is clear from the objectives of the statute, which are "[t]o provide for a legal framework for the prudential regulation and supervision of insurance business in the Republic that is consistent with the Constitution of the Republic of South Africa, 1996, and promotes the maintenance of a fair, safe and stable insurance market; to introduce a legal framework for microinsurance to promote financial inclusion; to replace certain parts of the Long-term Insurance Act, 1998, and the Short-term Insurance Act, 1998; and to provide for matters connected therewith". See also Millard (2018) 21 *Juta's Insurance L Bul 51*.

181 GN 639 in *GG* 41735 of 27-06-2018.

182 See GN 996 in *GG* 41928 of 28-09-2018.

183 The position for non-life insurance (long-term insurance), however, is different. Donnelly "Do you always get something out? The impact of the Insurance Act 18 of 2017 and revised policyholder protection rules on material misrepresentation and non-disclosure" 2018 *SALJ* 593 597 explains that section 59 of the LTIA was repealed by a second notice of commencement three months after the IA came into force (1 October 2018 (GN 1020 in *GG* 41947 of 28-09-2018)). The legislature simultaneously promulgated the second tranche of amendments to the Long-term PPRs (GN 997 in *GG* 41928 of 28-09-2018). This means that the Long-term PPRs currently contain a new rule 21 on misrepresentation, which became effective on 1 October 2018 and that the all-important aspect of non-disclosure in life insurance is currently regulated by subordinate legislation. It is not clear why this distinction is made between life and non-life insurance, such as marine insurance.

legal position is highly contentious, it is submitted that it better balances the rights of insurers and policyholders.

In the final instance, it submitted that it is patently evident that good faith in South African law is not a separate requirement for the validity of a contract and that breach of good faith alone rarely provides a suitable remedy, such as cancellation of a contract. The latest statutory framework stresses the idea that insurance contracts are contracts in good faith. However, the shift that has taken place is that the duty to disclose material information, which still rests on the policyholder, cannot be used as a weapon to repudiate as many claims as possible. Rather, the insurer has an active duty to guide a policyholder to understand which facts are likely to be material to the risk and why, thereby ensuring that the correct cover is sold at the correct price.[184]

CONCLUSION

It is accordingly clear that English law and South African law illustrate two significantly different lines of development. English law retained utmost good faith in marine insurance and South African law developed good faith from a pre-contractual duty to a statutory, shared responsibility between insurers and policyholders but with a very strong consumer-oriented focus. It is further submitted that the tried and trusted section 53(1)(a) of the STIA, the current GCC and the 2018 PPRs are aimed at personal and commercial insurance alike and do not "scale" the duty of good faith according to the size of the insurable interest or it being a commercial or personal one.

In terms of the duty of good faith, it appears as if the rigid and strict approach in England in codifying the duty of utmost good faith led to unfair results and generated much criticism, which necessitated law reform. The majority of law reforms evidently changed the remedy for non-compliance with the duty as well as the disclosure requirements of a policyholder, thereby constituting a fairer balance between insurers and policyholders, with more equitable results for both parties. This means that, in England, the duty of utmost good faith, although

---

184 Donnelly (n 183) 607.

retaining its essence as highlighted in the MIA, has developed through reform to achieve a fairer dispensation. The remedy and disclosure requirements in England now show a closer resemblance to those in South Africa.

In South Africa, the duty of good faith remains a common law, pre-contractual duty on both parties. In the past, misrepresentation was often used by insurers to avoid paying claims and prospective policyholders received no guidance as to what would generally be considered material to the risk to be insured. Save for the now repealed section 59 of the LTIA[185] and section 53 of the STIA, no other statutory measures existed until the FAIS Act was introduced and much more was made of the role of advisors and intermediaries at the pre-contractual stage, especially in ensuring that insurers take on the correct risks. It is only with the promulgation of the 2018 PPRs that it became patently clear that the age-old concept of good faith currently has a strong, statutory element to it in that, in England and in South Africa, various rules have been enacted to emphasise the duties of insurers to explain the importance of pre-contractual representations pertaining to the risk.[186] In both jurisdictions, marine and other insurance contracts are subject to consumer-oriented rules that better balance the parties' respective duties of good faith towards each other. This supports the conclusion that insurers (and insurance agents) must act in good faith as well. Furthermore, while the absence of good faith never provided an aggrieved party with a remedy in South Africa, the breach of any of the rules in the PPRs or the GCC does provide remedies, based on the effect of such breach.

In conclusion, it can be said that insurance business has changed dramatically from the decision in *Carter v Boehm*. Although utmost good faith is alive and well in England, it is submitted that the content of the doctrine has changed for the better. In South Africa, good faith in insurance continues to play an important role, albeit in a new and evolving statutory context.

---

185 Note that the content of section 59 has now been moved to rule 21 of the PPRs in terms of the LTIA and that it still corresponds with section 53 of the STIA.

186 Donnelly (n 183) 604.

www.ingramcontent.com/pod-product-compliance
Lightning Source LLC
Chambersburg PA
CBHW051334200326
41519CB00026B/7423